Microsoft® Office

Access 2007

Introductory Concepts and Techniques

Gary B. Shelly

Thomas J. Cashman

Philip J. Pratt

Mary Z. Last

THOMSON

COURSE TECHNOLOGY™

THOMSON COURSE TECHNOLOGY   25 THOMSON PLACE   BOSTON MA 02210

SHELLY CASHMAN SERIES®

Australia • Canada • Denmark • Japan • Mexico • New Zealand • Philippines • Puerto Rico • Singapore • South Africa • Spain • United Kingdom • United States

Microsoft Office Access 2007
Introductory Concepts and Techniques

Gary B. Shelly

Thomas J. Cashman

Philip J. Pratt

Mary Z. Last

Executive Editor
Alexandra Arnold

Senior Product Manager
Reed Curry

Associate Product Manager
Klenda Martinez

Editorial Assistant
Jon Farnham

Senior Marketing Manager
Joy Stark-Vancs

Marketing Coordinator
Julie Schuster

Print Buyer
Julio Esperas

Director of Production
Patty Stephan

Production Editor
Matthew Hutchinson

Developmental Editor
Amanda Brodkin

Proofreaders
John Bosco,
Kim Kosmatka

Indexer
Rich Carlson

QA Manuscript Reviewers
John Freitas, Serge Palladino,
Chris Scriver, Danielle Shaw,
Marianne Snow, Teresa Storch

Art Director
Bruce Bond

Cover and Text Design
Joel Sadagursky

Cover Photo
Jon Chomitz

Compositor
GEX Publishing Services

Printer
Banta Menasha

Microsoft® Office
Access 2007
Introductory Concepts and Techniques

Contents

Microsoft Office **Access 2007**

CHAPTER ONE
Creating and Using a Database

CHAPTER TWO
Querying a Database

CHAPTER THREE
Maintaining a Database

INTEGRATION FEATURE
Sharing Data Among Applications

Appendices

APPENDIX A

Project Planning Guidelines

APPENDIX B

Introduction to Microsoft Office 2007

APPENDIX C

Microsoft Office Access 2007 Help

APPENDIX D

Publishing Office 2007 Web Pages to a
Web Server

APPENDIX E

Customizing Microsoft Office Access 2007

APPENDIX F

Steps for the Windows XP User

APPENDIX G

Microsoft Business Certification Program

Preface

The Shelly Cashman Series® offers the finest textbooks in computer education. We are proud of the fact that our series of Microsoft Office 4.3, Microsoft Office 95, Microsoft Office 97, Microsoft Office 2000, Microsoft Office XP, and Microsoft Office 2003 textbooks have been the most widely used books in education. With each new edition of our Office books, we have made significant improvements based on the software and comments made by instructors and students.

Microsoft Office 2007 contains more changes in the user interface and feature set than all other previous versions combined. Recognizing that the new features and functionality of Microsoft Office 2007 would impact the way that students are taught skills, the Shelly Cashman Series development team carefully reviewed our pedagogy and analyzed its effectiveness in teaching today's Office student. An extensive customer survey produced results confirming what the series is best known for: its step-by-step, screen-by-screen instructions, its project-oriented approach, and the quality of its content.

We learned, though, that students entering computer courses today are different than students taking these classes just a few years ago. Students today read less, but need to retain more. They need not only to be able to perform skills, but to retain those skills and know how to apply them to different settings. Today's students need to be continually engaged and challenged to retain what they're learning.

As a result, we've renewed our commitment to focusing on the user and how they learn best. This commitment is reflected in every change we've made to our Office 2007 books.

Objectives of This Textbook

Microsoft Office Access 2007: Introductory Concepts and Techniques is intended for a course that includes an introduction to Access 2007. No experience with a computer is assumed, and no mathematics beyond the high school freshman level is required. The objectives of this book are:

- To teach the fundamentals of Microsoft Office Access 2007

- To expose students to practical examples of the computer as a useful tool

- To acquaint students with the proper procedures to create documents suitable for coursework, professional purposes, and personal use

- To help students discover the underlying functionality of Access 2007 so they can become more productive

- To develop an exercise-oriented approach that allows learning by doing

The Shelly Cashman Approach

Features of the Shelly Cashman Series Microsoft Office Access 2007 books include:

- **Project Orientation** Each chapter in the book presents a project with a practical problem and complete solution in an easy-to-understand approach.

- **Plan Ahead Boxes** The project orientation is enhanced by the inclusion of Plan Ahead boxes. These new features prepare students to create successful projects by encouraging them to think strategically about what they are trying to accomplish before they begin working.

- **Step-by-Step, Screen-by-Screen Instructions** Each of the tasks required to complete a project is clearly identified throughout the chapter. Now, the step-by-step instructions provide a context beyond point-and-click. Each step explains why students are performing a task, or the result of performing a certain action. Found on the screens accompanying each step, call-outs give students the information they need to know when they need to know it. Now, we've used color to distinguish the content in the call-outs. The Explanatory call-outs (in black) summarize what is happening on the screen and the Navigational call-outs (in red) show students where to click.

- **Q&A** Found within many of the step-by-step sequences, Q&As raise the kinds of questions students may ask when working through a step sequence and provide answers about what they are doing, why they are doing it, and how that task might be approached differently.

- **Experimental Steps** These new steps, within our step-by-step instructions, encourage students to explore, experiment, and take advantage of the features of the Office 2007 new user interface. These steps are not necessary to complete the projects, but are designed to increase the confidence with the software and build problem-solving skills.

- **Thoroughly Tested Projects** Unparalleled quality is ensured because every screen in the book is produced by the author only after performing a step, and then each project must pass Thomson Course Technology's Quality Assurance program.

- **Other Ways Boxes and Quick Reference Summary** The Other Ways boxes displayed at the end of most of the step-by-step sequences specify the other ways to do the task completed in the steps. Thus, the steps and the Other Ways box make a comprehensive reference unit. A Quick Reference Summary at the end of the book contains all of the tasks presented in the chapters, and all ways identified of accomplishing the tasks.

- **BTW** These marginal annotations provide background information, tips, and answers to common questions that complement the topics covered, adding depth and perspective to the learning process.

- **Integration of the World Wide Web** The World Wide Web is integrated into the Access 2007 learning experience by (1) BTW annotations that send students to Web sites for up-to-date information and alternative approaches to tasks; (2) a Microsoft Business Certification Program Web page so students can prepare for the certification examinations; (3) a Quick Reference Summary Web page that summarizes the ways to complete tasks (mouse, Ribbon, shortcut menu, and keyboard); and (4) the Learn It Online section at the end of each chapter, which has chapter reinforcement exercises, learning games, and other types of student activities.

- **End-of-Chapter Student Activities** Extensive student activities at the end of each chapter provide the student with plenty of opportunities to reinforce the materials learned in the chapter through hands-on assignments. Several new types of activities have been added that challenge the student in new ways to expand their knowledge, and to apply their new skills to a project with personal relevance.

Q&A

What is a maximized window?

A maximized window fills the entire screen. When you maximize a window, the Maximize button changes to a Restore Down button.

Other Ways

1. Click Italic button on Mini toolbar
2. Right-click selected text, click Font on shortcut menu, click Font tab, click Italic in Font style list, click OK button
3. Click Font Dialog Box Launcher, click Font tab, click Italic in Font style list, click OK button
4. Press CTRL+I

BTW

Minimizing the Ribbon
If you want to minimize the Ribbon, right-click the Ribbon and then click Minimize the Ribbon on the shortcut menu, double-click the active tab, or press CTRL+F1. To restore a minimized Ribbon, right-click the Ribbon and then click Minimize the Ribbon on the shortcut menu, double-click any top-level tab, or press CTRL+F1. To use commands on a minimized Ribbon, click the top-level tab.

Organization of This Textbook

Microsoft Office Access 2007: Introductory Concepts and Techniques consists of three chapters on Microsoft Office Access 2007, one special feature emphasizing Web-related topics, seven appendices, and a Quick Reference Summary.

End-of-Chapter Student Activities

A notable strength of the Shelly Cashman Series Microsoft Office 2007 books is the extensive student activities at the end of each chapter. Well-structured student activities can

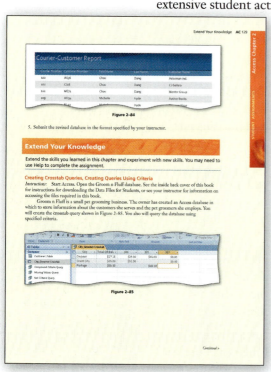

make the difference between students merely participating in a class and students retaining the information they learn. The activities in the Shelly Cashman Series Office books include the following.

CHAPTER SUMMARY A concluding paragraph, followed by a listing of the tasks completed within a chapter together with the pages on which the step-by-step, screen-by-screen explanations appear.

LEARN IT ONLINE Every chapter features a Learn It Online section that is comprised of six exercises. These exercises include True/False, Multiple Choice, Short Answer, Flash Cards, Practice Test, and Learning Games.

APPLY YOUR KNOWLEDGE This exercise usually requires students to open and manipulate a file from the Data Files that parallels the activities learned in the chapter. To obtain a copy of the Data Files for Students, follow the instructions on the inside back cover of this text.

EXTEND YOUR KNOWLEDGE This exercise allows students to extend and expand on the skills learned within the chapter.

MAKE IT RIGHT This exercise requires students to analyze a document, identify errors and issues, and correct those errors and issues using skills learned in the chapter.

IN THE LAB Three all new in-depth assignments per chapter require students to utilize the chapter concepts and techniques to solve problems on a computer.

CASES AND PLACES Five unique real-world case-study situations, including Make It Personal, an open-ended project that relates to student's personal lives, and one small-group activity.

Instructor Resources CD-ROM

The Shelly Cashman Series is dedicated to providing you with all of the tools you need to make your class a success. Information about all supplementary materials is available through your Thomson Course Technology representative or by calling one of the following telephone numbers: Colleges, Universities, and Continuing Ed departments, 1-800-648-7450; High Schools, 1-800-824-5179; and Career Colleges, Business, Government, Library and Resellers, 1-800-477-3692.

The Instructor Resources CD-ROM for this textbook include both teaching and testing aids. The contents of each item on the Instructor Resources CD-ROM (ISBN 1-4239-1226-8) are described on the following pages.

INSTRUCTOR'S MANUAL The Instructor's Manual consists of Microsoft Access files, which include chapter objectives, lecture notes, teaching tips, classroom activities, lab activities, quick quizzes, figures and boxed elements summarized in the chapters, and a glossary page. The new format of the Instructor's Manual will allow you to map through every chapter easily.

LECTURE SUCCESS SYSTEM The Lecture Success System consists of intermediate files that correspond to certain figures in the book, allowing you to step through the creation of a project in a chapter during a lecture without entering large amounts of data.

SYLLABUS Sample syllabi, which can be customized easily to a course, are included. The syllabi cover policies, class and lab assignments and exams, and procedural information.

FIGURE FILES Illustrations for every figure in the textbook are available in electronic form. Use this ancillary to present a slide show in lecture or to print transparencies for use in lecture with an overhead projector. If you have a personal computer and LCD device, this ancillary can be an effective tool for presenting lectures.

POWERPOINT PRESENTATIONS PowerPoint Presentations is a multimedia lecture presentation system that provides slides for each chapter. Presentations are based on chapter objectives. Use this presentation system to present well-organized lectures that are both interesting and knowledge based. PowerPoint Presentations provides consistent coverage at schools that use multiple lecturers.

SOLUTIONS TO EXERCISES Solutions are included for the end-of-chapter exercises, as well as the Chapter Reinforcement exercises. Rubrics and annotated solution files, as described below, are also included.

RUBRICS AND ANNOTATED SOLUTION FILES The grading rubrics provide a customizable framework for assigning point values to the laboratory exercises. Annotated solution files that correspond to the grading rubrics make it easy for you to compare students' results with the correct solutions whether you receive their homework as hard copy or via e-mail.

TEST BANK & TEST ENGINE In the ExamView test bank, you will find our standard question types (40 multiple-choice, 25 true/false, 20 completion) and new objective-based question types (5 modified multiple-choice, 5 modified true/false and 10 matching). Critical Thinking questions are also included (3 essays and 2 cases with 2 questions each) totaling the test bank to 112 questions for every chapter with page number references, and when appropriate, figure references. A version of the test bank you can print also is included. The test bank comes with a copy of the test engine, ExamView, the ultimate tool for your objective-based testing needs. ExamView is a state-of-the-art test builder that is easy to use. ExamView enables you to create paper-, LAN-, or Web-based tests from test banks designed specifically for your Thomson Course Technology textbook. Utilize the ultra-efficient QuickTest Wizard to create tests in less than five minutes by taking advantage of Thomson Course Technology's question banks, or customize your own exams from scratch.

LAB TESTS/TEST OUT The Lab Tests/Test Out exercises parallel the In the Lab assignments and are supplied for the purpose of testing students in the laboratory on the material covered in the chapter or testing students out of the course.

DATA FILES FOR STUDENTS All the files that are required by students to complete the exercises are included. You can distribute the files on the Instructor Resources CD-ROM to your students over a network, or you can have them follow the instructions on the inside back cover of this book to obtain a copy of the Data Files for Students.

ADDITIONAL ACTIVITIES FOR STUDENTS These additional activities consist of Chapter Reinforcement Exercises, which are true/false, multiple-choice, and short answer questions that help students gain confidence in the material learned.

Assessment & Training Solutions

SAM 2007

SAM 2007 helps bridge the gap between the classroom and the real world by allowing students to train and test on important computer skills in an active, hands-on environment.

SAM 2007's easy-to-use system includes powerful interactive exams, training or projects on critical applications such as Word, Excel, Access, PowerPoint, Outlook, Windows, the Internet, and much more. SAM simulates the application environment, allowing students to demonstrate their knowledge and think through the skills by performing real-world tasks.

Designed to be used with the Shelly Cashman series, SAM 2007 includes built-in page references so students can print helpful study guides that match the Shelly Cashman series textbooks used in class. Powerful administrative options allow instructors to schedule exams and assignments, secure tests, and run reports with almost limitless flexibility.

Student Edition Labs

Our Web-based interactive labs help students master hundreds of computer concepts, including input and output devices, file management and desktop applications, computer ethics, virus protection, and much more. Featuring up-to-the-minute content, eye-popping graphics, and rich animation, the highly interactive Student Edition Labs offer students an alternative way to learn through dynamic observation, step-by-step practice, and challenging review questions.

Online Content

Blackboard is the leading distance learning solution provider and class-management platform today. Thomson Course Technology has partnered with Blackboard to bring you premium online content. Instructors: Content for use with *Microsoft Office 2007: Introductory Concepts and Techniques, Windows Vista Edition* is available in a Blackboard Course Cartridge and may include topic reviews, case projects, review questions, test banks, practice tests, custom syllabi, and more.

Thomson Course Technology also has solutions for several other learning management systems. Please visit http://www.course.com today to see what's available for this title.

Workbook for Microsoft Office 2007: Introductory Concepts and Techniques

This highly popular supplement (ISBN 1-4188-4335-0) includes a variety of activities that help students recall, review, and master the concepts presented. The Workbook complements the end-of-chapter material with an outline; a self-test consisting of true/false, multiple-choice, short answer, and matching questions; and activities calculated to help students develop a deeper understanding of the information presented.

CourseCasts Learning on the Go. Always Available...Always Relevant.

Want to keep up with the latest technology trends relevant to you? Visit our site to find a library of podcasts, CourseCasts, featuring a "CourseCast of the Week," and download them to your portable media player at http://coursecasts.course.com.

Our fast-paced world is driven by technology. You know because you are an active participant — always on the go, always keeping up with technological trends, and always learning new ways to embrace technology to power your life.

Ken Baldauf, a faculty member of the Florida State University (FSU) Computer Science Department, is responsible for teaching technology classes to thousands of FSU students each year. He knows what you know; he knows what you want to learn. He is also an expert in the latest technology and will sort through and aggregate the most pertinent news and information so you can spend your time enjoying technology, rather than trying to figure it out.

Visit us at http://coursecasts.course.com to learn on the go!

CourseNotes

Course Technology's CourseNotes are six-panel quick reference cards that reinforce the most important and widely used features of a software application in a visual and user-friendly format. CourseNotes will serve as a great reference tool during and after the student completes the course. CourseNotes for Microsoft Office 2007, Word 2007, Excel 2007, Access 2007, PowerPoint 2007, Windows Vista, and more are available now!

To the Student . . . Getting the Most Out of Your Book

Welcome to *Microsoft Office Access 2007: Introductory Concepts and Techniques*. You can save yourself a lot of time and gain a better understanding of the Office 2007 programs if you spend a few minutes reviewing the figures and callouts in this section.

1 PROJECT ORIENTATION
Each chapter's project presents a practical problem and shows the solution in the first figure of the chapter. The project orientation lets you see firsthand how problems are solved from start to finish using application software and computers.

2 PROJECT PLANNING GUIDELINES AND PLAN AHEAD BOXES
Overall planning guidelines at the beginning of a chapter and Plan Ahead boxes throughout encourage you to think critically about how to accomplish the next goal before you actually begin working.

3 CONSISTENT STEP-BY-STEP, SCREEN-BY-SCREEN PRESENTATION
Chapter solutions are built using a step-by-step, screen-by-screen approach. This pedagogy allows you to build the solution on a computer as you read through the chapter. Generally, each step includes an explanation that indicates the result of the step.

4 MORE THAN JUST STEP-BY-STEP
BTW annotations in the margins of the book, Q&As in the steps, and substantive text in the paragraphs provide background information, tips, and answers to common questions that complement the topics covered, adding depth and perspective. When you finish with this book, you will be ready to use the Office programs to solve problems on your own. Experimental steps provide you with opportunities to step out on your own to try features of the programs, and pick up right where you left off in the chapter.

5 OTHER WAYS BOXES AND QUICK REFERENCE SUMMARY
Other Ways boxes that follow many of the step sequences and a Quick Reference Summary at the back of the book explain the other ways to complete the task presented, such as using the mouse, Ribbon, shortcut menu, and keyboard.

6 EMPHASIS ON GETTING HELP WHEN YOU NEED IT
The first project of each application and Appendix C show you how to use all the elements of Office Help. Being able to answer your own questions will increase your productivity and reduce your frustrations by minimizing the time it takes to learn how to complete a task.

7 REVIEW, REINFORCEMENT, AND EXTENSION
After you successfully step through a project in a chapter, a section titled Chapter Summary identifies the tasks with which you should be familiar. Terms you should know for test purposes are bold in the text. The SAM Training feature provides the opportunity for addional reinforcement on important skills covered in each chapter. The Learn It Online section at the end of each chapter offers reinforcement in the form of review questions, learning games, and practice tests. Also included are exercises that require you to extend your learning beyond the book.

8 LABORATORY EXERCISES
If you really want to learn how to use the programs, then you must design and implement solutions to problems on your own. Every chapter concludes with several carefully developed laboratory assignments that increase in complexity.

About Our New Cover Look

Learning styles of students have changed, but the Shelly Cashman Series' dedication to their success has remained steadfast for over 30 years. We are committed to continually updating our approach and content to reflect the way today's students learn and experience new technology.

This focus on the user is reflected in our bold new cover design, which features photographs of real students using the Shelly Cashman Series in their courses. Each book features a different user, reflecting the many ages, experiences, and backgrounds of all of the students learning with our books. When you use the Shelly Cashman Series, you can be assured that you are learning computer skills using the most effective courseware available.

Microsoft Office Access 2007

1 | Creating and Using a Database

Objectives

You will have mastered the material in this chapter when you can:

- Describe databases and database management systems
- Design a database to satisfy a collection of requirements
- Start Access
- Describe the features of the Access window
- Create a database
- Create a table and add records

- Close a table
- Close a database and quit Access
- Open a database
- Print the contents of a table
- Create and print custom reports
- Create and use a split form
- Use the Access Help system

1 | Creating and Using a Database

What Is Microsoft Office Access 2007?

Microsoft Office Access 2007, usually referred to as simply Access, is a database management system. A database management system, such as Access, is a software tool that allows you to use a computer to create a database; add, change, and delete data in the database; sort the data in the database; retrieve data in the database; and create forms and reports using the data in the database. The term **database** describes a collection of data organized in a manner that allows access, retrieval, and use of that data. Some of the key features in Access are:

- **Data entry and update** Access provides easy mechanisms for adding, changing, and deleting data, including the capability of making mass changes in a single operation.
- **Queries (questions)** Access makes it possible to ask complex questions concerning the data in the database and then receive instant answers.
- **Forms** Access allows the user to produce attractive and useful forms for viewing and updating data.
- **Reports** Access includes report creation tools that make it easy to produce sophisticated reports for presenting data.
- **Web support** Access allows you to save objects, reports, and tables in HTML format so they can be viewed using a browser. You also can import and export documents in XML format as well as share data with others using SharePoint Services.

This latest version of Access has many new features to help you be more productive. Like the other Office applications, it features a new, improved interface utilizing the Ribbon. The new Navigation Pane makes navigating among the various objects in a database easier and more intuitive than in the past. The new version includes several professionally designed templates that you can use to quickly create a database. Sorting and filtering has been enhanced in this version. The new Layout view allows you to make changes to the design of forms and reports at the same time you are browsing the data. Datasheet view also has been enhanced to make creating tables more intuitive. Split form, a new form object, combines both a datasheet and a form as a single unit. Memo fields now support rich text, and there is a new Attachment data type. Using the Attachment data type, a field can contain an attached file, such as a document, image, or spreadsheet.

Project Planning Guidelines

> The process of developing a database that communicates specific information requires careful analysis and planning. As a starting point, establish why the database is needed. Once the purpose is determined, analyze the intended users of the database and their unique needs. Then, gather information about the topic and decide what to include in the database. Finally, determine the database design and style that will be most successful at delivering the message. Details of these guidelines are provided in Appendix A. In addition, each project in this book provides practical applications of these planning considerations.

Project — Database Creation

JSP Recruiters is a recruiting firm that specializes in job placement for health care professionals. Because the recruiters at JSP have previous experience in the health care industry, the firm is able to provide quality candidates for employment in hospitals, clinics, medical laboratories, doctors' offices, and other health care facilities.

JSP Recruiters works with clients in need of health care professionals. It assigns each client to a specific recruiter. The recruiter works with the client to determine the necessary qualifications for each job candidate. The recruiter then contacts and does a preliminary review of the qualifications for each candidate before setting up a job interview between the client and the candidate. If the candidate is hired, the client pays a percentage of the new employee's annual salary to the recruiting firm, which then distributes a percentage of that client fee to the recruiter.

To ensure that operations run smoothly, JSP Recruiters organizes data on its clients and recruiters in a database, managed by Access. In this way, JSP keeps its data current and accurate while the firm's management can analyze the data for trends and produce a variety of useful reports.

In Access, a database consists of a collection of tables, each of which contains information on a specific subject. Figure 1–1 shows the database for JSP Recruiters. It consists of two tables. The Client table (Figure 1–1a) contains information about the clients to whom JSP provides services. The Recruiter table (Figure 1–1b) contains information about the recruiters to whom these clients are assigned.

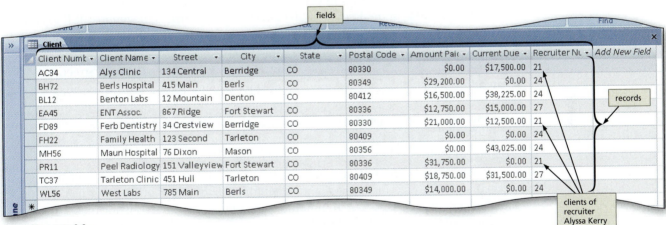

(a) Client Table

Client Number	Client Name	Street	City	State	Postal Code	Amount Paid	Current Due	Recruiter Number
AC34	Alys Clinic	134 Central	Berridge	CO	80330	$0.00	$17,500.00	21
BH72	Berls Hospital	415 Main	Berls	CO	80349	$29,200.00	$0.00	24
BL12	Benton Labs	12 Mountain	Denton	CO	80412	$16,500.00	$38,225.00	24
EA45	ENT Assoc.	867 Ridge	Fort Stewart	CO	80336	$12,750.00	$15,000.00	27
FD89	Ferb Dentistry	34 Crestview	Berridge	CO	80330	$21,000.00	$12,500.00	21
FH22	Family Health	123 Second	Tarleton	CO	80409	$0.00	$0.00	24
MH56	Maun Hospital	76 Dixon	Mason	CO	80356	$0.00	$43,025.00	24
PR11	Peel Radiology	151 Valleyview	Fort Stewart	CO	80336	$31,750.00	$0.00	21
TC37	Tarleton Clinic	451 Hull	Tarleton	CO	80409	$18,750.00	$31,500.00	27
WL56	West Labs	785 Main	Berls	CO	80349	$14,000.00	$0.00	24

(b) Recruiter Table

Recruiter Number	Last Name	First Name	Street	City	State	Postal Code	Rate	Commission
21	Kerry	Alyssa	261 Pointer	Tourin	CO	80416	0.10	$17,600.00
24	Reeves	Camden	3135 Brill	Denton	CO	80412	0.10	$19,900.00
27	Fernandez	Jaime	265 Maxwell	Charleston	CO	80380	0.09	$9,450.00
34	Lee	Jan	1827 Oak	Denton	CO	80413	0.08	$0.00

Figure 1–1

The rows in the tables are called **records**. A record contains information about a given person, product, or event. A row in the Client table, for example, contains information about a specific client.

The columns in the tables are called fields. A **field** contains a specific piece of information within a record. In the Client table, for example, the fourth field, City, contains the city where the client is located.

The first field in the Client table is the Client Number. JSP Recruiters assigns a number to each client. As is common to the way in which many organizations format client numbers, JSP Recruiters calls it a *number*, although it actually contains letters. The JSP client numbers consist of two uppercase letters followed by a two-digit number.

These numbers are unique; that is, no two clients are assigned the same number. Such a field can be used as a **unique identifier**. This simply means that a given client number will appear only in a single record in the table. Only one record exists, for example, in which the client number is BH72. A unique identifier also is called a **primary key**. Thus, the Client Number field is the primary key for the Client table.

The next seven fields in the Client table are Client Name, Street, City, State, Postal Code, Amount Paid, and Current Due. Note that the default width of the columns cuts off the names of some of the columns. The Amount Paid column contains the amount that the client has paid JSP Recruiters year to date (YTD) prior to the current period. The Current Due column contains the amount due to JSP for the current period. For example, client BL12 is Benton Labs. The address is 12 Mountain in Denton, Colorado. The postal code is 80412. The client has paid $16,500 for recruiting services so far this year. The amount due for the current period is $38,225.

JSP assigns each client a single recruiter. The last column in the Client table, Recruiter Number, gives the number of the client's recruiter.

The first field in the Recruiter table, Recruiter Number, is the number JSP Recruiters assigns to the recruiter. These numbers are unique, so Recruiter Number is the primary key of the Recruiter table.

The other fields in the Recruiter table are Last Name, First Name, Street, City, State, Postal Code, Rate, and Commission. The Rate field contains the percentage of the client fee that the recruiter earns, and the Commission field contains the total amount that JSP has paid the recruiter so far this year. For example, Recruiter 27 is Jaime Fernandez. His address is 265 Maxwell in Charleston, Colorado. The Postal Code is 80380. His commission rate is .09 (9%), and his commission is $9,450.

The recruiter number appears in both the Client table and the Recruiter table. It relates clients and recruiters. For example, in the Client table, you see that the recruiter number for client BL12 is 24. To find the name of this recruiter, look for the row in the Recruiter table that contains 24 in the Recruiter Number column. After you have found it, you know the client is assigned to Camden Reeves. To find all the clients assigned to Camden Reeves, you must look through the Client table for all the clients that contain 24 in the Recruiter Number column. His clients are BH72 (Berls Hospital), BL12 (Benton Labs), FH22 (Family Health), MH56 (Maun Hospital), and WL56 (West Labs).

The last recruiter in the Recruiter table, Jan Lee, has not been assigned any clients yet; therefore, her recruiter number, 34, does not appear on any row in the Client table.

Overview

As you read this chapter, you will learn how to create the database shown in Figure 1–1 on the previous page by performing these general tasks:
- Design the database.
- Create a new blank database.

- Create a table and add the records.
- Preview and print the contents of a table.
- Create a second table and add the records.
- Create four reports.
- Create a form.

**Plan
Ahead**

Database design guidelines.

Database design refers to the arrangement of data into tables and fields. In the example in this chapter the design is specified, but in many cases, you will have to determine the design based on what you want the system to accomplish.

When designing a database, the actions you take and the decisions you make will determine the tables and fields that will be included in the database. As you create a database, such as the project shown in Figure 1–1 on page AC 3, you should follow these general guidelines:

1. **Identify the tables.** Examine the requirements for the database in order to identify the main objects that are involved. There will be a table for each object you identified.

   In one database, for example, the main objects might be departments and employees. Thus, there would be two tables: one for departments and the other for employees. In another database, the main objects might be clients and recruiters. In this case, there would also be two tables: one for clients and the other for recruiters. In still another database, the main objects might be books, publishers, and authors. Here there would be three tables: one for books, a second for publishers, and a third for authors.

2. **Determine the primary keys.** Recall that the primary key is the unique identifier for records in the table. For each table, determine the unique identifier, if there is one. For a Department table, for example, the unique identifier might be the Department Code. For a Book table, the unique identifier might be the ISBN number.

3. **Determine the additional fields.** The primary key will be a field or combination of fields in a table. There typically will be many additional fields, each of which contains a type of data. Examine the project requirements to determine these additional fields. For example, in an Employee table, the additional fields might include such fields as Employee Name, Street Address, City, State, Postal Code, Date Hired, Salary, and so on.

4. **Determine relationships among the tables.** Examine the list of tables you have created to see which tables are related. When you determine two tables are related, include matching fields in the two tables. For example, in a database containing employees and departments, there is a relationship between the two tables because one department can have many employees assigned to it. Department Code could be the matching field in the two tables.

5. **Determine data types for the fields.** For each field, determine the type of data the field can contain. One field, for example, might contain only numbers. Another field might contain currency amounts, while a third field might contain only dates. Some fields contain text data, meaning any combination of letters, numbers and special characters (!, ;, ', &, and so on). For example, in an Employee table, the Date Hired field would contain dates, the Salary field would contain currency amounts, and the Hours Worked field would contain numbers. The other fields in the Employee table would contain text data, such as Employee Name and Department Code.

6. **Identify and remove any unwanted redundancy. Redundancy** is the storing of a piece of data in more than one place. Redundancy usually, but not always, causes problems, such as wasted space, difficulties with update, and possible data inconsistency. Examine each table you have created to see if it contains redundancy and, if so, determine whether the redundancy causes these problems. If it does, remove the redundancy by splitting the table into two tables. For example, you may have a single table of employees. In addition to typical employee data (name, address, earnings, and so on), the table might contain Department Number and Department Name. If so, the Department Name could repeat multiple times.

(continued)

**Plan
Ahead**

(continued)

Every employee whose department number is 12, for example, would have the same department name. It would be better to split the table into two tables, one for Employees and one for Department. In the Department table, the Department Name is stored only once.

7. **Determine a location for the database. The database you have designed will be stored in a single file. You need to determine a location in which to store the file.**

When necessary, more specific details concerning the above guidelines are presented at appropriate points in the chapter. The chapter also will identify the actions performed and decisions made regarding these guidelines during the creation of the database shown in Figure 1–1 on page AC 3.

BTW

Database Design
For more information on database design methods and for techniques for identifying and eliminating redundancy, visit the Access 2007 Database Design Web page (scsite.com/ac2007/dbdesign).

Designing a Database

This section illustrates the database design process by showing how you would design the database for JSP Recruiters from a set of requirements. In this section, you will use a commonly accepted shorthand to represent the tables and fields that make up the database as well as the primary keys for the tables. For each table, you give the name of the table followed by a set of parentheses. Within the parentheses is a list of the fields in the table separated by columns. You underline the primary key. For example,

Product (Product Code, Description, On Hand, Price)

represents a table called Product. The Product table contains four fields: Product Code, Description, On Hand, and Price. The Product Code field is the primary key.

Database Requirements

JSP Recruiters needs to maintain information on both clients and recruiters. It currently keeps this data in the two Word tables and two Excel workbooks shown in Figure 1–2. They use Word tables for address information and Excel workbooks for financial information.

Client Number	Client Name	Street	City	State	Postal Code
AC34	Alys Clinic	134 Central	Berridge	CO	80330
BH72	Berls Hospital	415 Main	Berls	CO	80349
BL12	Benton Labs	12 Mountain	Denton	CO	80412
EA45	ENT Assoc.	867 Ridge	Fort Stewart	CO	80336
FD89	Ferb Dentistry	34 Crestview	Berridge	CO	80330
FH22	Family Health	123 Second	Tarleton	CO	80409
MH56	Maun Hospital	76 Dixon	Mason	CO	80356
PR11	Peel Radiology	151 Valleyview	Fort Stewart	CO	80336
TC37	Tarleton Clinic	451 Hull	Tarleton	CO	80409
WL56	West Labs	785 Main	Berls	CO	80349

**(a)
Client Address
Information
(Word Table)**

Figure 1–2

(b) Client Financial Information (Excel Workbook)

	A	B	C	D
1	Client Number	Client Name	Amount Paid	Current Due
2	AC34	Alys Clinic	$0.00	$17,500.00
3	BH72	Berls Hospital	$29,200.00	$0.00
4	BL12	Benton Labs	$16,500.00	$38,225.00
5	EA45	ENT Assoc.	$12,750.00	$15,000.00
6	FD89	Ferb Dentistry	$21,000.00	$12,500.00
7	FH22	Family Health	$0.00	$0.00
8	MH56	Maun Hospital	$0.00	$43,025.00
9	PR11	Peel Radiology	$31,750.00	$0.00
10	TC37	Tarleton Clinic	$18,750.00	$31,500.00
11	WL56	West Labs	$14,000.00	$0.00

(c) Recruiter Address Information (Word Table)

Recruiter Number	Last Name	First Name	Street	City	State	Postal Code
21	Kerry	Alyssa	261 Pointer	Tourin	CO	80416
24	Reeves	Camden	3135 Brill	Denton	CO	80412
27	Fernandez	Jaime	265 Maxwell	Charleston	CO	80380
34	Lee	Jan	1827 Oak	Denton	CO	80413

(d) Recruiter Financial Information (Excel Workbook)

	A	B	C	D	E
1	Recruiter Number	Last Name	First Name	Rate	Commission
2	21	Kerry	Alyssa	0.10	$17,600.00
3	24	Reeves	Camden	0.10	$19,900.00
4	27	Fernandez	Jaime	0.09	$9,450.00
5	34	Lee	Jan	0.08	$0.00

Figure 1–2 (continued)

For clients, JSP needs to maintain address data. It currently keeps this address data in a Word table (Figure 1–2a). It also maintains financial data for each client. This includes the amount paid and the current due from the client. It keeps these amounts along with the client name and number in the Excel workbook shown in Figure 1–2b.

JSP keeps recruiter address data in a Word table as shown in Figure 1–2c. Just as with clients, it keeps financial data for recruiters, including their rate and commission, in a separate Excel workbook, as shown in Figure 1–2d.

Finally, it keeps track of which clients are assigned to which recruiters. Currently, for example, clients AC34 (Alys Clinic), FD89 (Ferb Dentistry), and PR11 (Peel Radiology) are assigned to recruiter 21 (Alyssa Kerry). Clients BH72 (Berls Hospital), BL12 (Benton Labs), FH22 (Family Health), MH56 (Maun Hospital), and WL56 (West Labs) are assigned to recruiter 24 (Camden Reeves). Clients EA45 (ENT Assoc.) and TC37 (Tarleton Clinic) are assigned to recruiter 27 (Jaime Fernandez). JSP has an additional recruiter, Jan Lee, whose number has been assigned as 34, but who has not yet been assigned any clients.

Naming Tables and Fields

In designing your database, you must name the tables and fields. Thus, before beginning the design process, you must understand the rules for table and field names, which are:

1. Names can be up to 64 characters in length.
2. Names can contain letters, digits, and spaces, as well as most of the punctuation symbols.
3. Names cannot contain periods (.), exclamation points (!), accent graves (`), or square brackets ([ ]).
4. The same name cannot be used for two different fields in the same table.

Naming Fields
Access 2007 has a number of reserved words, words that have a special meaning to Access. You cannot use these reserved words as field names. For example, Name is a reserved word and could not be used in the Client table to describe a client's name. For a complete list of reserved words in Access 2007, consult Access Help.

The approach to naming tables and fields used in this text is to begin the names with an uppercase letter and to use lowercase for the other letters. In multiple-word names, each word begins with an uppercase letter, and there is a space between words (for example, Client Number). You should know that there are other approaches. Some people omit the space (ClientNumber). Still others use an underscore in place of the space (Client_Number). Finally, some use an underscore in place of a space, but use the same case for all letters (CLIENT_NUMBER or client_number).

Identifying the Tables

Now that you know the rules for naming tables and fields, you are ready to begin the design process. The first step is to identify the main objects involved in the requirements. For the JSP Recruiters database, the main objects are clients and recruiters. This leads to two tables, which you must name. Reasonable names for these two tables are:

Client

Recruiter

Determining the Primary Keys

The next step is to identify the fields that will be the primary keys. Client numbers uniquely identify clients, and recruiter numbers uniquely identify recruiters. Thus, the primary key for the Client table is the client number, and the primary key for the Recruiter table is the recruiter number. Reasonable names for these fields would be Client Number and Recruiter Number, respectively. Adding these primary keys to the tables gives:

Client (<u>Client Number</u>)

Recruiter (<u>Recruiter Number</u>)

Database Design Language (DBDL)
DBDL is a commonly accepted shorthand representation for showing the structure of a relational database. You write the name of the table and then within parentheses you list all the columns in the table. If the columns continue beyond one line, indent the subsequent lines.

Determining Additional Fields

After identifying the primary keys, you need to determine and name the additional fields. In addition to the client number, the Client Address Information shown in Figure 1–2a on page AC 6 contains the client name, street, city, state, and postal code. These would be fields in the Client table. The Client Financial Information shown in Figure 1–2b also contains the client number and client name, which are already included in the Client table. The financial information also contains the amount paid and the current due. Adding the amount paid and current due fields to those already identified in the Client table and assigning reasonable names gives:

Client (<u>Client Number</u>, Client Name, Street, City, State, Postal Code,
    Amount Paid, Current Due)

Similarly, examining the Recruiter Address Information in Figure 1–2c on page AC 7 adds the last name, first name, street, city, state, and postal code fields to the Recruiter table. In addition to the recruiter number, last name, and first name, the Recruiter Financial Information in Figure 1–2d would add the rate and commission. Adding these fields to the Recruiter table and assigning reasonable names gives:

Recruiter (<u>Recruiter Number</u>, Last Name, First Name, Street, City, State, Postal Code, Rate, Commission)

Determining and Implementing Relationships Between the Tables

Plan Ahead

Determine relationships among the tables.

The most common type of relationship you will encounter between tables is the **one-to-many relationship**. This means that each row in the first table may be associated with *many* rows in the second table, but each row in the second table is associated with only *one* row in the first. The first table is called the "one" table and the second is called the "many" table. For example, there may be a relationship between departments and employees, in which each department can have many employees, but each employee is assigned to only one department. In this relationship, there would be two tables, Department and Employee. The Department table would be the "one" table in the relationship. The Employee table would be the "many" table.

To determine relationships among tables, you can follow these general guidelines:

1. Identify the "one" table.

2. Identify the "many" table.

3. Include the primary key from the "one" table as a field in the "many" table.

According to the requirements, each client has one recruiter, but each recruiter can have many clients. Thus, the Recruiter table is the "one" table, and the Client table is the "many" table. To implement this one-to-many relationship between recruiters and clients, add the Recruiter Number field (the primary key of the Recruiter table) to the Client table. This produces:

Client (<u>Client Number</u>, Client Name, Street, City, State, Postal Code, Amount Paid, Current Due, Recruiter Number)

Recruiter (<u>Recruiter Number</u>, Last Name, First Name, Street, City, State, Postal Code, Rate, Commission)

Determining Data Types for the Fields

Each field has a **data type**. This indicates the type of data that can be stored in the field. Three of the most commonly used data types are:

1. **Text** — The field can contain any characters. A maximum number of 255 characters is allowed in a field whose data type is Text.

2. **Number** — The field can contain only numbers. The numbers either can be positive or negative. Fields are assigned this type so they can be used in arithmetic operations. Fields that contain numbers but will not be used for arithmetic operations usually are assigned a data type of Text.

3. **Currency** — The field can contain only monetary data. The values will appear with currency symbols, such as dollar signs, commas, and decimal points, and with

BTW

Currency Symbols
To show the symbol for the Euro (€) instead of the dollar sign, change the Format property for the field whose data type is currency. To change the default symbols for currency, change the settings in the operating system using the Control Panel.

two digits following the decimal point. Like numeric fields, you can use currency fields in arithmetic operations. Access assigns a size to currency fields automatically.

Table 1–1 shows the other data types that are available.

Table 1–1 Additional Data Types	
Data Type	**Description**
Memo	Field can store a variable amount of text or combinations of text and numbers where the total number of characters may exceed 255.
Date/Time	Field can store dates and times.
AutoNumber	Field can store a unique sequential number that Access assigns to a record. Access will increment the number by 1 as each new record is added.
Yes/No	Field can store only one of two values. The choices are Yes/No, True/False, or On/Off.
OLE Object	Field can store an OLE object, which is an object linked to or embedded in the table.
Hyperlink	Field can store text that can be used as a hyperlink address.
Attachment	Field can contain an attached file. Images, spreadsheets, documents, charts, and so on can be attached to this field in a record in the database. You can view and edit the attached file.

In the Client table, because the Client Number, Client Name, Street, City, and State can all contain letters, their data types should be Text. The data type for Postal Code is Text instead of Number, because postal codes are not used in arithmetic operations. You do not add postal codes or find an average postal code, for example. The Amount Paid and Current Due fields both contain monetary data, so their data types should be Currency.

Similarly, in the Recruiter table, the data type for the Recruiter Number, Last Name, First Name, Street, City, State, and Postal Code fields all should be Text. The Commission field contains monetary amounts, so its data type should be Currency. The Rate field contains a number that is not a currency amount, so its data type should be Number.

Identifying and Removing Redundancy

Redundancy means storing the same fact in more than one place. It usually results from placing too many fields in a table — fields that really belong in separate tables — and often causes serious problems. If you had not realized there were two objects, clients and recruiters, for example, you might have placed all the data in a single Client table. Figure 1–3 shows a portion of this table with some sample data. Notice that the data for a given Recruiter (number, name, address, and so on) occurs on more than one record. The data for Camden Reeves is repeated in the figure.

Client Table

clients of recruiter 24

name of recruiter 24 appears more than once

Client Number	Client Name	Street	...	Recruiter Number	Last Name	First Name	...
AC34	Alys Clinic	134 Central	...	21	Kerry	Alyssa	...
BH72	Berls Hospital	415 Main	...	24	Reeves	Camden	...
BL12	Benton Labs	12 Mountain	...	24	Reeves	Camden	...
...	...	...	...	...	...	...	...

Figure 1–3

Storing this data on multiple records is an example of redundancy, which causes several problems, including:

1. Wasted storage space. The name of Recruiter 24 (Camden Reeves), for example, should be stored only once. Storing this fact several times is wasteful.

2. More difficult database updates. If, for example, Camden Reeves's name is spelled wrong and needs to be changed in the database, his name would need to be changed in several different places.

3. A possibility of inconsistent data. There is nothing to prohibit the recruiter's last name from being Reeves on client BH72's record and Reed on client BL12's record. The data would be inconsistent. In both cases, the recruiter number is 24, but the last names are different.

The solution to the problem is to place the redundant data in a separate table, one in which the data no longer will be redundant. If, for example, you place the data for recruiters in a separate table (Figure 1–4), the data for each recruiter will appear only once.

Client Table

Client Number	Client Name	Street	...	Recruiter Number
AC34	Alys Clinic	134 Central	...	21
BH72	Berls Hospital	415 Main	...	24
BL12	Benton Labs	12 Mountain	...	24
...	...	...	...	...

clients of recruiter 24

Recruiter Table

Recruiter Number	Last Name	First Name	...
21	Kerry	Alyssa	...
24	Reeves	Camden	...
...	...	...	...

name of recruiter 24 appears only once

Figure 1–4

Notice that you need to have the recruiter number in both tables. Without it, there would be no way to tell which recruiter is associated with which client. The remaining recruiter data, however, was removed from the Client table and placed in the Recruiter table. This new arrangement corrects the problems of redundancy in the following ways:

1. Because the data for each recruiter is stored only once, space is not wasted.

2. Changing the name of a recruiter is easy. You have only to change one row in the Recruiter table.

3. Because the data for a recruiter is stored only once, inconsistent data cannot occur. Designing to omit redundancy will help you to produce good and valid database designs.

You should always examine your design to see if it contains redundancy. If it does, you should decide whether you need to remove the redundancy by creating a separate table.

Postal Codes
Some organizations with many customers spread throughout the country will, in fact, have a separate table of postal codes, cities, and states. If you call such an organization to place an order, they typically will ask you for your postal code (or ZIP code), rather than asking for your city, state, and postal code. They then will indicate the city and state that correspond to that postal code and ask you if that is correct.

If you examine your design, you'll see that there is one area of redundancy (see the data in Figure 1–1 on page AC 3). Cities and states are both repeated. Every client whose postal code is 80330, for example, has Berridge as the city and CO as the state. To remove this redundancy, you would create a table whose primary key is Postal Code and that contains City and State as additional fields. City and State would be removed from the Client table. Having City, State, and Postal Code in a table is very common, however, and usually you would not take such action. There is no other redundancy in your tables.

Starting Access

If you are using a computer to step through the project in this chapter, and you want your screen to match the figures in this book, you should change your screen's resolution to 1024×768. For information about how to change a computer's resolution, read Appendix E.

Note: If you are using Windows XP, see Appendix F for alternate steps.

To Start Access

The following steps, which assume Windows Vista is running, start Access based on a typical installation. You may need to ask your instructor how to start Access for your computer.

1

• Click the Start button on the Windows Vista taskbar to display the Start menu.

• Click All Programs at the bottom of the left pane on the Start menu to display the All Programs list.

• Click Microsoft Office in the All Programs list to display the Microsoft Office list (Figure 1–5).

Figure 1–5

2
- Click Microsoft Office Access 2007 to start Access and display the Getting Started with Microsoft Office Access screen (Figure 1–6).

- If the Access window is not maximized, click the Maximize button next to the Close button on its title bar to maximize the window.

What is a maximized window?

A maximized window fills the entire screen. When you maximize a window, the Maximize button changes to a Restore Down button.

Figure 1–6

Creating a Database

In Access, all the tables, reports, forms, and queries that you create are stored in a single file called a database. Thus, before creating any of these objects, you first must create the database that will hold them. You can use either the Blank Database option or a template to create a new database. If you already know the tables and fields you want in your database, you would use the Blank Database option. If not, you can use a template. Templates can guide you by suggesting some commonly used databases. If you choose to create a database using a template, you would use the following steps.

To Create a Database Using a Template

1. If the template you wish to use is not already visible on the Getting Started with Microsoft Office Access page, double-click the links in the Template Categories pane to display the desired template.

2. Click the template you wish to use.

3. Enter a file name (or accept the suggested file name) and select a location for the database.

4. Click the Create button to create the database or the Download button to download the database and create the database, if necessary.

     When you create a database, the computer places it on a storage medium, such as a USB flash drive, CD, or hard disk. A saved database is referred to as a **file**. A **file name** is the name assigned to a file when it is saved.

BTW

Naming Files
File names can be a maximum of 260 characters including the file extension. The file extension for Access 2007 is .accdb. You can use either uppercase or lowercase letters in file names.

<table>
<tr><td>Plan
Ahead</td><td>Determine where to create the database.
When creating a database, you must decide which storage medium to use.

If you always work on the same computer and have no need to transport your database to a different location, then your computer's hard drive will suffice as a storage location. It is a good idea, however, to save a backup copy of your database on a separate medium in case the file becomes corrupted, or the computer's hard drive fails.

If you plan to work on your database in various locations or on multiple computers, then you can consider saving your projects on a portable medium, such as a USB flash drive or CD. The projects in this book are stored on a USB flash drive, which saves files quickly and reliably and can be reused. CDs are easily portable and serve as good backups for the final versions of projects because they generally can save files only one time.</td></tr>
</table>

To Create a Database

Because you already know the tables and fields you want in the JSP Recruiters database, you would use the Blank Database option rather than using a template. The following steps create a database, using the file name JSP Recruiters, on a USB flash drive.

Note: If you are using Windows XP, see Appendix F for alternate steps.

- With a USB flash drive connected to one of the computer's USB ports, click Blank Database to create a new blank database (Figure 1–7).

Figure 1–7

2

- Repeatedly press the DELETE key to delete the default name of Database1.

- Type JSP Recruiters in the File Name text box to replace the default file name of Database1 (your screen may show Database1.accdb). Do not press the ENTER key after typing the file name (Figure 1–8).

Q&A

What characters can I use in a file name?

A file name can have a maximum of 260 characters, including spaces. The only invalid characters are the backslash (\), slash (/), colon (:), asterisk (*), question mark (?), quotation mark ("), less than symbol (<), greater than symbol (>), and vertical bar (|).

3

- Click the 'Browse for a location to put your database' button to display the File New Database dialog box.

- If the Navigation Pane is not displayed in the Save As dialog box, click the Browse Folders button to expand the dialog box.

- If a Folders list is displayed below the Folders button, click the Folders button to remove the Folders list (Figure 1-9).

Q&A

Do I have to save to a USB flash drive?

No. You can save to any device or folder. A **folder** is a specific location on a storage medium. You can save to the default folder or a different folder. You also can create your own folders, which is explained later in this book.

Figure 1–8

Figure 1–9

• If Computer is not displayed in the Favorite Links section, drag the top or bottom edge of the Save As dialog box until Computer is displayed.

• Click Computer in the Favorite Links section to display a list of available drives (Figure 1–10).

• If necessary, scroll until UDISK 2.0 (E:) appears in the list of available drives.

Q&A Why is my list of drives arranged and named differently?

The size of the Save As dialog box and your computer's configuration determine how the list is displayed and how the drives are named.

Figure 1–10

Q&A How do I save the file if I am not using a USB flash drive?

Use the same process, but select your desired save location in the Favorite Links section.

• Double-click UDISK 2.0 (E:) in the Computer list to select the USB flash drive, Drive E in this case, as the new save location (Figure 1–11).

Q&A What if my USB flash drive has a different name or letter?

It is very likely that your USB flash drive will have a different name and drive letter and be connected to a different port. Verify that the device in your Computer list is correct.

Figure 1–11

• Click the OK button to select the USB flash drive as the location for the database and to return to the Getting Started with Microsoft Office Access screen (Figure 1–12).

Figure 1–12

7

- Click the Create button to create the database on the USB flash drive with the file name, JSP Recruiters (Figure 1–13).

Q&A How do I know that the JSP Recruiters database is created?

The name of the database appears in the title bar.

Figure 1–13

8

- If a Field List appears, click its Close button to remove the Field List from the screen (Figure 1–14).

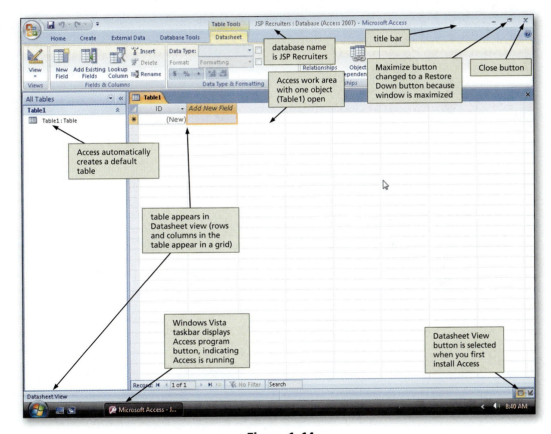

Figure 1–14

Other Ways

1. Click Office Button, click Save, type file name, click Computer, select drive or folder, click Save button

2. Press CTRL+S or press SHIFT+F12, type file name, click Computer, select drive or folder, click Save button

The Access Window

The Access window consists of a variety of components to make your work more efficient and documents more professional. These include the Navigation Pane, Access work area, Ribbon, Mini toolbar and shortcut menus, Quick Access Toolbar, and Office Button. Some of these components are common to other Microsoft Office 2007 programs; others are unique to Access.

Navigation Pane and Access Work Area

You work on objects such as tables, forms, and reports in the **Access work area**. In the work area in Figure 1–14 on the previous page, a single table, Table1, is open in the work area. Figure 1–15 shows a work area with multiple objects open. **Object tabs** for the open objects appear at the top of the work area. You can select one of the open objects by clicking its tab. In the figure, the Client Form is the selected object. To the left of the work area is the Navigation Pane. The Navigation Pane contains a list of all the objects in the database. You use this pane to open an object. You also can customize the way objects are displayed in the Navigation Pane.

Figure 1–15

The Access work area in Figure 1–15 contains an insertion point, mouse pointer, scroll bar, and status bar. Other elements that may appear in the work area are discussed later in this and subsequent chapters.

Insertion Point The **insertion point** is a blinking vertical bar that indicates where text, graphics, and other items will be inserted. As you type, the insertion point moves to the right.

Mouse Pointer The **mouse pointer** becomes different shapes depending on the task you are performing in Access and the pointer's location on the screen. The mouse pointer in Figure 1–15 is the shape of an I-beam.

Scroll Bar   You use a **scroll bar** to display different portions of a database object in the Access window. At the right edge of the window is a **vertical scroll bar**. If an object is too wide to fit in the Access window, a **horizontal scroll bar** also appears at the bottom of the window. On a scroll bar, the position of the **scroll box** reflects the location of the portion of the database object that is displayed in the Access window. A **scroll arrow** is located at each end of a scroll bar. To scroll through, or display different portions of the object in the Access window, you can click a scroll arrow or drag the scroll box.

Status Bar   The **status bar**, located at the bottom of the Access window above the Windows Vista taskbar, presents information about the database object, the progress of current tasks, and the status of certain commands and keys; it also provides controls for viewing the object. As you type text or perform certain commands, various indicators may appear on the status bar.

The left edge of the status bar in Figure 1–15 shows that the form object is open in Form view. Toward the right edge are View buttons, which you can use to change the view that is currently displayed.

Ribbon

The **Ribbon**, located near the top of the Access window, is the control center in Access (Figure 1–16a). The Ribbon provides easy, central access to the tasks you perform while creating a database object. The Ribbon consists of tabs, groups, and commands. Each **tab** surrounds a collection of groups, and each group contains related commands.

When you start Access, the Ribbon displays four top-level tabs: Home, Create, External Data, and Database Tools. The **Home tab**, called the primary tab, contains the more frequently used commands. To display a different tab on the Ribbon, click the top-level tab. That is, to display the Create tab, click Create on the Ribbon. To return to the Home tab, click Home on the Ribbon. The tab currently displayed is called the **active tab**.

To allow more space in the Access work area, some users prefer to minimize the Ribbon, which hides the groups on the Ribbon and displays only the top-level tabs (Figure 1–16b). To use commands on a minimized Ribbon, click the top-level tab.

Each time you start Access, the Ribbon appears the same way it did the last time you used Access. The chapters in this book, however, begin with the Ribbon appearing as it did at the initial installation of the software. If you are stepping through this chapter on a computer and you want your Ribbon to match the figures in this book, read Appendix E.

BTW

Minimizing the Ribbon
If you want to minimize the Ribbon, right-click the Ribbon and then click Minimize the Ribbon on the shortcut menu, double-click the active tab, or press CTRL+F1. To restore a minimized Ribbon, right-click the Ribbon and then click Minimize the Ribbon on the shortcut menu, double-click any top-level tab, or press CTRL+F1. To use commands on a minimized Ribbon, click the top-level tab.

(a) Ribbon at Initial Installation (Default Ribbon)

(b) Minimized Ribbon

Figure 1–16

In addition to the top-level tabs, Access displays other tabs, called **contextual tabs**, when you perform certain tasks or work with objects such as datasheets. If you are working with a table in Datasheet view, for example, the Table Tools tab and its related subordinate Datasheet tab appear (Figure 1–17). When you are finished working with the table, the Table Tools and Datasheet tabs disappear from the Ribbon. Access determines when contextual tabs should appear and disappear based on tasks you perform. Some contextual tabs have more than one related subordinate tab.

Figure 1–17

Figure 1–18

Commands on the Ribbon include buttons, boxes (text boxes, check boxes, etc.), and galleries (Figure 1–18). A **gallery** is a set of choices, often graphical, arranged in a grid or in a list. You can scroll through choices on an in-Ribbon gallery by clicking the gallery's scroll arrows. Or, you can click a gallery's More button to view more gallery options on the screen at a time. Some buttons and boxes have arrows that, when clicked, also display a gallery; others always cause a gallery to be displayed when clicked. Many galleries support **live preview**, which is a feature that allows you to point to a gallery choice and see its effect in the database object — without actually selecting the choice.

Some commands on the Ribbon display an image to help you remember their function. When you point to a command on the Ribbon, all or part of the command glows in shades of yellow and orange, and an Enhanced ScreenTip appears on the screen. An **Enhanced ScreenTip** is an on-screen note that provides the name of the command, available keyboard shortcut(s), a description of the command, and sometimes instructions for how to obtain help about the command (Figure 1–19). Enhanced ScreenTips are more detailed than a typical ScreenTip, which usually only displays the name of the command.

The lower-right corner of some groups on the Ribbon has a small arrow, called a **Dialog Box Launcher**, which, when clicked, displays a dialog box or a task pane with additional options for the group (Figure 1–20). When presented with a dialog box, you make selections and must close the dialog box before returning to the database object. A **task pane**, by contrast, is a window that can remain open and visible while you work in the database object.

Figure 1–19

Figure 1–20

Mini Toolbar and Shortcut Menus

The **Mini toolbar**, which appears automatically based on tasks you perform, contains commands related to changing the appearance of text in a database object. All commands on the Mini toolbar also exist on the Ribbon. The purpose of the Mini toolbar is to minimize mouse movement. For example, if you want to use a command that currently is not displayed on the active tab, you can use the command on the Mini toolbar — instead of switching to a different tab to use the command.

When the Mini toolbar appears, it initially is transparent (Figure 1–21a). If you do not use the transparent Mini toolbar, it disappears from the screen. To use the Mini toolbar, move the mouse pointer into the toolbar, which causes the Mini toolbar to change from a transparent to bright appearance (Figure 1–21b).

A **shortcut menu**, which appears when you right-click an object, is a list of frequently used commands that relate to the right-clicked object. When you right-click a table, for example, a shortcut menu appears with commands related to the table (Figure 1–21c).

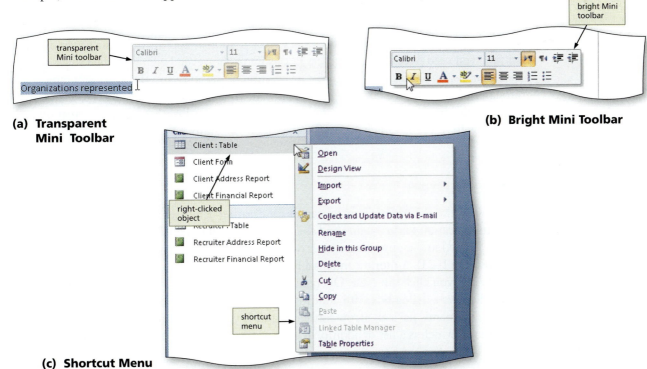

(a) **Transparent Mini Toolbar**

(b) **Bright Mini Toolbar**

(c) **Shortcut Menu**

Figure 1–21

Quick Access Toolbar

The **Quick Access Toolbar**, located by default above the Ribbon, provides easy access to frequently used commands (Figure 1–22a). The commands on the Quick Access Toolbar always are available, regardless of the task you are performing. Initially, the Quick Access Toolbar contains the Save, Undo, and Redo commands. If you click the Customize Quick Access Toolbar button, Access provides a list of commands you quickly can add to and remove from the Quick Access Toolbar (Figure 1–22b).

You also can add other commands to or delete commands from the Quick Access Toolbar so that it contains the commands you use most often. As you add commands to the Quick Access Toolbar, its commands may interfere with the title of the database object on the title bar. For this reason, Access provides an option of displaying the Quick Access Toolbar below the Ribbon (Figure 1–22c).

Figure 1–22

Each time you start Access, the Quick Access Toolbar appears the same way it did the last time you used Access. The chapters in this book, however, begin with the Quick Access Toolbar appearing as it did at the initial installation of the software. If you are stepping through this chapter on a computer, and you want your Quick Access Toolbar to match the figures in this book, you should reset your Quick Access Toolbar. For more information about how to reset the Quick Access Toolbar, read Appendix E.

Office Button

While the Ribbon is a control center for creating database objects, the **Office Button** is a central location for managing and sharing database objects. When you click the Office Button, located in the upper-left corner of the window, Access displays the Office Button menu (Figure 1–23). A **menu** contains a list of commands.

When you click the New, Open, and Print commands on the Office Button menu, Access displays a dialog box with additional options. The Save As, Print, Manage, and Publish commands have an arrow to their right. If you point to this arrow, Access displays a **submenu**, which is a list of additional commands associated with the selected command (Figure 1–24). For the Save As, Print, Manage, and Publish commands that do not display a dialog box when clicked, you can point either to the command or the arrow to display the submenu.

Office Button

list of recently created Office documents appears here

Office Button menu

Figure 1–23

submenu

pointing to the arrow to the right of a command causes a submenu to be displayed

for the Manage and Publish commands, pointing to the command or to the arrow causes a submenu to be displayed

Figure 1–24

Key Tips

If you prefer using the keyboard instead of the mouse, you can press the ALT key on the keyboard to display a **Key Tip badge**, or keyboard code icon, for certain commands (Figure 1–25). To select a command using the keyboard, press its displayed code letter, or **Key Tip**. When you press a Key Tip, additional Key Tips related to the selected command may appear. For example, to select the New command on the Office Button menu, press the ALT key, then press the F key, then press the N key.

To remove the Key Tip badges from the screen, press the ALT key or the ESC key until all Key Tip badges disappear, or click the mouse anywhere in the Access window.

Key Tip badges appear when you press ALT key on keyboard

Figure 1–25

Creating a Table

When you first create your database, Access automatically creates a table for you. You can immediately begin defining the fields. If, for whatever reason, you do not have this table or inadvertently delete it, you can create the table by clicking Create on the Ribbon and then clicking the Table button on the Create tab. In either case, you are ready to define the fields.

To Define the Fields in a Table

With the table already created, the next step is to define the fields in the table and to assign them data types. The fields in the Client table are Client Number, Client Name, Street, City, State, Postal Code, Amount Paid, Current Due, and Recruiter Number. The data type for the Amount Paid and Current Due fields is Currency. The data type for all other fields is Text. The following steps define the fields in the table.

1

• Right-click Add New Field to display a shortcut menu (Figure 1–26).

Q&A Why don't I delete the ID field first, before adding other fields?

You cannot delete the primary key in Datasheet view; you only can delete it in Design view. After adding the other fields, you will move to Design view, delete the ID field, and then make the Client Number the primary key.

Q&A Why does my shortcut menu look different?

You right-clicked within the column instead of right-clicking the column heading.

Figure 1–26

2

• Click Rename Column on the shortcut menu to display an insertion point.

• Type Client Number to assign a name to the new field.

• Press the DOWN ARROW key to complete the addition of the field (Figure 1–27).

Q&A Why doesn't the whole name appear?

The default column size is not large enough for Client Number to appear in its entirety. Later in this book, you will learn how to resize columns so that the entire name can appear.

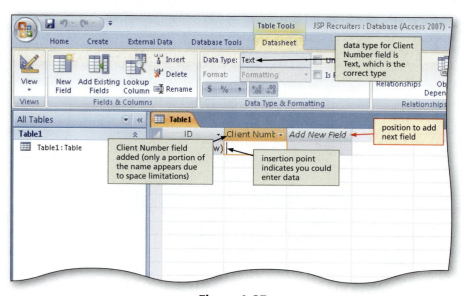

Figure 1–27

3

- Right-click Add New Field to display a shortcut menu, click Rename Column on the shortcut menu to display an insertion point, type `Client Name` to assign a name to the new field, and then press the DOWN ARROW key to complete the addition of the field.

Q&A

Did I have to press the DOWN ARROW key? Couldn't I have just moved to the next field or pressed the ENTER key?

You could have pressed the TAB key or the ENTER key to move to the column heading for the next field. Pressing the DOWN ARROW key, however, completes the entry of the Client Number field and allows you to ensure that the column is assigned the correct data type.

- Using the same technique add the fields in the Client table up through and including the Amount Paid field.

- Click the Data Type box arrow to display the Data Type box menu (Figure 1–28).

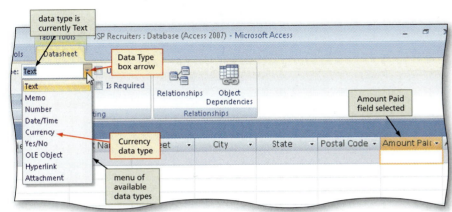

Figure 1–28

4

- Click Currency to select Currency as the data type for the Amount Paid field (Figure 1–29).

Q&A

Why does Currency appear twice?

The second Currency is the format, which indicates how the data will be displayed. For the Currency data type, Access automatically sets the format to Currency, which is usually what you would want. You could change it to something else, if desired, by clicking the arrow and selecting the desired format.

Figure 1–29

5

- Click the right scroll arrow to shift the fields to the left and display the Add New Field column (Figure 1–30).

Figure 1–30

6
- Make the remaining entries from the Client table structure shown in Figure 1–31 to complete the structure. Be sure to select Currency as the data type for the Current Due field.

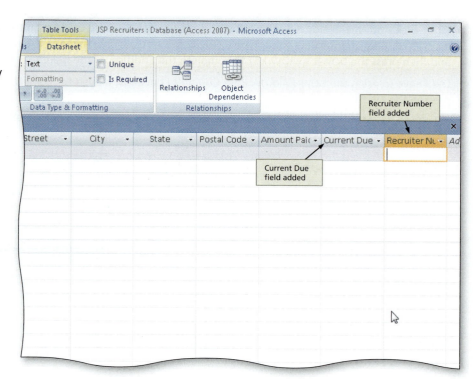

Figure 1–31

BTW

Creating a Table: Table Templates
Access includes table templates that assist you in creating some commonly used tables and fields. To use a template, click Create on the Ribbon and then click the Table Templates button on the Create tab. Click the desired template, make any adjustments you wish to the table that Access creates, and then save the table.

Making Changes to the Structure

When creating a table, check the entries carefully to ensure they are correct. If you discover a mistake while still typing the entry, you can correct the error by repeatedly pressing the BACKSPACE key until the incorrect characters are removed. Then, type the correct characters. If you do not discover a mistake until later, you can use the following techniques to make the necessary changes to the structure:

- To undo your most recent change, click the Undo button on the Quick Access Toolbar. If there is nothing that Access can undo, this button will be dim, and clicking it will have no effect.
- To delete a field, right-click the column heading for the field (the position containing the field name), and then click Delete Column on the shortcut menu.
- To change the name of a field, right-click the column heading for the field, click Rename Column on the shortcut menu, and then type the desired field name.
- To insert a field as the last field, right-click the Add New Field column heading, click Rename Column on the shortcut menu, type the desired field name, click the down arrow, and then ensure the correct data type is already selected.
- To insert a field between existing fields, right-click the column heading for the field that will follow the new field, and then click Insert Column on the shortcut menu. You then proceed just as you do when you insert a field as the last field.

As an alternative to these steps, you may want to start over. To do so, click the Close button for the window containing the table, and then click the No button in the Microsoft Office Access dialog box. Click Create on the Ribbon and then click the Table button to create a table. You then can repeat the process you used earlier to define the fields in the table.

To Save a Table

The Client table structure now is complete. The final step is to save and close the table within the database. At this time, you should give the table a name.

The following steps save the table, giving it the name, Client.

1
- Click the Save button on the Quick Access Toolbar to save the structure of the table (Figure 1–32).

Q&A I have an extra row between the row containing the field names and the row that begins with the asterisk. What happened? Is this a problem? If so, how do I fix it?

You inadvertently added a record to the table by pressing some key after you pressed the DOWN ARROW key. Even pressing the Spacebar would add a record. You now have a record you do not want and it will cause problems when you attempt to assign a different primary key. To fix it, you need to delete the record, which you will do in Step 3.

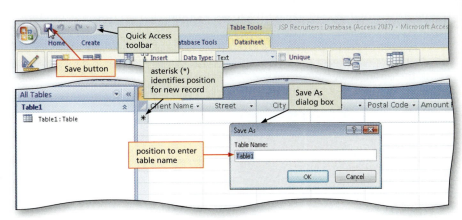

Figure 1–32

2
- Type `Client` to change the name to be assigned to the table (Figure 1–33).

Figure 1–33

3
- Click the OK button to save the structure with the name, Client (Figure 1–34).

- If you have an additional record between the field names and the asterisk, click the record selector (the box at the beginning of the record), press the DELETE key, and then click the Yes button when Access asks you if you want to delete the record.

Figure 1–34

Other Ways	
1. Click Office Button, click Save on the Office Button menu	2. Right-click tab for table, click Save on shortcut menu
	3. Press CTRL+S

To Change the Primary Key

To change the primary key, you must first delete the ID field that Access created automatically. You then can designate the Client Number field as the primary key. To delete the ID field, the table must appear in Design view rather than Datasheet view. You also can designate the Client Number field as the primary key within Design view. As you define or modify the fields, the **row selector**, the small box or bar that, when you click it, selects the entire row, indicates the field you currently are describing. The following steps move to Design view and then change the primary key.

- Click the Design View button on the status bar to move to Design view.

- Confirm that your data types match those shown in the figure. Make any necessary corrections to the data types (Figure 1-35).

Q&A Did I have to save the table before moving to Design view?

Yes. If you had not saved it yourself, Access would have asked you to save it.

Figure 1–35

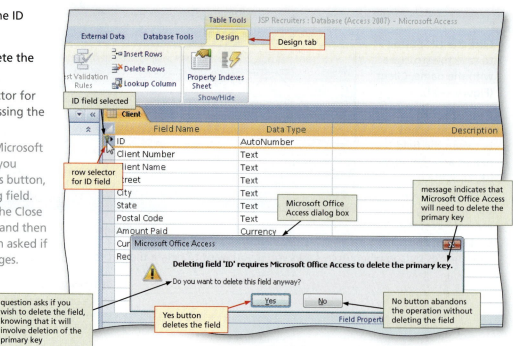

- Click the row selector for the ID field to select the field.

- Press the DELETE key to delete the field (Figure 1–36).

Q&A What if I click the row selector for the wrong field before pressing the DELETE key?

Click the No button in the Microsoft Office Access dialog box. If you inadvertently clicked the Yes button, you have deleted the wrong field. You can fix this by clicking the Close button for the Client table, and then clicking the No button when asked if you want to save your changes.

Figure 1–36

3

- Click the Yes button to complete the deletion of the field.

- With the Client Number field selected, click the Primary Key button to designate the Client Number field as the primary key.

- Click the Save button to save the changes (Figure 1–37).

Q&A

When I attempted to save the table I got an error message that indicates index or primary key cannot contain a null value. What did I do wrong and how do I fix it?

You inadvertently added a record to the table by pressing some key after you pressed the DOWN ARROW key. To fix it, click the OK button (you will need to do it twice) and then click the Primary Key button to remove the primary key. Click the Save button to save the table and then click the View button near the upper-left corner of the screen to return to datasheet view. Click the little box immediately to the left of the record you added and press the DELETE key. Click the Yes button when Access asks if it is OK to delete the record. Click the View button again and continue with these steps.

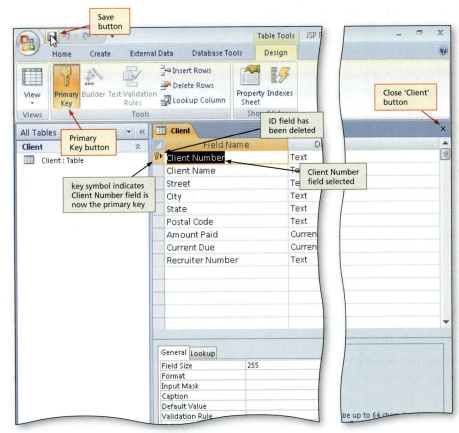

Figure 1–37

4

- Close the Client table by clicking the Close 'Client' button (Figure 1–38).

Figure 1–38

To Add Records to a Table

Creating a table by building the structure and saving the table is the first step in a two-step process. The second step is to add records to the table. To add records to a table, the table must be open. When making changes to tables, you work in Datasheet view. In **Datasheet view**, the table is represented as a collection of rows and columns called a **datasheet**.

You often add records in phases. You may, for example, not have enough time to add all the records in one session. The following steps open the Client table in Datasheet view and then add the first two records in the Client table (Figure 1–39).

Client Numb ▾	Client Name ▾	Street ▾	City ▾	State ▾	Postal Code ▾	Amount Paic ▾	Current Due ▾	Recruiter Nu ▾
AC34	Alys Clinic	134 Central	Berridge	CO	80330	$0.00	$17,500.00	21
BH72	Berls Hospital	415 Main	Berls	CO	80349	$29,200.00	$0.00	24

Figure 1–39

- Right-click the Client table in the Navigation Pane to display the shortcut menu (Figure 1–40).

Figure 1–40

• Click Open on the shortcut menu to open the Client table in Datasheet view.

Q&A

What if I want to return to Design view?

There are two ways to get to Design view. You could click Design View on the shortcut menu. Alternatively, you could click Open on the shortcut menu to open the table in Datasheet view and then click the Design View button on the Access status bar.

• Click the Shutter Bar Open/Close Button to hide the Navigation Pane (Figure 1–41).

Figure 1–41

• Click in the Client Number field and type AC34 to enter the first client number. Be sure you type the letters in uppercase so they are entered in the database correctly (Figure 1–42).

Figure 1–42

4

- Press the TAB key to complete the entry for the Client Number field.

- Enter the client name, street, city, state, and postal code by typing the following entries, pressing the TAB key after each one: Alys Clinic as the client name, 134 Central as the street, Berridge as the city, CO as the state, and 80330 as the postal code.

- Type 0 to enter the amount paid (Figure 1–43).

Do I need to type a dollar sign?

You do not need to type dollar signs or commas. In addition, because the digits to the right of the decimal point are both zeros, you do not need to type either the decimal point or the zeros.

Figure 1–43

5

- Press the TAB key to complete the entry for the Amount Paid field.

- Type 17500 to enter the current due amount and then press the TAB key to move to the next field.

- Type 21 as the Recruiter number to complete data entry for the record (Figure 1–44).

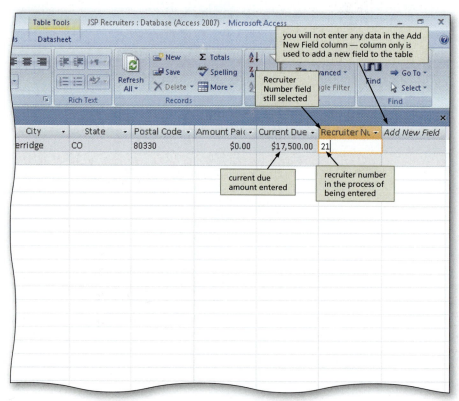

Figure 1–44

6

- Press the TAB key to complete the entry of the first record (Figure 1–45).

Q&A

How and when do I save the record?

As soon as you have entered or modified a record and moved to another record, the original record is saved. This is different from other applications. The rows entered in an Excel worksheet, for example, are not saved until the entire worksheet is saved.

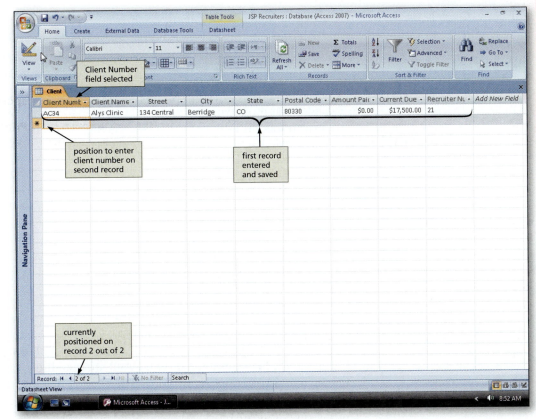

Figure 1–45

7

- Use the techniques shown in Steps 3 through 6 to enter the data for the second record in the Client table (Figure 1–46).

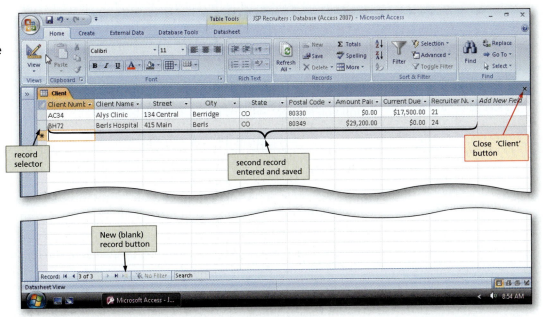

Figure 1–46

BTW

Undo and Redo
You also can undo multiple actions. To see a list of recent actions that you can undo, click the down arrow next to the Undo button on the Quick Access Toolbar. To redo the most recent action, click the Redo button on the Quick Access Toolbar. You also can redo multiple actions by clicking the down arrow next to the button.

BTW

Cut, Copy, and Paste
Just as in other Office applications, you can use buttons in the Clipboard group on the Home tab to cut, copy, and paste data. To cut data, select the data to be cut and click the Cut button. To copy data, select the data and click the Copy button. To paste data, select the desired location and click the Paste button.

BTW

AutoCorrect Options
Using the Office AutoCorrect feature, you can create entries that will replace abbreviations with spelled-out names and phrases automatically. For example, you can create the abbreviated entry *dbms* for *database management system*. Whenever you type dbms followed by a space or punctuation mark, Access automatically replaces dbms with database management system. To specify AutoCorrect rules and exceptions to the rules, click Access Options on the Office Button menu and then click Proofing in the Access Options dialog box.

Making Changes to the Data

Check your entries carefully to ensure they are correct. If you make a mistake and discover it before you press the TAB key, correct it by pressing the BACKSPACE key until the incorrect characters are removed and then typing the correct characters. If you do not discover a mistake until later, you can use the following techniques to make the necessary corrections to the data:

- To undo your most recent change, click the Undo button on the Quick Access Toolbar. If there is nothing that Access can undo, this button will be dim, and clicking it will have no effect.

- To add a record, click the New (blank) record button, shown in Figure 1–46 on the previous page, and then add the record. Do not worry about it being in the correct position in the table. Access will reposition the record based on the primary key, in this case, the Client Number.

- To delete a record, click the Record selector, shown in Figure 1–46, for the record to be deleted. Then press the DELETE key to delete the record, and click the Yes button when Access asks you to verify that you do indeed wish to delete the record.

- To change the contents of one or more fields in a record, the record must be on the screen. If it is not, use any appropriate technique, such as the UP ARROW and DOWN ARROW keys or the vertical scroll bar, to move to it. If the field you want to correct is not visible on the screen, use the horizontal scroll bar along the bottom of the screen to shift all the fields until the one you want appears. If the value in the field is currently highlighted, you can simply type the new value. If you would rather edit the existing value, you must have an insertion point in the field. You can place the insertion point by clicking in the field or by pressing F2. Once you have produced an insertion point, you can use the arrow keys, the DELETE key, and the BACKSPACE key in making the correction. You also can use the INSERT key to switch between Insert and Overtype mode. When you have made the change, press the TAB key to move to the next field.

If you cannot determine how to correct the data, you may find that you are "stuck" on the record. Access neither allows you to move to any other record until you have made the correction, nor allows you to close the table. If you encounter this situation, simply press the ESC key. Pressing the ESC key will remove from the screen the record you are trying to add. You then can move to any other record, close the table, or take any other action you desire.

AutoCorrect

Not visible in the Access window, the **AutoCorrect** feature of Access works behind the scenes, correcting common mistakes when you complete a text entry in a cell. AutoCorrect makes three types of corrections for you:

1. Corrects two initial capital letters by changing the second letter to lowercase.

2. Capitalizes the first letter in the names of days.

3. Replaces commonly misspelled words with their correct spelling. For example, it changes the misspelled word *recieve* to *receive* when you complete the entry. AutoCorrect will correct the spelling automatically of more than 400 commonly misspelled words.

To Close a Table

It is a good idea to close a table as soon as you have finished working with it. It keeps the screen from getting cluttered and prevents you from making accidental changes to the data in the table. The following steps close the Client table.

1
- Click the Close 'Client' button, shown in Figure 1–46 on page AC 33, to close the table (Figure 1–47).

Figure 1–47

Other Ways

1. Right-click tab for table, click Close on shortcut menu

Quitting Access

If you save the object on which you are currently working and then quit Access, all Access windows close. If you have made changes to an object since the last time the object was saved, Access displays a dialog box asking if you want to save the changes you made before it closes that window. The dialog box contains three buttons with these resulting actions:

- Yes button — Saves the changes and then quits Access
- No button — Quits Access without saving changes
- Cancel button — Closes the dialog box and redisplays the database without saving the changes

If no changes have been made to any object since the last time the object was saved, Access will close all windows without displaying any dialog boxes.

To Quit Access

You saved your changes to the table and did not make any additional changes. You are ready to quit Access. The following step quits Access.

1 Click the Close button on the right side of the Access title bar, shown in Figure 1–47 on the previous page, to quit Access.

Starting Access and Opening a Database

Once you have created and later closed a database, you will need to open it in the future in order to use it. Opening a database requires that Access is running on your computer.

Note: If you are using Windows XP, see Appendix F for alternate steps.

To Start Access

The following steps, which assume Windows Vista is running, start Access.

1 Click the Start button on the Windows Vista taskbar to display the Start menu.

2 Click All Programs at the bottom of the left pane on the Start menu to display the All Programs list and then click Microsoft Office in the All Programs list to display the Microsoft Office list.

3 Click Microsoft Office Access 2007 on the Microsoft Office submenu to start Access and display the Getting Started with Microsoft Office Access window (Figure 1–48).

4 If the Access window is not maximized, click the Maximize button on its title bar to maximize the window.

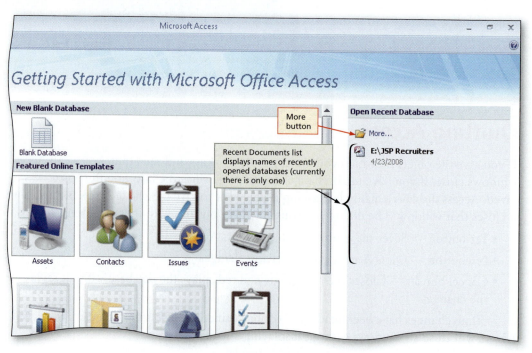

Figure 1–48

To Open a Database from Access

Note: If you are using Windows XP, see Appendix F for alternate steps.

Earlier in this chapter you created your database on a USB flash drive using the file name, JSP Recruiters. There are two ways to open the file containing your database. If the file you created appears in the Recent Documents list, you could click it to open the file. If not, you can use the More button to open the file. The following steps use the More button to open the JSP Recruiters database from the USB flash drive.

1

- With your USB flash drive connected to one of the computer's USB ports, click the More button, shown in Figure 1–48, to display the Open dialog box.

- If the Folders list is displayed below the Folders button, click the Folders button to remove the Folders list.

- If necessary, click Computer in the Favorite Links section.

- Double-click UDISK 2.0 (E:) to select the USB flash drive, Drive E in this case, as the new open location.

- Click JSP Recruiters to select the file name (Figure 1–49).

Q&A

How do I open the file if I am not using a USB flash drive?

Use the same process, but be certain to select your device in the Look in list. You might need to open multiple folders.

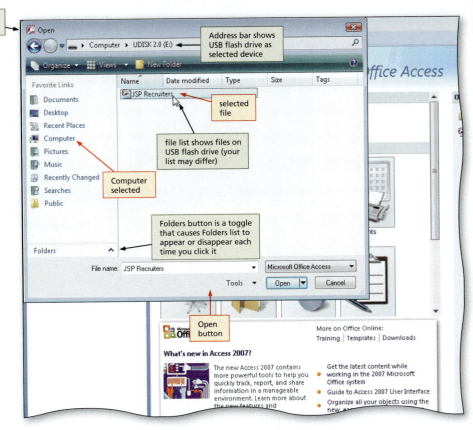

Figure 1–49

2

- Click the Open button to open the database (Figure 1–50).

Q&A

Why do I see the Access icon and name on the Windows Vista taskbar?

When you open an Access database, an Access program button is displayed on the taskbar. If the contents of a button cannot fit in the allotted button space, an ellipsis appears. If you point to a program button, its entire contents appear in a ScreenTip, which in this case would be the program name followed by the file name.

Figure 1–50

3

- If a Security Warning appears, as shown in Figure 1–50 on the previous page, click the Options button to display the Microsoft Office Security Options dialog box (Figure 1–51).

4

- Click the 'Enable this content' option button.

- Click the OK button to enable the content.

Q&A

When would I want to disable the content?

You would want to disable the content if you suspected that your database might contain harmful content or damaging macros. Because you are the one who created the database and no one else has used it, you should have no such suspicions.

Figure 1–51

Other Ways

1. Click Office Button, double-click file name in Recent Documents list

2. Press CTRL+O, select file name, press ENTER

To Add Additional Records to a Table

You can add records to a table that already contains data using a process almost identical to that used to add records to an empty table. The only difference is that you place the insertion point after the last data record before you enter the additional data. To do so, use the **Navigation buttons**, which are buttons used to move within a table, found near the lower-left corner of the screen when a table is open. The purpose of each of the Navigation buttons is described in Table 1–2.

Table 1–2 Navigation Buttons in Datasheet View

Button	Purpose
First record	Moves to the first record in the table
Previous record	Moves to the previous record
Next record	Moves to the next record
Last record	Moves to the last record in the table
New (blank) record	Moves to the end of the table to a position for entering a new record

The following steps add the remaining records (Figure 1–52) to the Client table.

Client Numb ▾	Client Name ▾	Street ▾	City ▾	State ▾	Postal Code ▾	Amount Paic ▾	Current Due ▾	Recruiter Nu ▾
BL12	Benton Labs	12 Mountain	Denton	CO	80412	$16,500.00	$38,225.00	24
EA45	ENT Assoc.	867 Ridge	Fort Stewart	CO	80336	$12,750.00	$15,000.00	27
FD89	Ferb Dentistry	34 Crestview	Berridge	CO	80330	$21,000.00	$12,500.00	21
FH22	Family Health	123 Second	Tarleton	CO	80409	$0.00	$0.00	24
MH56	Maun Hospital	76 Dixon	Mason	CO	80356	$0.00	$43,025.00	24
PR11	Peel Radiology	151 Valleyview	Fort Stewart	CO	80336	$31,750.00	$0.00	21
TC37	Tarleton Clinic	451 Hull	Tarleton	CO	80409	$18,750.00	$31,500.00	27
WL56	West Labs	785 Main	Berls	CO	80349	$14,000.00	$0.00	24

Figure 1–52

• If the Navigation Pane is hidden, click the Shutter Bar Open/Close Button, shown in Figure 1–51, to show the Navigation Pane (Figure 1–53).

Figure 1–53

• Right-click the Client table in the Navigation Pane to display a short-cut menu.

• Click Open on the shortcut menu to open the Client table in Datasheet view.

• Hide the Navigation Pane by clicking the Shutter Bar Open/Close button (Figure 1–54).

Figure 1–54

3

• Click the New (blank) record button to move to a position to enter a new record (Figure 1–55).

Why click the New (blank) record button? Could you just click the Client Number on the first open record and then add the record?

You could click the Client Number on the first open record, provided that record appears on the screen. With only two records in the table, this is not a problem. Once a table contains more records than will fit on the screen, it is easier to click the New (blank) record button.

Figure 1–55

4

• Add the records shown in Figure 1–52 on the previous page, using the same techniques you used to add the first two records (Figure 1–56).

5

• Click the Close 'Client' button to close the table.

Figure 1–56

Other Ways

1. Click New button in Records group on Ribbon

2. Press CTRL+PLUS SIGN (+)

Previewing and Printing the Contents of a Table

When working with a database, you often will need to print a copy of the table contents. Figure 1–57 shows a printed copy of the contents of the Client table. (Yours may look slightly different, depending on your printer.) Because the Client table is wider substantially than the screen, it also will be wider than the normal printed page in portrait orientation. **Portrait orientation** means the printout is across the width of the page.

Client Number	Client Name	Street	City	State	Postal Code	Amount Paid	Current Due	Recruiter Numb
AC34	Alys Clinic	134 Central	Berridge	CO	80330	$0.00	$17,500.00	21
BH72	Berls Hospital	415 Main	Berls	CO	80349	$29,200.00	$0.00	24
BL12	Benton Labs	12 Mountain	Denton	CO	80412	$16,500.00	$38,225.00	24
EA45	ENT Assoc.	867 Ridge	Fort Stewart	CO	80336	$12,750.00	$15,000.00	27
FD89	Ferb Dentistry	34 Crestview	Berridge	CO	80330	$21,000.00	$12,500.00	21
FH22	Family Health	123 Second	Tarleton	CO	80409	$0.00	$0.00	24
MH56	Maun Hospital	76 Dixon	Mason	CO	80356	$0.00	$43,025.00	24
PR11	Peel Radiology	151 Valleyview	Fort Stewart	CO	80336	$31,750.00	$0.00	21
TC37	Tarleton Clinic	451 Hull	Tarleton	CO	80409	$18,750.00	$31,500.00	27
WL56	West Labs	785 Main	Berls	CO	80349	$14,000.00	$0.00	24

Client   4/23/2008

Figure 1–57

Landscape orientation means the printout is across the length (height) of the page. Thus, to print the wide database table, use landscape orientation. If you are printing the contents of a table that fit on the screen, you will not need landscape orientation. A convenient way to change to landscape orientation is to preview what the printed copy will look like by using Print Preview. This allows you to determine whether landscape orientation is necessary and, if it is, to change the orientation easily to landscape. In addition, you also can use Print Preview to determine whether any adjustments are necessary to the page margins.

To Preview and Print the Contents of a Table

The following steps use Print Preview to preview and then print the Client table.

1

- If the Navigation Pane is hidden, show the Navigation Pane by clicking the Shutter Bar Open/ Close Button.

- Be sure the Client table is selected (Figure 1–58).

Q&A

Why do I have to be sure the Client table is selected? It is the only object in the database.

Figure 1–58

There is no issue when the database contains only one object. Ensuring that the correct object is selected is a good habit to form, however, to make sure that the object you print is the one you want.

2

- Click the Office Button to display the Office Button menu.

- Point to the Print command arrow to display the Print submenu (Figure 1–59).

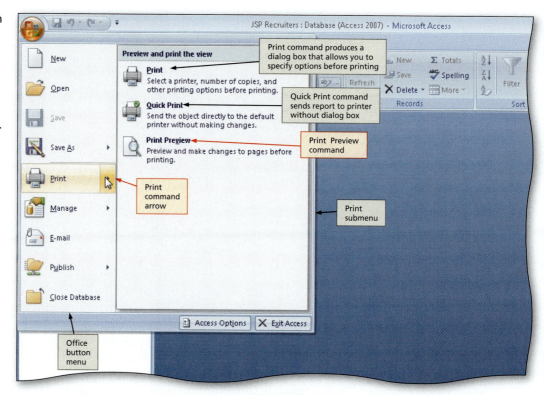

Figure 1–59

3

- Click Print Preview on the Print submenu to display a preview of the report (Figure 1–60).

Q&A I can't read the report. Can I magnify a portion of the report?

Yes. Point the mouse pointer, whose shape will change to a magnifying glass, at the portion of the report that you wish to magnify, and then click. You can return the view of the report to the one shown in the figure by clicking a second time.

Figure 1–60

4

- Click the mouse pointer in the position shown in Figure 1–60 to magnify the upper-right section of the report (Figure 1–61).

Q&A

My report was already magnified in a different area. How can I see the area shown in the figure?

There are two ways. You can use the scroll bars to move to the desired portion of the report. You also can click the mouse pointer anywhere in the report to produce a screen like the one in Figure 1–60, and then click in the location shown in the figure.

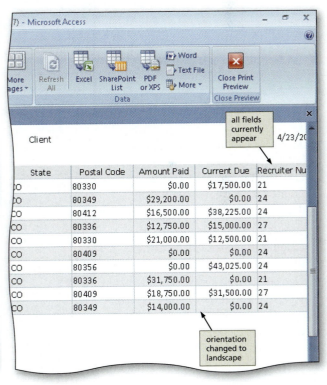

	Client Name	Street	City	State	Postal Code
umber	Alys Clinic	134 Central	Berridge	CO	80330
	Berls Hospital	415 Main	Berls	CO	80349
	Benton Labs	12 Mountain	Denton	CO	80412
	ENT Assoc.	867 Ridge	Fort Stewart	CO	80336
	Ferb Dentistry	34 Crestview	Berridge	CO	80330
	Family Health	123 Second	Tarleton	CO	80409
	Maun Hospital	76 Dixon	Mason	CO	80356
	Peel Radiology	151 Valleyview	Fort Stewart	CO	80336

Figure 1–61

5

- Click the Landscape button to change to landscape orientation (Figure 1–62).

6

- Click the Print button on the Print Preview tab to print the report.

- When the printer stops, retrieve the hard copy of the Client table.

- Click the Close 'Client' button to close the Print Preview window.

Q&A

How can I print multiple copies of my document other than clicking the Print button multiple times?

Click the Office Button, point to the arrow next to Print on the Office Button menu, click Print on the Print submenu, increase the number in the Number of Copies: box, and then click the OK button.

Q&A

How can I print a range of pages rather than printing the whole report?

Click the Office Button, point to the arrow next to Print on the Office Button menu, click Print on the Print submenu, click the Pages option button in the Print Range box, enter the desired page range, and then click the OK button.

State	Postal Code	Amount Paid	Current Due	Recruiter Nu
CO	80330	$0.00	$17,500.00	21
CO	80349	$29,200.00	$0.00	24
CO	80412	$16,500.00	$38,225.00	24
CO	80336	$12,750.00	$15,000.00	27
CO	80330	$21,000.00	$12,500.00	21
CO	80409	$0.00	$0.00	24
CO	80356	$0.00	$43,025.00	24
CO	80336	$31,750.00	$0.00	21
CO	80409	$18,750.00	$31,500.00	27
CO	80349	$14,000.00	$0.00	24

Figure 1–62

Other Ways

1. Press CTRL+P, press ENTER

Creating Additional Tables

The JSP Recruiters database contains two tables, the Client table and the Recruiter table. You need to create the Recruiter table and add records to it. Because you already used the default table that Access created when you created the database, you will need to first create the table. You can then add fields as you did with the Client table.

To Create an Additional Table

The fields to be added are Recruiter Number, Last Name, First Name, Street, City, State, Postal Code, Rate, and Commission. The data type for the Rate field is Number, and the data type for the Commission field is Currency. The data type for all other fields is Text. The following steps create the Recruiter table.

1
- Click Create on the Ribbon to display the Create tab (Figure 1–63).

Figure 1–63

2
- Click the Table button on the Create tab to create a new table (Figure 1–64).

Q&A

Could I save the table now so I can assign it the name I want, rather than Table1?

You certainly can. Be aware, however, that you will still need to save it again once you have added all your fields.

Figure 1–64

- Right-click Add New Field to display a shortcut menu.

- Click Rename Column on the short-cut menu to display an insertion point.

- Type `Recruiter Number` to assign a name to the new field.

- Press the DOWN ARROW key to complete the addition of the field.

- Using the same technique, add the Last Name, First Name, Street, City, State, Postal Code, and Rate fields.

- Click the Data Type box arrow to display the Data Type box menu (Figure 1–65).

Figure 1–65

- Click Number on the Data Type box menu to select the Number data type and assign the Number data type to the Rate field.

- Add the Commission field and assign it the Currency data type.

- Click the Save button to display the Save As dialog box (Figure 1–66).

Figure 1–66

- Type `Recruiter` to assign a name to the table.

- Click the OK button (Figure 1–67).

Figure 1–67

To Modify the Primary Key and Field Properties

Fields whose data type is Number often require you to change the field size. Table 1–3 shows the possible field sizes for Number fields.

Table 1–3 Field Sizes for Number Fields	
Field Size	**Description**
Byte	Integer value in the range of 0 to 255.
Integer	Integer value in the range of -32,768 to 32,767.
Long Integer	Integer value in the range of -2,147,483,648 to 2,147,483,647.
Single	Numeric values with decimal places to seven significant digits — requires four bytes of storage.
Double	Numeric values with decimal places to more accuracy than Single — requires eight bytes of storage.
Replication ID	Special identifier required for replication.
Decimal	Numeric values with decimal places to more accuracy than Single — requires 12 bytes of storage.

Because the values in the Rate field have decimal places, only Single, Double, or Decimal would be possible choices. The difference between these choices concerns the amount of accuracy. Double is more accurate than Single, for example, but requires more storage space. Because the rates are only two decimal places, Single is a perfectly acceptable choice.

In addition to changing the field size, you should also change the format to Fixed (a fixed number of decimal places) and the number of decimal places to 2.

The following steps move to Design view, delete the ID field, and make the Recruiter Number field the primary key. They then change the field size of the Rate field to Single, the format to Fixed, and the number of decimal places to 2.

1

• Click the Design View button on the status bar to move to Design view (Figure 1–68).

Figure 1–68

2

- Click the row selector for the ID field to select the field.

- Press the DELETE key to delete the field.

- Click the Yes button to complete the deletion of the field.

- With the Recruiter Number field selected, click the Primary Key button to designate the Recruiter Number field as the primary key.

- Click the row selector for the Rate field to select the field (Figure 1–69).

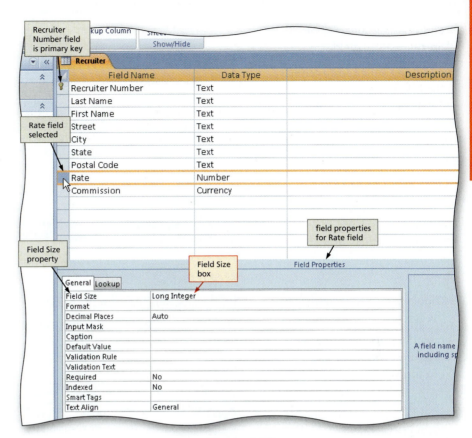

Figure 1–69

3

- Click the Field Size box to display the Field Size box arrow.

- Click the Field Size box arrow to display the Field Size box menu (Figure 1–70).

Q&A

What would happen if I left the field size set to Integer?

If the field size is Integer, no decimal places can be stored. Thus a value of .10 would be stored as 0. If you enter your rates and the values all appear as 0, chances are you did not change the field size.

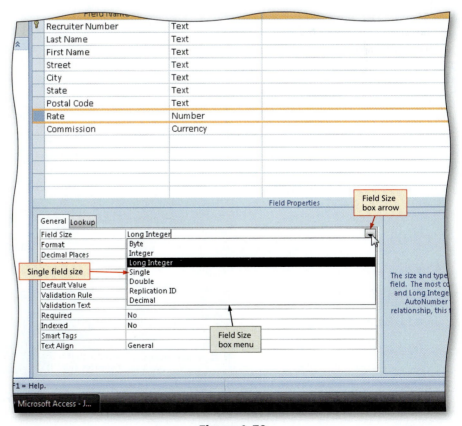

Figure 1–70

4

- Click Single to select single precision as the field size.

- Click the Format box to display the Format box arrow (Figure 1–71).

- Click the Format box arrow to open the Format box menu.

Figure 1–71

5

- Click Fixed to select fixed as the format.

- Click the Decimal Places box to display the Decimal Places box arrow.

- Click the Decimal Places box arrow to enter the number of decimal places.

- Click 2 to select 2 as the number of decimal places.

- Click the Save button to save your changes (Figure 1–72).

Q&A

What is the purpose of the error checking button?

You changed the number of decimal places. The error checking button gives you a quick way of making the same change everywhere Rate appears. So far, you have not added any data, nor have you created any forms or reports that use the Rate field, so no such changes are necessary.

Figure 1–72

6

- Close the Recruiter table by clicking the Close 'Recruiter' button (Figure 1–73).

Figure 1–73

To Add Records to an Additional Table

The following steps add the records shown in Figure 1–74 to the Recruiter table.

Recruiter Nu ▾	Last Name ▾	First Name ▾	Street ▾	City ▾	State ▾	Postal Code ▾	Rate ▾	Commission ▾
21	Kerry	Alyssa	261 Pointer	Tourin	CO	80416	0.10	$17,600.00
24	Reeves	Camden	3135 Brill	Denton	CO	80412	0.10	$19,900.00
27	Fernandez	Jaime	265 Maxwell	Charleston	CO	80380	0.09	$9,450.00
34	Lee	Jan	1827 Oak	Denton	CO	80413	0.08	$0.00

Figure 1–74

1

- Open the Recruiter table in Datasheet view by right-clicking the Recruiter table in the Navigation Pane and then clicking Open on the shortcut menu.

- Enter the Recruiter data from Figure 1–74 (Figure 1–75).

Experiment

- Click in the Rate field on any of the records. Be sure the Datasheet tab is selected. Click the Format box arrow and then click each of the formats in the Format box menu to see the effect on the values in the Rate field. When finished, click Fixed in the Format box menu.

Figure 1–75

2

- Click the Close 'Recruiter' button to close the table and remove the datasheet from the screen.

Creating a Report

JSP Recruiters needs the following reports. You will create the four reports shown in Figure 1–76 in this section.

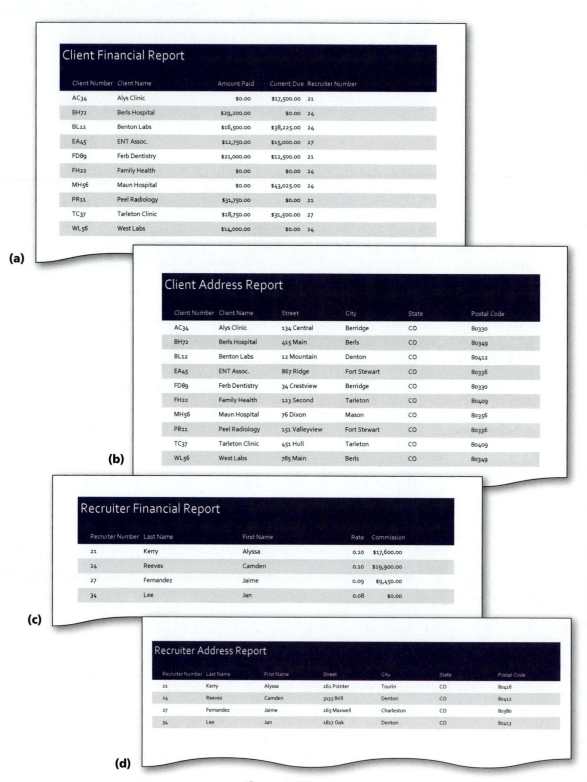

Figure 1–76

To Create a Report

You will first create the report shown in Figure 1–76a. The records in the report are sorted (ordered) by Client Number. To ensure that the records appear in this order, you will specify that the records are to be sorted on the Client Number field. The following steps create the report in Figure 1–76a.

1

- Be sure the Client table is selected in the Navigation Pane.

- Click Create on the Ribbon to display the Create tab.

- Click the Report Wizard button to display the Report Wizard dialog box (Figure 1–77).

Q&A What would have happened if the Recruiter table were selected instead of the Client table?

The list of available fields would have contained fields from the Recruiter table rather than the Client table.

Q&A If the list contained Recruiter table fields, how could I make it contain Client table fields?

Click the arrow in the Tables/Queries box and then click the Client table in the list that appears.

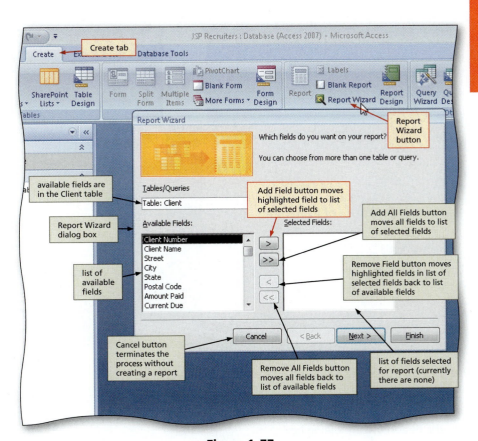

Figure 1–77

2

- Click the Add Field button to add the Client Number field.

- Click the Add Field button to add the Client Name field.

- Click the Amount Paid field, and then click the Add Field button to add the Amount Paid field.

- Click the Add Field button to add the Current Due field.

- Click the Add Field button to add the Recruiter Number field (Figure 1–78).

Figure 1–78

3

- Click the Next button to display the next Report Wizard screen (Figure 1–79).

Q&A What is grouping?

Grouping means creating separate collections of records sharing some common characteristic. For example, you might want to group clients in the same Postal code or that have the same recruiter.

Q&A What if I realize that I have selected the wrong fields?

You can click the Back button to return to the previous screen and then correct the list of fields. You also could click the Cancel button and start over.

Figure 1–79

4

- Because you will not specify any grouping, click the Next button in the Report Wizard dialog box to display the next Report Wizard screen.

- Click the box arrow in the text box labeled 1 to display a list of available fields for sorting (Figure 1–80).

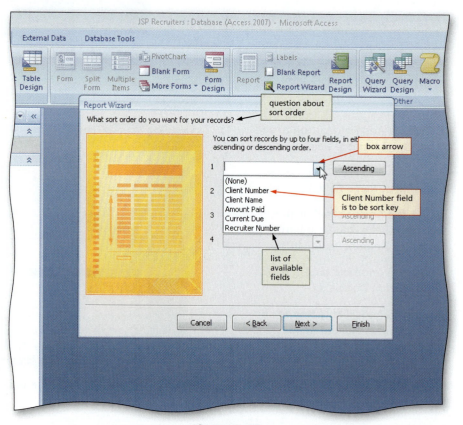

Figure 1–80

5

• Click the Client Number field to
select the field as the sort key
(Figure 1–81).

What if I want Descending order?

Click the Ascending button next to
the sort key to change Ascending
order to Descending. If you decide
you want Ascending after all, click
the button a second time.

Figure 1–81

6

• Click the Next button to display
the next Report Wizard screen
(Figure 1–82).

 Experiment

• Click different layouts and
orientations and observe the effect
on the sample report. When you
have finished experimenting, click
the Tabular option button for
the layout and the Portrait option
button for the orientation.

Figure 1–82

- Make sure that Tabular is selected as the Layout. (If it is not, click the Tabular option button to select Tabular layout.)

- Make sure Portrait is selected as the Orientation. (If it is not, click the Portrait option button to select Portrait orientation.)

- Click the Next button to display the next Report Wizard screen (Figure 1–83).

Experiment

- Click different styles and observe the effect on the sample report. When you have finished experimenting, click the Module style.

Figure 1–83

- Be sure the Module style is selected. (If it is not, click Module to select the Module style.)

- Click the Next button to display the next Report Wizard screen (Figure 1–84).

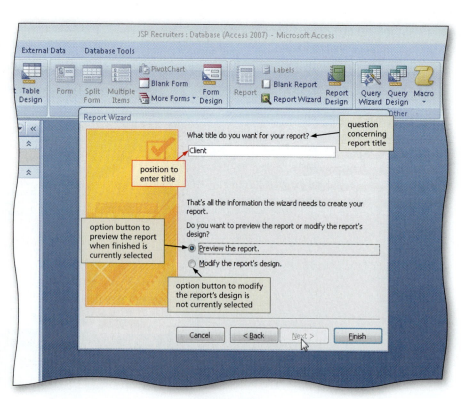

Figure 1–84

9

- Erase the current title, and then type `Client Financial Report` as the new title (Figure 1–85).

Q&A How do I erase the title?

You can highlight the existing title and then press the DELETE key. You can click at the end of the title and repeatedly press the BACKSPACE key. You can click at the beginning of the title and repeatedly press the DELETE key.

Q&A Could I just click after the word, Client, press the Spacebar, and then type Financial Report?

Yes. In general, you can edit the current title to produce the new title using the method with which you are most comfortable.

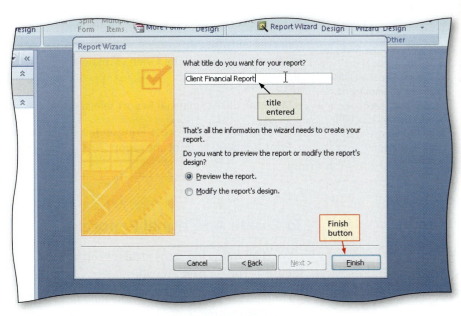

Figure 1–85

- Click the Finish button to produce the report (Figure 1–86).

10

- Click the Close 'Client Financial Report' button to remove the report from the screen.

Q&A Why didn't I have to save the report?

The Report Wizard saves the report automatically.

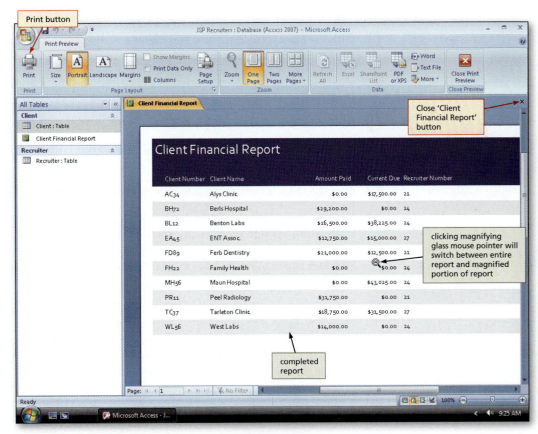

Figure 1–86

BTW

Quick Reference
For a table that lists how to complete the tasks covered in this book using the mouse, Ribbon, shortcut menu, and keyboard, see the Quick Reference Summary at the back of this book, or visit the Access 2007 Quick Reference Web page (scsite.com/ac2007/qr).

To Print a Report

Once you have created a report, you can print it at any time. The printed layout will reflect the layout you created. The data in the report will always reflect current data. The following step prints the Client Financial Report.

- With the Client Financial Report selected in the Navigation Pane, click the Office Button.

- Point to the arrow next to Print on the Office Button menu and then click Quick Print on the Print submenu to print the report.

To Create Additional Reports

The following steps produce the reports shown in Figure 1–76b, Figure 1–76c, and Figure 1–76d on page AC 50.

1 If necessary, click Create on the Ribbon to display the Create tab, and then click the Report Wizard button to display the Report Wizard dialog box.

2 Add the Client Number, Client Name, Street, City, State, and Postal Code fields by clicking each field and then clicking the Add Field button.

3 Click the Next button to move to the screen asking about grouping, and then click the Next button a second time to move to the screen asking about sort order.

4 Click the box arrow in the text box labeled 1, click the Client Number field to select the field as the sort key, and then click the Next button.

5 Make sure that Tabular is selected as the Layout and that Portrait is selected as the Orientation, and then click the Next button.

6 Make sure the Module style is selected, and then click the Next button.

7 Enter `Client Address Report` as the title and click the Finish button to produce the report.

8 Click the Close 'Client Address Report' button to close the Print Preview window.

9 Click the Recruiter table in the Navigation Pane, and then use the techniques shown in Steps 1 through 8 to produce the Recruiter Financial Report. The report is to contain the Recruiter Number, Last Name, First Name, Rate, and Commission fields. It is to be sorted by Recruiter Number. It is to have tabular layout, portrait orientation, and the Module Style. The title is to be Recruiter Financial Report.

10 With the Recruiter table selected in the Navigation Pane, use the techniques shown in Steps 1 through 8 to produce the Recruiter Address Report. The report is to contain the Recruiter Number, Last Name, First Name, Street, City, State, and Postal Code fields. It is to be sorted by Recruiter Number. It is to have tabular layout, landscape orientation, and the Module Style. The title is to be Recruiter Address Report.

11 Click the Close 'Recruiter Address Report' button to close the Print Preview window.

Using a Form to View Data

In Datasheet view, you can view many records at once. If there are many fields, however, only some of the fields in each record might be visible at a time. In **Form view**, where data is displayed in a form on the screen, you usually can see all the fields, but only for one record. To get the advantages from both, many database management systems allow you to easily switch between Datasheet view and Form view while maintaining position within the database. In Access 2007, you can view both a datasheet and a form simultaneously using a split form.

To Create a Split Form

A **split form** combines both a datasheet and a form, thus giving the advantages of both views. The following steps create a split form.

1
- Select the Client table in the Navigation Pane.
- If necessary, click Create on the Ribbon to display the Create tab (Figure 1–87).

Figure 1–87

2
- Click the Split Form button to create a split form. If a Field List appears, click its Close button to remove the Field List from the screen (Figure 1–88).

Q&A

Is the form automatically saved the way the report was created when I used the Report Wizard?

No. You must take specific action if you wish to save the form.

Figure 1–88

Click the Save button to display the Save As dialog box (Figure 1–89).

Figure 1–89

Type Client Form as the form name, and then click the OK button to save the form.

If the form appears in Layout view, click the Form View button on the Access status bar to display the form in Form view (Figure 1–90).

How can I recognize Layout view?

There are three ways. The left end of the Status bar will contain the words Layout View. There will be shading around the outside of the selected field in the form. The Layout View button will be selected in the right end of the Status bar.

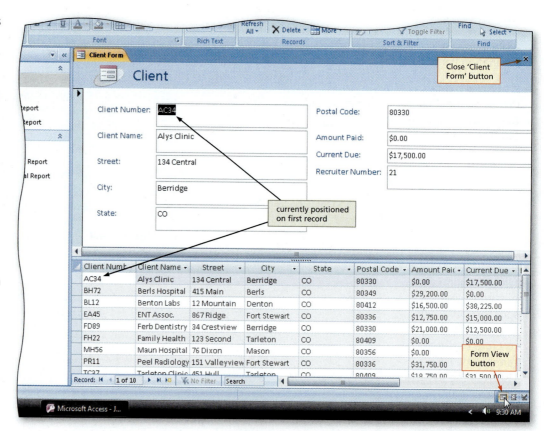

Figure 1–90

To Use a Split Form

After you have saved a form, you can use it at any time by right-clicking the form in the Navigation Pane and then clicking Open in the shortcut menu. If you plan to use the form to enter data, you must ensure you are viewing the form in Form view.

1

● Click the Next Record button four times to move to record 5 (Figure 1–91).

Q&A I inadvertently closed the form at the end of the previous steps. What should I do?

Right-click the form in the Navigation Pane and then click Open on the shortcut menu.

Q&A Do I have to take any special action for the form to be positioned on the same record as the datasheet?

No. The advantage to the split form is that changing the position on either the datasheet or the form automatically changes the position on the other.

Figure 1–91

2

● Click the Postal Code field on the second record in the data-sheet to select the second record in both the datasheet and the form (Figure 1–92).

🔍 Experiment

● Click several fields in various records in the datasheet and observe the effect on the form.

3

● Click the Close 'Client Form' button to remove the form from the screen.

Figure 1–92

BTW

Certification
The Microsoft Certified Application Specialist (MCAS) program provides an opportunity for you to obtain a valuable industry credential — proof that you have the Access 2007 skills required by employers. For more information see Appendix G or visit the Access 2007 Certification Web page (scsite.com/ ac2007/cert).

Changing Document Properties

Access helps you organize and identify your databases by using **database properties,** which are the details about a file. Database properties, also known as **metadata,** can include such information as the project author, title, or subject. **Keywords** are words or phrases that further describe the database. For example, a class name or database topic can describe the file's purpose or content.

Five different types of document properties exist, but the more common ones used in this book are standard and automatically updated properties. **Standard properties** are associated with all Microsoft Office documents and include author, title, and subject. **Automatically updated properties** include file system properties, such as the date you create or change a file, and statistics, such as the file size.

To Change Database Properties

The Database Properties dialog box contains areas where you can view and enter document properties. You can view and change information in this dialog box at any time while you are working on your database. It is a good idea to add your name and class name as database properties. The following steps use the Properties dialog box to change database properties.

1

• Click the Office Button to display the Office Button menu.

• Point to Manage on the Office Button menu to display the Manage submenu (Figure 1–93).

Q&A What other types of actions besides changing properties can you take to prepare a database for distribution?

The Manage submenu provides commands to compact and repair a database as well as to back up a database.

Figure 1–93

2

• Click Database Properties on the Manage submenu to display the JSP Recruiters.accdb Properties dialog box (Figure 1–94).

Q&A Why are some of the document properties in my Properties dialog box already filled in?

The person who installed Microsoft Office 2007 on your computer or network may have set or customized the properties.

Figure 1–94

3

- If necessary, click the Summary tab.

- Click the Author text box and then type your name as the Author property. If a name already is displayed in the Author text box, delete it before typing your name.

- Click the Subject text box, if necessary delete any existing text, and then type your course and section as the Subject property.

- Click the Keywords text box, if necessary delete any existing text, and then type `Healthcare, Recruiter` as the Keywords property (Figure 1–95).

What types of properties does Access collect automatically?

Access records such details as when the database was created, when it was last modified, total editing time, and the various objects contained in the database.

Figure 1–95

4

- Click the OK button to save your changes and remove the JSP Recruiters.accdb Properties dialog box from the screen.

Access Help

At any time while using Access, you can find answers to questions and display information about various topics through **Access Help**. Used properly, this form of assistance can increase your productivity and reduce your frustrations by minimizing the time you spend learning how to use Access.

This section introduces you to Access Help. Additional information about using Access Help is available in Appendix C.

To Search for Access Help

Using Access Help, you can search for information based on phrases, such as create a form or change a data type, or key terms, such as copy, save, or format. Access Help responds with a list of search results displayed as links to a variety of resources. The following steps, which use Access Help to search for information about creating a form, assume you are connected to the Internet.

1
- Click the Microsoft Office Access Help button near the upper-right corner of the Access window to open the Access Help window.

- Type create a form in the 'Type words to search for' text box at the top of the Access Help window (Figure 1–96).

Figure 1–96

2
- Press the ENTER key to display the search results.

- Click the Maximize button on the Access Help window title bar to maximize the Help window unless it is already maximized (Figure 1–97).

Q&A | Where is the Access window with the JSP Recruiters database?

Access is open in the background, but the Access Help window sits on top of the Microsoft Access window. When the Access Help window is closed, the database will reappear.

Figure 1–97

3

- Click the 'Create a split form' link to display information regarding creating a split form (Figure 1–98).

Q&A

What is the purpose of the buttons at the top of the Access Help window?

Use the buttons in the upper-left corner of the Access Help window to navigate through the Help system, change the display, show the Access Help table of contents, and print the contents of the window.

4

- Click the Close button on the Access Help window title bar to close the Access Help window and make the database active.

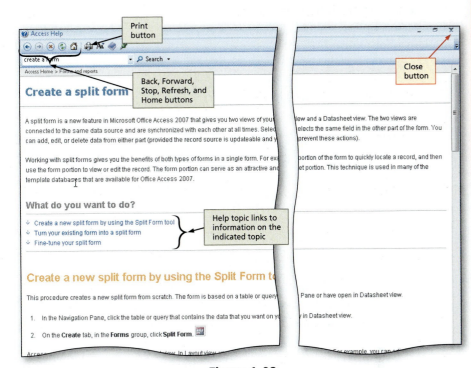

Figure 1–98

Other Ways
1. Press F1

To Quit Access

You saved all your changes and are ready to quit Access. The following step quits Access.

1 Click the Close button on the right side of the Access title bar to quit Access.

Chapter Summary

In this chapter you have learned to design a database, create an Access database, create tables and add records to them, print the contents of tables, create reports, and create forms. The items listed below include all the new Access skills you have learned in this chapter.

1. Start Access (AC 12)
2. Create a Database Using a Template (AC 13)
3. Create a Database (AC 14)
4. Define the Fields in a Table (AC 24)
5. Create a Table Using a Template (AC 26)
6. Save a Table (AC 27)
7. Change the Primary Key (AC 28)
8. Add Records to a Table (AC 30)
9. Close a Table (AC 35)
10. Quit Access (AC 36)
11. Start Access (AC 36)
12. Open a Database from Access (AC 37)
13. Add Additional Records to a Table (AC 38)
14. Preview and Print the Contents of a Table (AC 41)
15. Create an Additional Table (AC 44)
16. Modify the Primary Key and Field Properties (AC 46)
17. Add Records to an Additional Table (AC 49)
18. Create a Report (AC 51)
19. Print a Report (AC 56)

If you have a SAM user profile, you may have access to hands-on instruction, practice, and assessment. Log in to your SAM account (http://sam2007.course.com) to launch any assigned training activities or exams that relate to the skills covered in this chapter.

Learn It Online

Test your knowledge of chapter content and key terms.

Instructions: To complete the Learn It Online exercises, start your browser, click the Address bar, and then enter the Web address scsite.com/ac2007/learn. When the Access 2007 Learn It Online page is displayed, click the link for the exercise you want to complete and then read the instructions.

Chapter Reinforcement TF, MC, and SA
A series of true/false, multiple choice, and short answer questions that test your knowledge of the chapter content.

Flash Cards
An interactive learning environment where you identify chapter key terms associated with displayed definitions.

Practice Test
A series of multiple choice questions that test your knowledge of chapter content and key terms.

Who Wants To Be a Computer Genius?
An interactive game that challenges your knowledge of chapter content in the style of a television quiz show.

Wheel of Terms
An interactive game that challenges your knowledge of chapter key terms in the style of the television show *Wheel of Fortune*.

Crossword Puzzle Challenge
A crossword puzzle that challenges your knowledge of key terms presented in the chapter.

Apply Your Knowledge

Reinforce the skills and apply the concepts you learned in this chapter.

Changing Data, Creating a Form, and Creating a Report
Instructions: Start Access. Open the The Bike Delivers database. See the inside back cover of this book for instructions for downloading the Data Files for Students, or see your instructor for information on accessing the files required in this book.

The Bike Delivers uses motorbikes to provide courier services for local businesses. The Bike Delivers has a database that keeps track of its couriers and customers. The database has two tables. The Customer table (Figure 1–99a) contains data on the customers who use the services of The Bike Delivers. The Courier table (Figure 1–99b) contains data on the individuals employed by The Bike Delivers.

(a) Customer Table

(b) Courier Table

Figure 1–99

Perform the following tasks:

1. Open the Customer table and change the Courier Number for customer KL55 to 113.

2. Close the Customer table.

3. Create a split form for the Courier table. Use the name Courier for the form.

4. Open the form you created and change the street address for Michelle Hyde to 65 Park.

5. Close the Courier form.

6. Create the report shown in Figure 1–100 for the Customer table. The report uses the Module style.

7. Change the database properties, as specified by your instructor. Submit the revised database in the format specified by your instructor.

Figure 1–100

Extend Your Knowledge

Extend the skills you learned in this chapter and experiment with new skills. You may need to use Help to complete the assignment.

Changing Formats and Creating Grouped and Sorted Reports

Instructions: Start Access. Open the Camden Scott College database. See the inside back cover of this book for instructions for downloading the Data Files for Students, or see your instructor for information on accessing the files required in this book.

Continued >

Extend Your Knowledge *continued*

Camden Scott College is a small liberal arts college. The Human Resources Director has created an Access database in which to store information about candidates applying for faculty positions. You will make some changes to the Candidate table so that it looks like that shown in Figure 1–101 and create a report that both groups records and sorts them in ascending order.

Figure 1–101

Perform the following tasks:

1. Open the Candidate table in Datasheet view and change the column heading for the ID field to Candidate ID.

2. Save the change and open the table in Design view.

3. Select a format for the App Date field that will produce the look shown in Figure 1–101.

4. Change the data type for the Documentation field so that it will match that shown in Figure 1–101.

5. Save the changes.

6. Open the table in Datasheet view. The Human Resources department has received an application from Edward Klinger. Edward applied for the same position as Sarah Klinger on the same date as Sarah. Edward's phone number is 610-555-1111. He did submit all his documentation with his application. Add this record.

7. Add the Quick Print button to the Quick Access Toolbar.

8. Create a report for the Candidate table that lists the Department Code, App Date, Last Name, and First Name. Group the report by Department Code. Sort the report by App Date, Last Name, and then First Name. Choose your own report style and use Candidate by Department as the title of the report.

9. Remove the Quick Print button from the Quick Access Toolbar.

10. Change the database properties, as specified by your instructor. Submit the revised database in the format specified by your instructor.

Make It Right

Analyze a database and correct all errors and/or improve the design.

Correcting Errors in the Table Structure

Instructions: Start Access. Open the SciFi Scene database. See the inside back cover of this book for instructions for downloading the Data Files for Students, or see your instructor for information on accessing the files required in this book.

SciFi Scene is a database containing information on science fiction books. The Book table shown in Figure 1–102 contains a number of errors in the table structure. You are to correct these errors before any additional records can be added to the table. Book Code, not ID, is the primary key for the Book table. The column heading Titel is misspelled. The On Hand field represents the number of books on hand. The field will be used in arithmetic operations. Only whole numbers should be stored in the field. The Price field represents the price of the book. The current data type does not reflect this information.

Change the database properties, as specified by your instructor. Submit the revised database in the format specified by your instructor.

Figure 1–102

In the Lab

Design, create, modify, and/or use a database using the guidelines, concepts, and skills presented in this chapter. Labs are listed in order of increasing difficulty.

Lab 1: Creating the JMS TechWizards Database

Problem: JMS TechWizards is a local company that provides technical services to several small businesses in the area. The company currently keeps its records in two Excel workbooks. One Excel workbook (Figure 1–103a) contains information on the clients that JMS TechWizards serves. The other Excel workbook (Figure 1–103b) contains information on the technicians that JMS employs. JMS would like to store this data in a database and has asked for your help.

(a) Client Data (Excel Workbook)

(b) Technician Data (Excel Workbook)

Figure 1–103

Continued >

In the Lab *continued*

Instructions: Perform the following tasks:

1. Create a new database in which to store all the objects related to the technical services data. Call the database JMS TechWizards.

2. Create a table in which to store the data related to clients. Use the name Client for the table. The fields for the Client table are: Client Number, Client Name, Street, City, State, Postal Code, Telephone Number, Billed, Paid, and Technician Number. Client Number is the primary key. The Billed and Paid fields are currency data type.

3. Create a table in which to store the data related to technicians. Use the name Technician for the table. The fields for the Technician table are: Technician Number, Last Name, First Name, Street, City, State, Postal Code, Hourly Rate, and YTD Earnings. The primary key for the Technician table is Technician Number. Hourly rate and YTD Earnings are currency data type.

4. Add the data from the Client workbook in Figure 1–103a to the Client table.

5. Add the data from the Technician workbook in Figure 1–103b to the Technician table.

6. Create and save the reports shown in Figure 1–104a for the Client table and Figure 1–104b for the Technician table.

7. Change the database properties, as specified by your instructor. Submit the revised database in the format specified by your instructor.

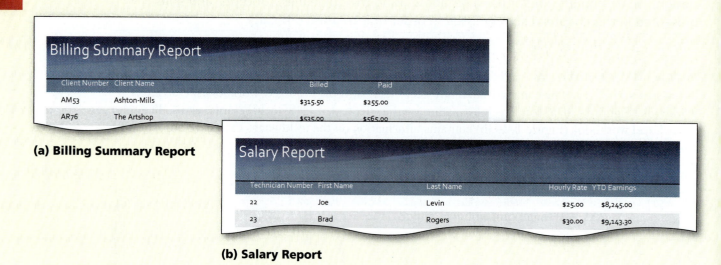

(a) Billing Summary Report

(b) Salary Report

Figure 1–104

In the Lab

Lab 2: Creating the Hockey Fan Zone Database

Problem: Your town has a minor league hockey team. The team store sells a variety of items with the team logo. The store purchases the items from suppliers that deal in specialty items for sports teams. Currently, the information about the items and suppliers is stored in the Excel workbook shown in Figure 1–105. You work part-time at the store, and your boss has asked you to create a database that will store the item and supplier information. You have already determined that you need two tables: an Item table and a Supplier table in which to store the information.

Instructions: Perform the following tasks:

1. Design a new database in which to store all the objects related to the items for sale. Call the database Hockey Fan Zone.

2. Use the information shown in Figure 1–105 to determine the primary keys and determine additional fields. Then, determine the relationships among tables and the data types.

3. Create the Item table using the information shown in Figure 1–105.

4. Create the Supplier table using the information shown in Figure 1–105.

5. Add the appropriate data to the Item table.

6. Add the appropriate data to the Supplier table.

7. Create a split form for the Item table. Use the name Item for the form.

8. Create the report shown in Figure 1–106 for the Item table.

9. Change the database properties, as specified by your instructor. Submit the database in the format specified by your instructor.

	A	B	C	D	E	F	G	H
1	Item Number	Description	On Hand	Cost	Selling Price	Supplier Code	Supplier Name	Telephone Number
2	3663	Ball Cap	30	$11.15	$18.95	LG	Logo Goods	517-555-3853
3	3683	Bumper Sticker	50	$0.95	$1.50	MN	Mary's Novelties	317-555-4747
4	4563	Earrings	10	$4.50	$7.00	LG	Logo Goods	517-555-3853
5	4593	Foam Finger	25	$2.95	$5.00	LG	Logo Goods	517-555-3853
6	5923	Jersey	12	$21.45	$24.75	AC	Ace Clothes	616-555-9228
7	6189	Koozies	35	$2.00	$4.00	MN	Mary's Novelties	317-555-4747
8	6343	Note Cube	7	$5.75	$8.00	MN	Mary's Novelties	317-555-4747
9	7810	Tee Shirt	32	$9.50	$14.95	AC	Ace Clothes	616-555-9228
10	7930	Visor	9	$11.95	$17.00	LG	Logo Goods	517-555-3853
11								

Figure 1–105

Inventory Status Report

Item Number	Description	On Hand	Cost
3663	Ball Cap	30	$11.15
3683	Bumper Sticker	50	$0.95
4563	Earrings	10	$4.50
4593	Foam Finger	25	$2.95
5923	Jersey	12	$21.45
6189	Koozies	35	$2.00
6343	Note Cube	7	$5.75
7810	Tee Shirt	32	$9.50
7930	Visor	9	$11.95

Figure 1–106

In the Lab

Lab 3: Creating the Ada Beauty Supply Database

Problem: A distribution company supplies local beauty salons with items needed in the beauty industry. The distributor employs sales representatives who receive a base salary as well as a commission on sales. Currently, the distributor keeps data on customers and sales reps in two Word documents and two Excel workbooks.

Instructions: Using the data shown in Figure 1–107 on the next page, design the Ada Beauty Supply database. Use the database design guidelines in this chapter to help you in the design process.

Continued >

In the Lab *continued*

Customer Number	Customer Name	Street	Telephone
AM23	Amy's Salon	223 Johnson	555-2150
BB34	Bob the Barber	1939 Jackson	555-1939
BL15	Blondie's	3294 Devon	555-7510
CM09	Cut Mane	3140 Halsted	555-0604
CS12	Curl n Style	1632 Clark	555-0804
EG07	Elegante	1805 Boardway	555-1404
JS34	Just Cuts	2200 Lawrence	555-0313
LB20	Le Beauty	13 Devon	555-5161
NC25	Nancy's Place	1027 Wells	555-4210
RD03	Rose's Day Spa	787 Monroe	555-7657
TT21	Tan and Tone	1939 Congress	555-6554

(a) Customer Address Information (Word table)

	A	B	C	D	E
1	Customer Number	Customer Name	Balance	Amount Paid	Sales Rep Num
2	AM23	Amy's Salon	$195.00	$1,695.00	44
3	BB34	Bob the Barber	$150.00	$0.00	51
4	BL15	Blondie's	$555.00	$1,350.00	49
5	CM09	Cut Mane	$295.00	$1,080.00	51
6	CS12	Curl n Style	$145.00	$710.00	49
7	EG07	Elegante	$0.00	$1,700.00	44
8	JS34	Just Cuts	$360.00	$700.00	49
9	LB20	Le Beauty	$200.00	$1,250.00	51
10	NC25	Nancy's Place	$240.00	$550.00	44
11	RD03	Rose's Day Spa	$0.00	$975.00	51
12	TT21	Tan and Tone	$160.00	$725.00	44

(c) Customer Financial Information (Excel Workbook)

Sales Rep Number	Last Name	First Name	Street	City	State	Postal Code
44	Jones	Pat	43 Third	Lawncrest	WA	98084
49	Gupta	Pinn	678 Hillcrest	Manton	WA	98085
51	Ortiz	Gabe	982 Victoria	Lawncrest	WA	98084
55	Sinson	Terry	45 Elm	Manton	WA	98084

(b) Sales Rep Address Information (Word table)

	A	B	C	D	E	F
1	Sales Rep Number	Last Name	First Name	Salary	Comm Rate	Commission
2	44	Jones	Pat	$ 23,000.00	0.05	$613.50
3	49	Gupta	Pinn	$ 24,000.00	0.06	$616.60
4	51	Ortiz	Gabe	$ 22,500.00	0.05	$492.75
5	55	Sinson	Terry	$ 20,000.00	0.05	$0.00

(d) Sales Rep Financial Information (Excel Workbook)

Figure 1–107

When you have completed the database design, create the database, create the tables, and add the data to the appropriate tables. Be sure to determine the correct data types.

Finally, prepare the Customer Status Report shown in Figure 1–108a and the Sales Rep Salary Report shown in Figure 1–108b. Change the database properties, as specified by your instructor. Submit the database in the format specified by your instructor.

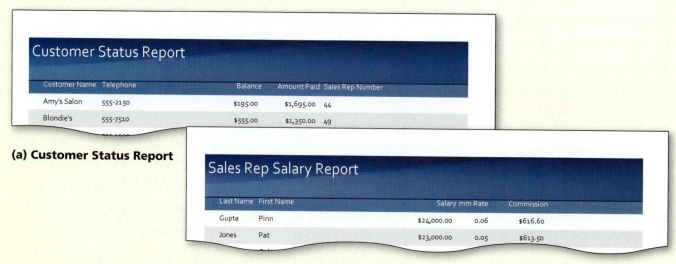

Customer Status Report

Customer Name	Telephone	Balance	Amount Paid	Sales Rep Number
Amy's Salon	555-2150	$195.00	$1,695.00	44
Blondie's	555-7510	$555.00	$1,350.00	49

(a) Customer Status Report

Sales Rep Salary Report

Last Name	First Name	Salary	mm Rate	Commission
Gupta	Pinn	$24,000.00	0.06	$616.60
Jones	Pat	$23,000.00	0.05	$613.50

(b) Sales Rep Salary Report

Figure 1–108

Cases and Places

Apply your creative thinking and problem solving skills to design and implement a solution.

• EASIER   •• MORE DIFFICULT

• 1: Design and Create an E-Commerce Database

Students often have very little money to furnish dorm rooms and apartments. You and two of your friends have decided to use the skills you learned in your e-commerce class to create a Web site specifically for college students to buy and sell used household furnishings.

Design and create a database to store the data that you need to manage this new business. Then create the necessary tables and enter the data from the Case 1-1 Second-Hand Goods document. See the inside back cover of this book for instructions for downloading the Data Files for Students, or see your instructor for information on accessing the files required in this book. Submit your assignment in the format specified by your instructor.

• 2: Design and Create a Rental Database

You are a part-time employee of BeachCondo Rentals. BeachCondo Rentals provides a rental service for condo owners who want to rent their units. The company rents units by the week. Currently, the company keeps information about its rentals in an Excel workbook.

Design and create a database to store the rental data. Then create the necessary tables and enter the data from the Case 1-2 BeachCondo Rentals workbook. See the inside back cover of this book for instructions for downloading the Data Files for Students, or see your instructor for information on accessing the files required in this book. Create an Available Rentals Report that lists the unit number, weekly rate, and owner number. Submit your assignment in the format specified by your instructor.

•• 3: Design and Create a Restaurant Database

Your school is sponsoring a conference that will draw participants from a wide geographical area. The conference director has asked for your help in preparing a database of restaurants that might be of interest to the participants. At a minimum, she needs to know the following: the type of restaurant (vegetarian, fast-food, fine dining, and so on), street address, telephone number, and opening and closing times and days. Because most of the participants will stay on campus, she also would like to know the approximate distance from campus. Additionally, she would like to know about any unique or special features the restaurants may have.

Design and create a database to meet the conference director's needs. Create the necessary tables, determine the necessary fields, enter some sample data, and prepare a sample report to show the director. Submit your assignment in the format specified by your instructor.

•• 4: Design and Create a Database to Help You Find a Job

Make It Personal

Conducting a job search requires careful preparation. In addition to preparing a resume and cover letter, you will need to research the companies for which you are interested in working and contact these companies to let them know of your interest and qualifications.

Microsoft Access includes a Contacts table template that can create a table that will help you keep track of your job contacts. Create a database to keep track of the companies that are of interest to you. Submit your assignment in the format specified by your instructor.

Continued >

STUDENT ASSIGNMENTS

Cases and Places *continued*

•• 5: Design a Database that Tracks Student Data

Working Together

Keeping track of students is an enormous task for school administrators. Microsoft Access can help school administrators manage student data. The Database Wizard includes a Students template that can create a database that will maintain many different types of data on students, such as allergies, medications, and emergency contact information.

Have each member of your team explore the features of the Database Wizard and determine individually which tables and fields should be included in a Students database. As a group, review your choices and decide on one common design. Prepare a short paper for your instructor that explains why your team chose the particular database design.

After agreeing on the database design, assign one member to create the database using the Database Wizard. Every other team member should contribute data and add the data to the database. Submit your assignment in the format specified by your instructor.

2 Querying a Database

Objectives

You will have mastered the material in this chapter when you can:

- Create queries using the Simple Query Wizard
- Print query results
- Create queries using Design view
- Include fields in the design grid
- Use text and numeric data in criteria
- Create and use parameter queries
- Save a query and use the saved query

- Use compound criteria in queries
- Sort data in queries
- Join tables in queries
- Create a report from a query
- Perform calculations in queries
- Calculate statistics in queries
- Create crosstab queries
- Customize the Navigation Pane

2 | Querying a Database

Introduction

A database management system such as Access offers many useful features, among them the capability of answering questions, the answers to which are found in the database. When you pose a question to Access, or any other database management system, the question is called a query. A **query** is simply a question presented in a way that Access can process.

Thus, to find the answer to a question, you first create a corresponding query using the techniques illustrated in this chapter. After you have created the query, you instruct Access to display the query results; that is, to perform the steps necessary to obtain the answer. Access then displays the answer in Datasheet view.

Project — Querying a Database

Organizations and individuals achieve several benefits from storing data in a database and using Access to manage the database. One of the most important benefits is the capability of easily finding the answers to questions such as those shown in Figure 2-1 and the following, which concern the data in the JSP Recruiters database:

1. What are the number, name, the amount paid, and the current due of client FD89?
2. Which clients' names begin with Be?
3. Which clients are located in Berridge?
4. Which clients have a current due of $0.00?
5. Which clients have an amount paid that is more than $20,000.00?
6. Which clients of recruiter 21 have an amount paid that is more than $20,000.00?
7. In what cities are all the clients located?
8. What is the total amount (amount paid + current due) for each client?
9. What is the client number and name of each client, and what is the number and name of the recruiter to whom each client is assigned?

In addition to these questions, JSP Recruiters needs to find information about clients located in a specific city, but they want to enter a different city each time they ask the question. A parameter query would enable this. The agency also has a special way it wants to summarize data. A crosstab query will present the data in the desired form.

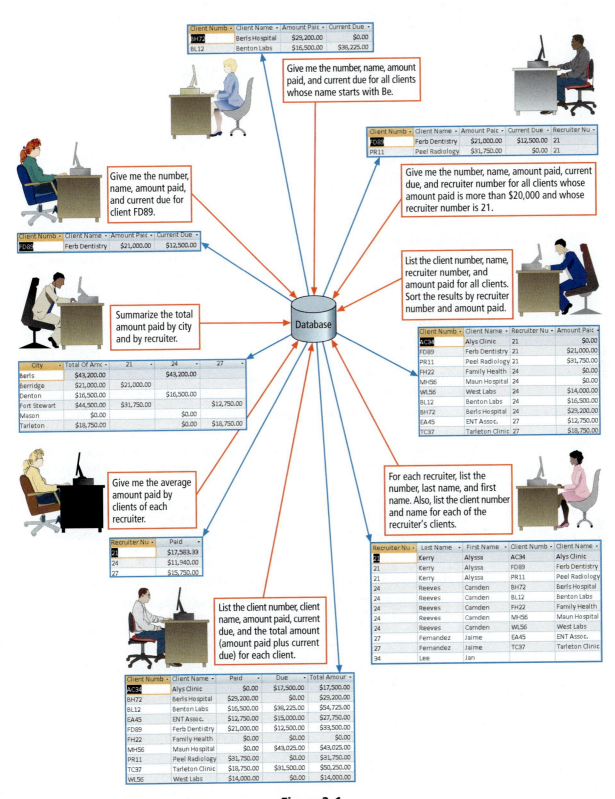

Figure 2–1

Overview

As you read this chapter, you will learn how to query a database by performing these general tasks:

- Create queries using the Simple Query Wizard and Design view
- Use criteria in queries
- Create and use parameter queries
- Sort data in queries
- Join tables in queries
- Perform calculations in queries
- Create crosstab queries

Plan Ahead

Query Design Guidelines

When posing a question to Access, you must design an appropriate query. In the process of designing a query, the decisions you make will determine the fields, tables, criteria, order, and special calculations included in the query. To design a query, you should follow these general guidelines:

1. **Identify the fields.** Examine the question or request to determine which fields from the tables in the database are involved. Examine the contents of these fields to make sure you understand how the data is stored.

2. **Identify restrictions.** Unless the question or request calls for all records, determine the restrictions, that is, the conditions records must satisfy in order to be included in the results.

3. **Determine whether special order is required.** Examine the question or request to determine whether the results must appear in some specific order.

4. **Determine whether more than one table is required.** If all the fields identified in Step 1 are in the same table, no special action is required. If this is not the case, identify all tables represented by those fields.

5. **Determine whether calculations are required.** Examine the question or request to determine whether, in addition to the fields determined in Step 1, calculations must be included. Results of mathematical operations typically are not stored in the database because they can be calculated easily when necessary. Such calculations include individual record calculations (for example, adding the values in two fields) or group calculations (for example, finding the total of the values in a particular field on all the records).

6. **If data is to be summarized, determine whether a crosstab query would be appropriate.** If data is to be grouped by two different types of information, you can use a crosstab query. You will need to identify the two types of information. One of the types will form the row headings and the other will form the column headings in the query results.

When necessary, more specific details concerning the above decisions and/or actions are presented at appropriate points in the chapter.

Starting Access

If you are using a computer to step through the project in this chapter and you want your screen to match the figures in this book, you should change your screen's resolution to 1024 × 768. For information about how to change a computer's resolution, read Appendix E.

To Start Access

The following steps, which assume Windows Vista is running, start Access.

Note: If you are using Windows XP, see Appendix F for alternate steps.

1 Click the Start button on the Windows Vista taskbar to display the Start menu.

2 Click All Programs at the bottom of the left Pane on the Start menu to display the All Programs list and then click Microsoft Office in the All Programs list to display the Microsoft Office list.

3 Click Microsoft Office Access 2007 on the Microsoft Office list to start Access and display the Getting Started with Microsoft Office Access window.

4 If the Access window is not maximized, click the Maximize button on its title bar to maximize the window.

To Open a Database

In Chapter 1, you created your database on a USB flash drive using the file name, JSP Recruiters. There are two ways to open the file containing your database. If the file you created appears in the Recent Documents list, you can click it to open the file. If not, you can use the More button to open the file. The following steps use the More button to open the JSP Recruiters database from the USB flash drive.

Note: If you are using Windows XP, see Appendix F for alternate steps.

1 With your USB flash drive connected to one of the computer's USB ports, click the More button to display the Open dialog box.

2 If the Folders list is displayed below the Folders button, click the Folders button to remove the Folders list.

3 If necessary, click Computer in the Favorite Links section and then double-click UDISK 2.0 (E:) to select the USB flash drive, Drive E in this case, as the new open location. (Your drive letter might be different.)

4 Click JSP Recruiters to select the file name.

5 Click the Open button to open the database.

6 If a Security Warning appears, click the Options button to display the Microsoft Office Security Options dialog box.

7 With the option button to enable this content selected, click the OK button to enable the content.

Creating Queries

Queries are simply questions, the answers to which are in the database. Access contains a powerful query feature. Through the use of this feature, you can find the answers to a wide variety of complex questions.

To Use the Simple Query Wizard to Create a Query

Once you have examined the question you wish to ask to determine the fields involved in the question, you can begin creating the query. If there are no restrictions involved in the query, nor any special order or calculations, you can use the Simple Query wizard. The following steps use the Simple Query wizard to create a query to display the number, name, and recruiter number of all clients.

1

- If the Navigation Pane is hidden, click the Shutter Bar Open/Close Button to show the Navigation Pane.

- Be sure the Client table is selected.

- Click Create on the Ribbon to display the Create tab.

- Click the Query Wizard button on the Create tab to display the New Query dialog box (Figure 2–2).

Figure 2–2

2

- Be sure Simple Query Wizard is selected, and then click the OK button to display the Simple Query Wizard dialog box (Figure 2–3).

Q&A

This looks like the screen I saw in the Report Wizard. Do I select fields in the same way?

Yes. In fact, you will see a similar screen in other wizards and you always select the fields just as you did in the Report Wizard.

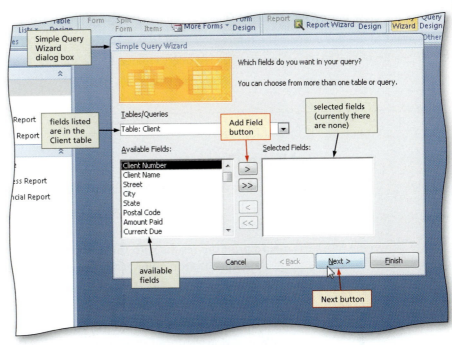

Figure 2–3

3

- Click the Add Field button to add the Client Number field.

- Click the Add Field button a second time to add the Client Name field.

- Click the Recruiter Number field, and then click the Add Field button to add the Recruiter Number field.

- Click the Next button.

- Be sure the title of the query is Client Query.

- Click the Finish button to create the query (Figure 2–4).

Figure 2–4

● Click the Close button for the Client Query to remove the query results from the screen.

If I want to use this query in the future, do I need to save the query?

Normally you would. The one exception is a query created by the wizard. The wizard automatically saves the query it creates.

Using Queries

After you have created and saved a query, you can use it in a variety of ways:

• To view the results of the query, open it by right-clicking the query in the Navigation Pane and clicking Open on the shortcut menu.

• To print the results with the query open, click the Office Button, point to Print on the Office Button menu, and then click Quick Print on the Print submenu.

• If you want to change the design of the query, right-click the query and then click Design View on the shortcut menu to open the query in Design view.

• To print the query without first opening it, be sure the query is selected in the Navigation Pane and then click the Office Button, point to Print on the Office Button menu, and then click Quick Print on the Print submenu.

You can switch between views of a query by using the View button (Figure 2–5). Clicking the arrow at the bottom of the button produces the View button menu as shown in the figure. You then click the desired view in the menu. The two views you will use in this chapter are Datasheet view (see the results) and Design view (change the design). You also can click the top part of the button, in which case, you will switch to the view identified by the icon on the button. In the figure, the button contains the icon for Design view, so clicking the button would change to Design view. For the most part, the icon on the button represents the view you want, so you can usually simply click the button.

Figure 2–5

To Use a Criterion in a Query

After you have determined the fields to be included in a query, you will determine whether there are any restrictions on the records that are to be included. For example, you might only want to include those clients whose recruiter number is 24. In such a case, you need to enter the 24 as a **criterion**, which is a condition that the records to be included must satisfy. To do so, you will open the query in Design view, enter the criterion below the appropriate field, and then view the results of the query. The following steps enter a criterion to include only the clients of recruiter 24 and then view the query results.

- Right-click Client Query to produce a shortcut menu (Figure 2–6).

Figure 2–6

- Click Design View on the shortcut menu to open the query in Design view (Figure 2–7). (Your field names may be enclosed in brackets.)

Figure 2–7

3

- Click the Criteria row in the Recruiter Number column of the grid, and then type 24 as the criterion (Figure 2–8).

Q&A

The Recruiter Number field is a text field. Do I need to enclose the value for a text field in quotation marks?

You could, but it is not necessary, because Access inserts the quotation marks for you automatically.

Figure 2–8

4

- Click the View button to display the results in Datasheet view (Figure 2–9).

Q&A

Could I click the View button arrow and then click Datasheet view?

Yes. If the icon representing the view you want appears on the View button, however, it is easier just to click the button.

Figure 2–9

5

- Close the Client Query window by clicking the Close 'Client Query' button.

- When asked if you want to save your changes, click the No button.

Q&A

If I saved the query, what would happen the next time I ran the query?

You would see only clients of recruiter 24.

Other Ways

1. Click Run button on Ribbon
2. Click Datasheet View button on status bar

To Print the Results of a Query

To print the results of a query, use the same techniques you learned in Chapter 1 on pages AC 41 and AC 42 to print the data in the table. The following steps print the current query results.

1 With the Client Query selected in the Navigation Pane, click the Office Button.

2 Point to Print on the Office Button menu.

3 Click Quick Print on the Print submenu.

To Create a Query in Design View

Most of the time you will use Design view to create queries. Once you have created a new query in Design view, you can specify fields, criteria, sorting, calculations, and so on. The following steps create a new query in Design view.

1

- Hide the Navigation Pane.

- Click Create on the Ribbon to display the Create tab.

- Click the Query Design button to create a new query (Figure 2–10).

Q&A

Is it necessary to hide the Navigation Pane?

No. It gives you more room for the query, however, so it is usually a good practice to hide it.

Figure 2–10

2

- With the Client table selected, click the Add button in the Show Table dialog box to add the Client table to the query.

- Click the Close button in the Show Table dialog box to remove the dialog box from the screen.

What if I inadvertently add the wrong table?

Right-click the table that you added in error and click Remove Table on the shortcut menu. You also can just close the query, indicate that you don't want to save it, and then start over.

- Drag the lower edge of the field box down far enough so all fields in the Client table appear (Figure 2–11).

How do I drag the lower edge?

Point to the lower edge, press and hold the left mouse button, move the mouse pointer to the new position for the lower edge, and then release the left mouse button. While the mouse pointer points to the lower edge of the field list, its shape changes to a double-headed arrow.

Is it essential that I resize the field box?

No. You can always scroll through the list of fields using the scroll bar. If you can resize the field box so all fields appear, it is usually more convenient.

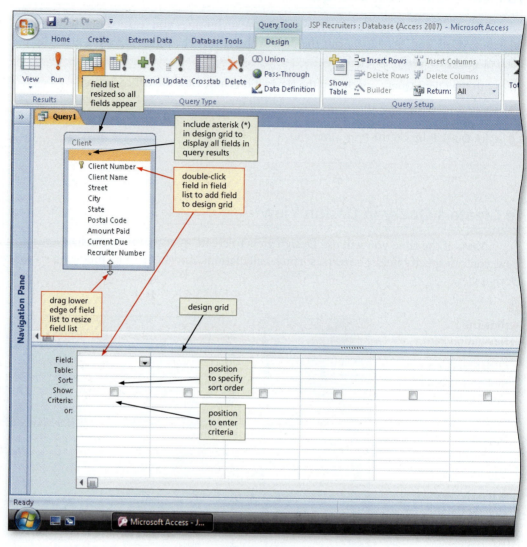

Figure 2–11

To Add Fields to the Design Grid

Once you have a new query displayed in Design view, you are ready to create the query by making entries in the design grid in the lower Pane of the window. You add the fields you want included in the Field row in the grid. Only the fields that appear in the design grid will be included in the results of the query. The following step includes the client number, client name, amount paid, and current due for all clients by adding only those fields in the design grid.

1

- Double-click the Client Number field in the field list to add the Client Number field to the query.

Q&A What if I add the wrong field?

Click just above the field name in the design grid to select the column and then press the DELETE key to remove the field.

- Double-click the Client Name field in the field list to add the Client Name field to the query.

- Add the Amount Paid field to the query by double-clicking the Amount Paid field in the field list.

- Add the Current Due field to the query (Figure 2–12).

Q&A What if I want to include all fields? Do I have to add each field individually?

No. Instead of adding individual fields, you can double-click the asterisk (*) to add the asterisk to the design grid.

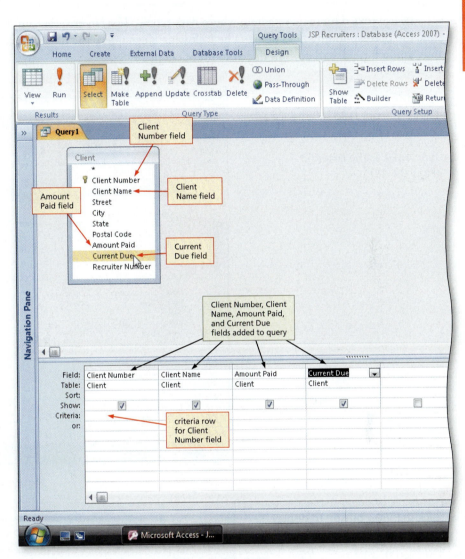

Figure 2–12

Entering Criteria

When you use queries, usually you are looking for those records that satisfy some criterion. In the simple query you created earlier, for example, you entered a criterion to restrict the records that were included to those on which the recruiter number was 24. In another query, you might want the name, amount paid, and current due amounts of the client whose number is FD89, for example, or of those clients whose names start with the letters, Be. You enter criteria in the Criteria row in the design grid below the field name to which the criterion applies. For example, to indicate that the client number must be FD89, you first must add the Client Number field to the design grid. You then would type FD89 in the Criteria row below the Client Number field.

To Use Text Data in a Criterion

To use **text data** (data in a field whose data type is Text) in criteria, simply type the text in the Criteria row below the corresponding field name. The following steps query the Client table and display the client number, client name, amount paid, and current due amount of client FD89.

1
- Click the Criteria row for the Client Number field to produce an insertion point.

- Type FD89 as the criterion (Figure 2–13).

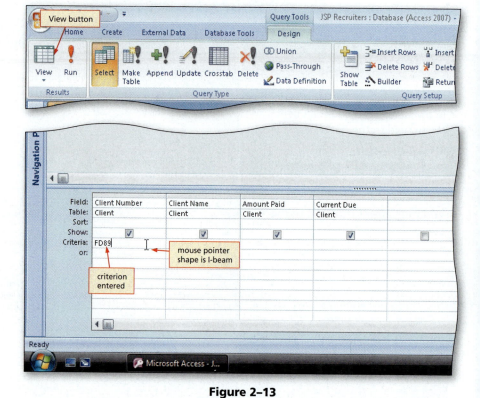

Figure 2–13

2
- Click the View button to display the query results (Figure 2–14).

Q&A
I noticed that there is a View button on both the Home tab and the Design tab. Do they both have the same effect?

Yes. Use whichever one you find most convenient.

Figure 2–14

To Use a Wildcard

Microsoft Access supports wildcards. **Wildcards** are symbols that represent any character or combination of characters. One common wildcard, the **asterisk (*)**, represents any collection of characters. Thus Be* represents the letters, Be, followed by any collection of characters. Another wildcard symbol is the **question mark (?)**, which represents any individual character. Thus T?m represents the letter, T, followed by any single character followed by the letter, m, such as Tim or Tom.

The following steps use a wildcard to find the number, name, and address of those clients whose names begin with Be. Because you do not know how many characters will follow the Be, the asterisk is appropriate.

1
- Click the View button to return to Design view.

- If necessary, click the Criteria row below the Client Number field to produce an insertion point.

- Use the DELETE or BACKSPACE key as necessary to delete the current entry.

- Click the Criteria row below the Client Name field to produce an insertion point.

- Type Be* as the criterion (Figure 2–15).

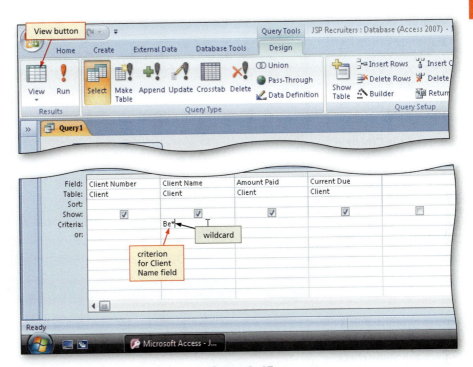

Figure 2–15

2
- View the query results by clicking the View button (Figure 2–16).

 Experiment

- Vary the case of the letters in the criteria and view the results to determine whether case makes a difference when entering a wildcard.

Figure 2–16

To Use Criteria for a Field Not Included in the Results

In some cases, you may have criteria for a particular field that should not appear in the results of the query. For example, you may want to see the client number, client name, address, and amount paid for all clients located in Berridge. The criteria involve the City field, which is not one of the fields to be included in the results.

To enter a criterion for the City field, it must be included in the design grid. Normally, this also would mean it would appear in the results. To prevent this from happening, remove the check mark from its Show check box in the Show row of the grid. The following steps display the client number, client name, amount paid, and current due for clients located in Berridge.

- Click the View button to return to Design view.

- Erase the criterion in the Client Name field.

- Include the City field in the query.

- Type `Berridge` as the criterion for the City field (Figure 2–17).

Figure 2–17

- Click the Show check box for the City field to remove the check mark (Figure 2–18).

Q&A

Could I have removed the check mark before entering the criterion?

Yes. The order in which you performed the two operations does not matter.

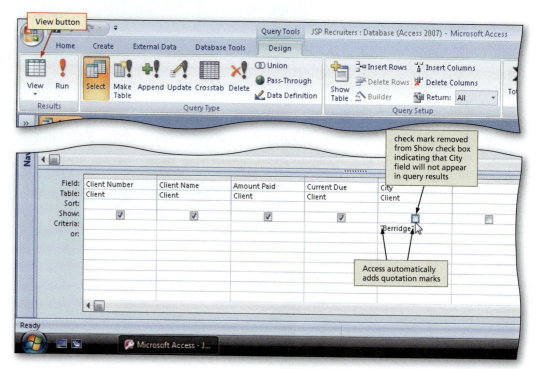

Figure 2–18

3
- View the query results (Figure 2–19).

Experiment
- Click the View button to return to Design view, enter a different city name, and view the results. Repeat this process with a variety of city names, including at least one city name that is not in the database.

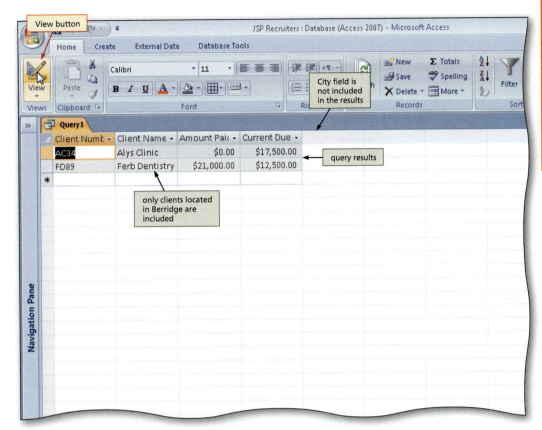

Figure 2–19

Creating a Parameter Query

If you wanted to find clients located in Fort Stewart rather than Berridge, you would either have to create a new query or modify the existing query by replacing Berridge with Fort Stewart as the criterion. Rather than giving a specific criterion when you first create the query, on occasion, you may want to be able to enter part of the criterion when you view the query results and then have the appropriate results appear. For example, to include all the clients located in Berridge, you could enter Berridge as a criterion in the City field. From that point on, every time you ran the query, only the clients in Berridge would appear.

A better way is to allow the user to enter the city at the time the user wants to view the results. Thus a user could view the query results, enter Berridge as the city and then see all the clients in Berridge. Later, the user could use the same query, but enter Fort Stewart as the city, and then see all the clients in Fort Stewart.

To enable this flexibility, you create a **parameter query**, which is a query that prompts for input whenever it is used. You enter a parameter, rather than a specific value, as the criterion. You create a parameter by enclosing a value in a criterion in square brackets. It is important that the value in the brackets does not match the name of any field. If you enter a field name in square brackets, Access assumes you want that particular field and does not prompt the user for input. For example, you could place [Enter City] as the criterion in the City field.

BTW

Removing a Table from a Query
If you add the wrong table to a query or have an extra table in the query, you can remove it by right-clicking the field list for the table and then clicking Remove Table on the shortcut menu.

To Create a Parameter Query

The following steps create a parameter query that prompts the user to enter a city, and then displays the client number, client name, amount paid, and current due for all clients located in that city.

1

- Return to Design view.

- Erase the current criterion in the City column, and then type [Enter City] as the new criterion (Figure 2–20).

Q&A What is the purpose of the square brackets?

The square brackets indicate that the text entered is not text that the value in the column must match. Without the brackets, for example, Access would search for records on which the city is Enter City.

Q&A What if I typed a field name in the square brackets?

Access would simply use the value in that field. In order to create a parameter query, it is essential that the text typed in the square brackets not be a field name.

Figure 2–20

2

- Click the View button to display the Enter Parameter Value dialog box (Figure 2–21).

Figure 2–21

3
- Type `Fort Stewart` as the parameter value in the Enter City text box and then click the OK button (Figure 2–22).

🔍 **Experiment**
- Try other characters between the square brackets. In each case, view the results. When finished, change the characters between the square brackets back to Enter City.

Figure 2–22

Each time you use this query, you will be asked to enter a city. Only clients in the city you enter will be included in the results.

To Save a Query

In many cases, you will want to repeatedly use the queries you construct. By saving the query, you eliminate the need to repeat all your entries. The following steps save the query you just have created and assign it the name Client-City Query.

1
- Click the Save button on the Quick Access Toolbar to open the Save As dialog box.

Q&A Can I also save from Design view?

Yes. You can save the query when you view it in Design view just as you can save the query when you view the query results in Datasheet view.

- Type `Client-City Query` in the Query Name text box (Figure 2–23).

Figure 2–23

2

• Click the OK button to save the query (Figure 2–24).

3

• Click the Close 'Client-City Query' button to close the query and remove it from the screen.

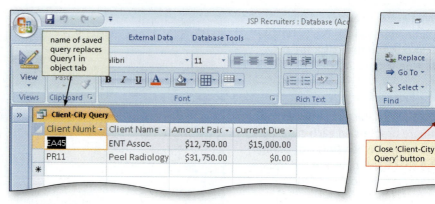

Figure 2–24

Other Ways

1. Right-click tab for query, click Save on shortcut menu
2. Press CTRL+S

To Use a Saved Query

Once you have saved a query, you can use and manipulate it at any time in the future by opening it. When you right-click the query in the Navigation Pane, Access displays a shortcut menu containing commands that allow you to open and change the design of the query. You also can print the results by clicking the Office Button, pointing to Print on the Office button menu, and then clicking Quick Print on the Print submenu.

The query always uses the data that is currently in the table. Thus, if changes have been made to the data since the last time you ran the query, the results of the query may be different. The following steps use the query named Client-City Query.

1

• Show the Navigation Pane.

• Right-click the Client-City Query to produce a shortcut menu.

• Click Open on the shortcut menu to open the query and display the Enter Parameter Value dialog box (Figure 2–25).

Q&A

What would have happened if there were no parameters?

You would immediately see the results without needing to furnish any additional information.

Figure 2–25

2

• Type Fort Stewart in the Enter City text box, and then click the OK button to display the results using Fort Stewart as the city as shown in Figure 2–24.

• Click the Close 'Client-City Query' button, shown in Figure 2–24, to close the query.

To Use a Number in a Criterion

To enter a number in a criterion, type the number without any dollar signs or commas. The following steps display all clients whose current due amount is $0.00.

1

- Hide the Navigation Pane.
- Click Create on the Ribbon to display the Create tab.
- Click the Query Design button to create a new query.
- With the Client table selected, click the Add button in the Show Table dialog box to add the Client table to the query.
- Click the Close button in the Show Table dialog box to remove the dialog box from the screen.
- Drag the lower edge of the field box down far enough so all fields in the Client table are displayed.
- Include the Client Number, Client Name, Amount Paid, and Current Due fields in the query.
- Type 0 as the criterion for the Current Due field (Figure 2–26).

 Q&A Do I need to enter a dollar sign and decimal point?

No. Access will interpret 0 as $0.00, because the data type for the Current Due field is currency.

Figure 2–26

2

- View the query results (Figure 2–27).

Q&A Why did Access display the results as $0.00 when I only entered 0?

Access uses the format for the field to determine how to display the result. In this case the format indicated that Access should include the dollar sign and decimal point.

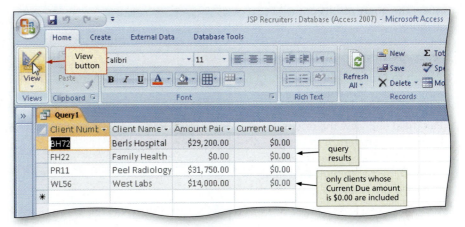

Figure 2–27

To Use a Comparison Operator in a Criterion

Unless you specify otherwise, Access assumes that the criteria you enter involve equality (exact matches). In the last query, for example, you were requesting those clients whose current due amount is equal to 0 (zero). If you want something other than an exact match, you must enter the appropriate **comparison operator**. The comparison operators are > (greater than), < (less than), >= (greater than or equal to), <= (less than or equal to), and NOT (not equal to).

The following steps use the > operator to find all clients whose amount paid is more than $20,000.00.

- Return to Design view.

- Erase the 0 in the Current Due column.

- Type >20000 as the criterion for the Amount Paid field (Figure 2–28).

Figure 2–28

- View the query results (Figure 2–29).

- Return to Design view. Try a different criterion involving a comparison operator in the Amount Paid field and view the results. When finished, return to Design view, enter the original criterion (>20000) in the Amount Paid field, and view the results.

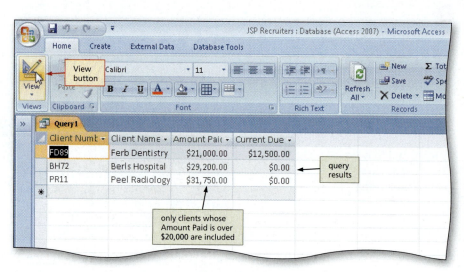

Figure 2–29

Using Compound Criteria

Often you will have more than one criterion that the data for which you are searching must satisfy. This type of criterion is called a **compound criterion**. Two types of compound criteria exist.

In an **AND criterion**, each individual criterion must be true in order for the compound criterion to be true. For example, an AND criterion would allow you to find those clients that have an amount paid greater than $20,000.00 and whose recruiter is recruiter 21.

Conversely, an **OR criterion** is true provided either individual criterion is true. An OR criterion would allow you to find those clients that have an amount paid greater than $20,000.00 or whose recruiter is recruiter 21. In this case, any client whose amount paid is greater than $20,000.00 would be included in the answer, regardless of whether the client's recruiter is recruiter 21. Likewise, any client whose recruiter is recruiter 21 would be included, regardless of whether the client had an amount paid greater than $20,000.00.

BTW

The BETWEEN Operator

The BETWEEN operator allows you to search for a range of values in one field. For example, to find all clients whose amount paid is between $10,000 and $20,000, you would enter Between 10000 and 20000 in the Criteria row for the Amount Paid field.

To Use a Compound Criterion Involving AND

To combine criteria with AND, place the criteria on the same line. The following steps use an AND criterion to find those clients whose amount paid is greater than $20,000.00 and whose recruiter is recruiter 21.

1

- Return to Design view.
- Include the Recruiter Number field in the query.
- Type 21 as the criterion for the Recruiter Number field (Figure 2–30).

Figure 2–30

- View the query results (Figure 2–31).

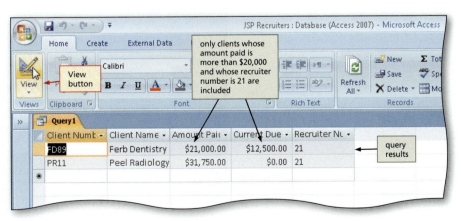

Figure 2–31

To Use a Compound Criterion Involving OR

To combine criteria with OR, the criteria must go on separate lines in the Criteria area of the grid. The following steps use an OR criterion to find those clients whose amount paid is greater than $20,000.00 or whose recruiter is recruiter 21 (or both).

- Return to Design view.

- If necessary, click the Criteria entry for the Recruiter Number field and then use the BACKSPACE key or the DELETE key to erase the entry ("21").

- Click the or: row (the row below the Criteria row) for the Recruiter Number field and then type 21 as the entry (Figure 2–32).

Figure 2–32

- View the query results (Figure 2–33).

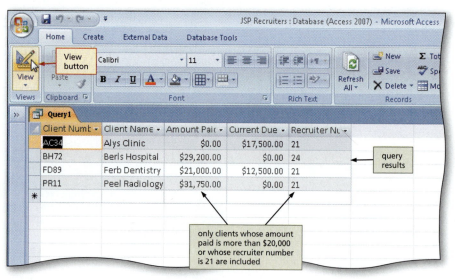

Figure 2–33

Sorting

In some queries, the order in which the records appear really does not matter. All you need to be concerned about are the records that appear in the results. It does not matter which one is first or which one is last.

In other queries, however, the order can be very important. You may want to see the cities in which clients are located and would like them arranged alphabetically. Perhaps you want to see the clients listed by recruiter number. Further, within all the clients of any given recruiter, you might want them to be listed by amount paid from largest amount to smallest.

To order the records in the answer to a query in a particular way, you **sort** the records. The field or fields on which the records are sorted is called the **sort key**. If you are sorting on more than one field (such as sorting by amount paid within recruiter number), the more important field (Recruiter Number) is called the **major key** (also called the **primary sort key**) and the less important field (Amount Paid) is called the **minor key** (also called the **secondary sort key**).

To sort in Microsoft Access, specify the sort order in the Sort row of the design grid below the field that is the sort key. If you specify more than one sort key, the sort key on the left will be the major sort key and the one on the right will be the minor key.

The following are guidelines related to sorting in queries.

Plan Ahead

Determine whether special order is required.

1. **Determine whether sorting is required.** Examine the query or request to see if it contains words such as "order" or "sort" that would imply that the order of the query results is important. If so, you need to sort the query.

2. **Determine the sort key(s).** If sorting is required, identify the field or fields on which the results are to be sorted. Look for words such as "ordered by" or "sort the results by," both of which would indicate that the specified field is a sort key.

3. **If using two sort keys, determine major and minor key.** If you are using two sort keys, determine which one is more important. That will be the major key. Look for words such as "sort by amount paid within recruiter number," which imply that the overall order is by recruiter number. Thus, the Recruiter Number field would be the major sort key and the Amount Paid field would be the minor sort key.

4. **Determine sort order.** Words such as "increasing," "ascending," or "low-to-high" imply Ascending order. Words such as "decreasing," "descending," or "high-to-low" imply Descending order. Sorting in alphabetical order implies Ascending order. If there are no words to imply a particular order, you would typically use Ascending.

5. **Determine restrictions.** Examine the query or request to see if there are any special restrictions. One common restriction is to exclude duplicates. Another common restriction is to list only a certain number of records, for example to list only the first five records.

To Clear the Design Grid

If the fields you want to include in the next query are different from those in the previous query, it is usually simpler to start with a clear grid, that is, one with no fields already in the design grid. You always can clear the entries in the design grid by closing the query and then starting over. A simpler approach to clearing the entries is to select all the entries and then press the DELETE key. The following steps return to Design view and clear the design grid.

- Return to Design view.

- Click just above the Client Number column heading in the grid to select the column.

Q&A
I clicked above the column heading, but the column is not selected. What should I do?

You didn't point to the correct location. Be sure the mouse pointer turns to a down-pointing arrow and then click again.

- Hold the SHIFT key down and click just above the Recruiter Number column heading to select all the columns (Figure 2–34).

clicking here selects first column

with first column already selected, clicking here while holding SHIFT key down selects all five columns

pressing DELETE key with all columns selected clears the grid

Figure 2–34

- Press the DELETE key to clear the design grid.

To Sort Data in a Query

If you have determined in the design process that a query is to be sorted, you must identify the sort key, that is, the field on which the results are to be sorted. In creating the query, you will need to specify the sort key to Access. The following steps sort the cities in the Client table by indicating that the City field is to be sorted. The steps specify Ascending sort order.

- Include the City field in the design grid.

- Click the Sort row below the City field, and then click the Sort row arrow to display a menu of possible sort orders (Figure 2–35).

City field included

Sort row

Sort row arrow

Ascending sort order

menu of available sort orders

Figure 2–35

2

● Click Ascending to select Ascending sort order (Figure 2–36).

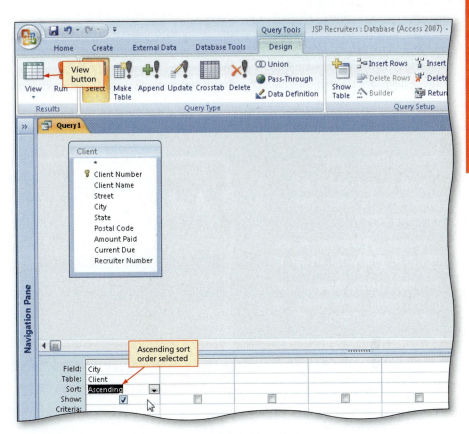

Figure 2–36

3

● View the query results (Figure 2–37).

Experiment

● Return to Design view and change the sort order to Descending. View the results. Return to Design view and change the sort order back to Ascending. View the results.

Q&A

Why do some cities appear more than once?

More than one client is located in those cities.

Figure 2–37

To Omit Duplicates

When you sort data, duplicates normally are included. In Figure 2–37 on the previous page, for example, Berridge appeared twice, as did Fort Stewart and Tarleton. These duplicates do not add any value, so you can eliminate them from the results. To eliminate duplicates, display the query's property sheet. A **property sheet** is a window containing the various properties of the object. To omit duplicates, you will use the property sheet to change the Unique Values property from No to Yes.

The following steps produce a sorted list of the cities in the Client table in which each city is listed only once.

- Return to Design view.

- Click the second field in the design grid (the empty field following City).

- If necessary, click Design on the Ribbon to display the Design tab.

- Click the Property Sheet button on the Design tab to display the property sheet (Figure 2–38).

Q&A

My property sheet looks different. What should I do?

If your sheet looks different, you clicked the wrong place and will have to close the property sheet and repeat this step.

Figure 2–38

❷

- Click the Unique Values property box, and then click the arrow that appears to produce a menu of available choices for Unique Values (Figure 2–39).

Figure 2–39

3

- Click Yes and then close the Query Properties sheet by clicking its Close button.

- View the query results (Figure 2–40).

query results

each city listed only once

Figure 2–40

To Sort on Multiple Keys

The following steps sort on multiple keys. Specifically, the data is to be sorted by amount paid (low to high) within recruiter number, which means that the Recruiter Number field is the major key and the Amount Paid field is the minor key.

1

- Return to Design view.

- Clear the design grid.

- Include the Client Number, Client Name, Recruiter Number, and Amount Paid fields in the query in this order.

- Select Ascending as the sort order for both the Recruiter Number field and the Amount Paid field (Figure 2–41).

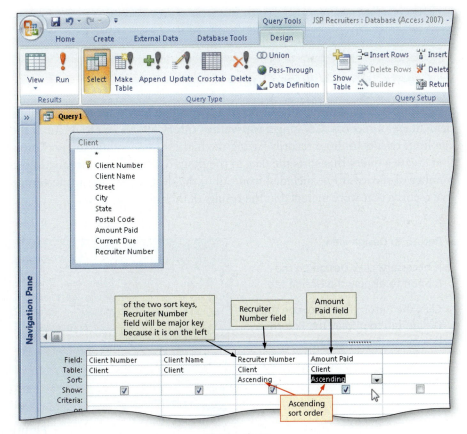

of the two sort keys, Recruiter Number field will be major key because it is on the left

Recruiter Number field

Amount Paid field

Ascending sort order

Figure 2–41

2

- View the query results (Figure 2–42).

🔍 **Experiment**

- Return to Design view and try other sort combinations for the Recruiter Number and Amount Paid fields, such as Ascending for Recruiter Number and Descending for Amount Paid. In each case, view the results to see the effect of the changes. When finished, select Ascending as the sort order for both fields.

Q&A What if the Amount Paid field is to the left of the Recruiter Number?

It is important to remember that the major sort key must appear to the left of the minor sort key in the design grid. If you attempted to sort by amount paid within recruiter number, but placed the Amount Paid field to the left of the Recruiter Number field, your results would be incorrect.

Figure 2–42

To Create a Top-Values Query

Rather than show all the results of a query, you may want to show only a specified number of records or a percentage of records. Creating a **top-values query** allows you to quantify the results. When you sort records, you can limit results to those records having the highest (descending sort) or lowest (ascending sort) values. To do so, first create a query that sorts the data in the desired order. Next, use the Return box on the Design tab to change the number of records to be included from All to the desired number or percentage. The following steps show the first five records that were included in the results of the previous query.

1

- Return to Design view.

- If necessary, click Design on the Ribbon to display the Design tab.

- Click the Return box arrow on the Design tab to display the Return box menu (Figure 2–43).

Figure 2–43

2

- Click 5 in the Return box menu to specify that the query results should contain the first five rows.

Q&A

Could I have typed the 5? What about other numbers that do not appear in the list?

Yes, you could have typed the 5. For numbers not appearing in the list, you must type the number.

- View the query results (Figure 2–44).

3

- Close the query by clicking the Close 'Query1' button.

- When asked if you want to save your changes, click the No button.

Q&A

Do I need to close the query before creating my next query?

Not necessarily. When you use a top-values query, however, it is important to change the value in the Return box back to All. If you do not change the Return value back to All, the previous value will remain in effect. Consequently, you may very well not get all the records you should in the next query. A good practice whenever you use a top-values query is to close the query as soon as you are done. That way, you will begin your next query from scratch, which guarantees that the value is set back to All.

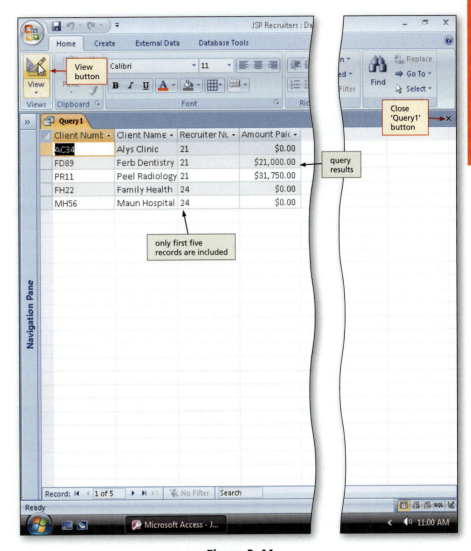

Figure 2–44

Joining Tables

In designing a query, you need to determine whether more than one table is required. If the question being asked involves data from both the Client and Recruiter tables, for example, both tables are required for the query. Such a query may require listing the number and name of each client along with the number and name of the client's recruiter. The client's name is in the Client table, whereas the recruiter's name is in the Recruiter table. Thus, this query cannot be completed using a single table; both the Client and Recruiter tables are required. You need to **join** the tables; that is, to find records in the two tables that have identical values in matching fields (Figure 2–45). In this example, you need to find records in the Client table and the Recruiter table that have the same value in the Recruiter Number fields.

Client table			
Client Number	**Name**	...	**Recruiter Number**
AC34	Alys Clinic	...	21
BH72	Berls Hospital	...	24
BL12	Benton Labs	...	24
EA45	ENT Assoc.	...	27
FD89	Ferb Dentistry	...	21
FH22	Family Health	...	24
MH56	Maun Hospital	...	24
PR11	Peel Radiology	...	21
TC37	Tarleton Clinic	...	27
WL56	West Labs	...	24

Give me the number and name of each client along with the number and name of each client's recruiter.

Recruiter table			
Recruiter Number	**Last Name**	**First Name**	...
21	Kerry	Alyssa	...
24	Reeves	Camden	...
27	Fernandez	Jaime	...
34	Lee	Jan	...

Join Types
BTW

The type of join that finds records from both tables that have identical values in matching fields is called an inner join. An inner join is the default join in Access. Outer joins are used to show all the records in one table as well as the common records; that is, the records that share the same value in the join field. In a left outer join, all rows from the table on the left are included. In a right outer join, all rows from the table on the right are included.

Join of Client and Recruiter tables						
Client Number	**Name**	...	**Recruiter Number**	**Last Name**	**First Name**	...
AC34	Alys Clinic	...	21	Kerry	Alyssa	...
BH72	Berls Hospital	...	24	Reeves	Camden	...
BL12	Benton Labs	...	24	Reeves	Camden	...
EA45	ENT Assoc.	...	27	Fernandez	Jaime	...
FD89	Ferb Dentistry	...	21	Kerry	Alyssa	...
FH22	Family Health	...	24	Reeves	Camden	...
MH56	Maun Hospital	...	24	Reeves	Camden	...
PR11	Peel Radiology	...	21	Kerry	Alyssa	...
TC37	Tarleton Clinic	...	27	Fernandez	Jaime	...
WL56	West Labs	...	24	Reeves	Camden	...

Figure 2–45

The following are guidelines related to joining tables.

Plan Ahead

Determine whether more than one table is required.

1. **Determine whether more than one table is required.** Examine the query or request to see if all the fields involved in the request are in one table. If the fields are in two (or more) tables, you need to join the tables.

2. **Determine the matching fields.** If joining is required, identify the matching fields in the two tables that have identical values. Look for the same column name in the two tables or for column names that are similar.

(continued)

(continued)

Plan Ahead

3. **Determine whether sorting is required**. Queries that join tables often are used as the basis for a report. If this is the case, it may be necessary to sort the results. For example, the Recruiter-Client Report is based on a query that joins the Recruiter and Client tables. The query is sorted by recruiter number and client number.

4. **Determine restrictions**. Examine the query or request to see if there are any special restrictions. For example, the query may only want clients whose current due amount is $0.00.

5. **Determine join properties**. Examine the query or request to see if you only want records from both tables that have identical values in matching fields. If you want to see records in one of the tables that do not have identical values, then you need to change the join properties. When two tables have fields with the same name, you also need to determine which table contains the field to be used in the query. For example, if you want to see all recruiters, even if they have no clients, then you should include the recruiter number from the Recruiter table in the design grid. If you want only records with identical values in matching fields, then it does not matter which matching field you select.

To Join Tables

If you have determined in the design process that you need to join tables, you will first bring field lists for both tables to the upper Pane of the Query window. Access will draw a line, called a **join line**, between matching fields in the two tables indicating that the tables are related. You then can select fields from either table. Access joins the tables automatically.

The first step is to create a new query and add the Recruiter table to the query. Then, add the Client table to the query. A join line will appear connecting the Recruiter Number fields in the two field lists. This join line indicates how the tables are related; that is, linked through these matching fields. (If you fail to give the matching fields the same name, Access will not insert the line. You can insert it manually, however, by clicking one of the two matching fields and dragging the mouse pointer to the other matching field.)

The following steps create a new query, add the Client table, and then select the appropriate fields.

1

- Click Create on the Ribbon to display the Create tab.

- Click the Query Design button to create a new query.

- Click the Recruiter table in the Show Table dialog box to select the table.

- Click the Add button to add a field list for the Recruiter table to the query (Figure 2–46).

Figure 2–46

2

- Click the Client table in the Show Table dialog box.

- Click the Add button to add a field list for the Client table.

- Close the Show Table dialog box by clicking the Close button.

- Expand the size of the field lists so all the fields in the Recruiter and Client tables appear (Figure 2–47).

I didn't get a join line. What should I do?

Ensure that the names of the matching fields are exactly the same, the data types are the same, and the matching field is the primary key in one of the two tables. If all of these are true and you still don't have a join line, you can produce one by pointing to one of the matching fields and dragging to the other matching field.

Figure 2–47

3

- In the design grid, include the Recruiter Number, Last Name, and First Name fields from the Recruiter table as well as the Client Number and Client Name fields from the Client table.

- Select Ascending as the sort order for both the Recruiter Number field and the Client Number field (Figure 2–48).

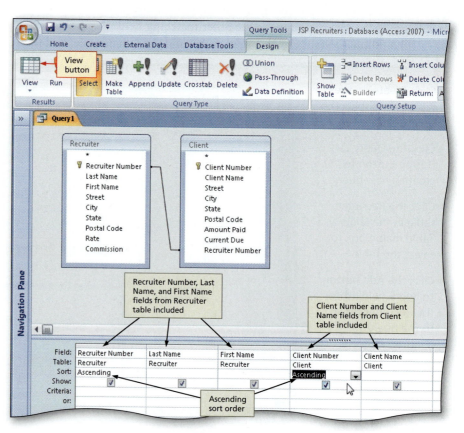

Figure 2–48

4
- View the query results (Figure 2–49).

Figure 2–49

To Save the Query

The following steps save the query.

1
- Click the Save button on the Quick Access Toolbar to display the Save As dialog box.
- Type `Recruiter-Client Query` as the query name (Figure 2–50).

2
- Click the OK button to save the query.

Figure 2–50

To Change Join Properties

Normally records that do not match do not appear in the results of a join query. A recruiter such as Jan Lee, for whom no clients currently exist, for example, would not appear. To cause such a record to be displayed, you need to change the **join properties**, which are the properties that indicate which records appear in a join, of the query, as in the following steps.

1

- Return to Design view.

- Right-click the join line to produce a shortcut menu (Figure 2–51).

Q&A

I don't see Join Properties on my shortcut menu. What should I do?

If Join Properties does not appear on your shortcut menu, you did not point to the appropriate portion of the join line. You will need to point to the correct portion and right-click again.

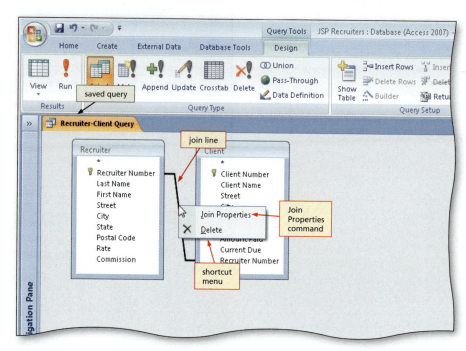

Figure 2–51

2

- Click Join Properties on the shortcut menu to display the Join Properties dialog box (Figure 2–52).

Q&A

How do the options in the Join Properties dialog box match the various types of joins described earlier?

Option button 1 gives an inner join, option button 2 gives a left join, and option button 3 gives a right join.

Figure 2–52

3

- Click option button 2 to include all records from the Recruiter table regardless of whether they match any clients.

- Click the OK button.

- View the query results by clicking the View button (Figure 2–53).

- Click the Save button on the Quick Access Toolbar.

🔎 **Experiment**

- Return to Design view, change the Join properties, and select option button 3. View the results to see the effect of this option. When done, return to Design view, change the Join properties, and once again select option button 2.

Figure 2–53

4

- Close the Recruiter-Client Query by clicking the Close 'Recruiter-Client Query' button. Click No if asked to save the changes to the query.

To Create a Report Involving a Join

The following steps create the report shown in Figure 2–54. The records in the report are sorted (ordered) by Client Number within Recruiter Number. To ensure that the records appear in this order, the steps specify that the Recruiter Number and Client Number fields are sort keys.

Recruiter-Client Report

Recruiter Number	Last Name	First Name	Client Number	Client Name
21	Kerry	Alyssa	AC34	Alys Clinic
21	Kerry	Alyssa	FD89	Ferb Dentistry
21	Kerry	Alyssa	PR11	Peel Radiology
24	Reeves	Camden	BH72	Berls Hospital
24	Reeves	Camden	BL12	Benton Labs
24	Reeves	Camden	FH22	Family Health
24	Reeves	Camden	MH56	Maun Hospital
24	Reeves	Camden	WL56	West Labs
27	Fernandez	Jaime	EA45	ENT Assoc.
27	Fernandez	Jaime	TC37	Tarleton Clinic
34	Lee	Jan		

Figure 2–54

● Show the Navigation Pane and be sure the Recruiter-Client Query is selected in the Navigation Pane.

Q&A I have two copies of Recruiter-Client Query. Does it matter which one I use?

No. There are two copies because the recruiter-Client Query involves two tables. It does not matter which one you select.

● Click Create on the Ribbon to display the Create tab.

● Click the Report Wizard button to display the Report Wizard dialog box (Figure 2–55).

Figure 2–55

● Click the Add All Fields button to add all the fields in the Recruiter-Client Query.

● Click the Next button to display the next Report Wizard screen (Figure 2–56).

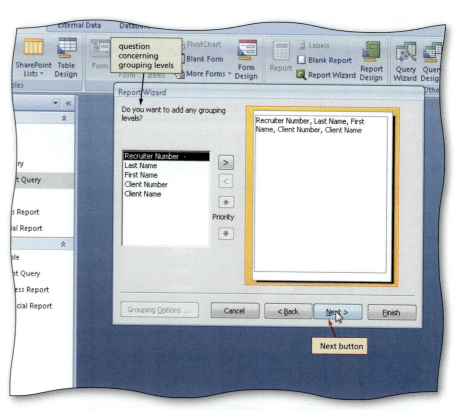

Figure 2–56

3

- Because you will not specify any grouping, click the Next button in the Report Wizard dialog box to display the next Report Wizard screen.

- Because you already specified the sort order in the query, click the Next button again to display the next Report Wizard screen.

- Make sure that Tabular is selected as the Layout and Portrait is selected as the Orientation.

- Click the Next button to display the next Report Wizard screen.

- Be sure the Module style is selected.

- Click the Next button to display the next Report Wizard screen.

Figure 2–57

- Erase the current title, and then type Recruiter-Client Report as the new title.

- Click the Finish button to produce the report (Figure 2–57).

4

- Click the Close button for the Recruiter-Client Report to remove the report from the screen.

To Print a Report

Once you have created a report, you can print it at any time. The layout will reflect the layout you created. The data in the report will always reflect current data. The following step prints the Recruiter-Client Report.

1 With the Recruiter-Client Report selected in the Navigation Pane, click the Office Button, point to Print on the Office button menu, and then click Quick Print on the Print submenu to print the report.

To Restrict the Records in a Join

Sometimes you will want to join tables, but you will not want to include all possible records. For example, you would like to create a report showing only those clients whose Amount Paid is greater than $20,000, but you do not want the Amount Paid field to appear in the results. In such cases, you will relate the tables and include fields just as you did before. You also will include criteria. To include only those clients whose amount paid is more than $20,000.00, you will include >20000 as a criterion for the Amount Paid field.

The following steps modify the Recruiter-Client query to restrict the records that will be included in the join.

- Open the Recruiter-Client Query in Design view and hide the Navigation Pane.

- Add the Amount Paid field to the query.

- Type >20000 as the criterion for the Amount Paid field and then click the Show check box for the Amount Paid field to remove the check mark (Figure 2–58).

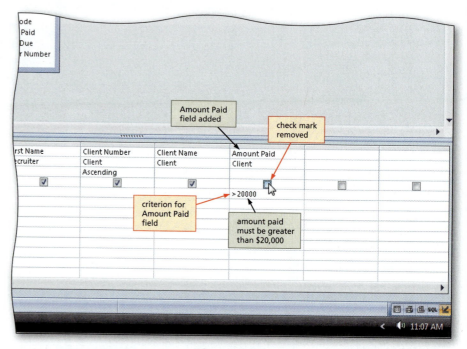

Figure 2–58

2

- View the query results (Figure 2–59).

3

- Close the query by clicking the Close 'Recruiter-Client Query' button.

- When asked if you want to save your changes, click the No button.

Figure 2–59

Calculations

If you have determined that a special calculation is required for a query, you then need to determine whether the calculation is an individual record calculation (for example, adding the values in two fields) or a group calculation (for example, finding the total of the values in a particular field on all the records).

JSP Recruiters may want to know the total amount (amount paid plus current due) from each client. This would seem to pose a problem because the Client table does not include a field for total amount. You can calculate it, however, because the total amount is equal to the amount paid plus the current due. A field that can be computed from other fields is called a **calculated field**. A calculated field is an individual record calculation.

JSP also may want to calculate the average amount paid for the clients of each recruiter. That is, they want the average for the clients of recruiter 21, the average for the clients of recruiter 24, and so on. This type of calculation is called a group calculation, because it involves groups of records. In this example, the clients of recruiter 21 would form one group, the clients of recruiter 24 would be a second, and the clients of recruiter 27 form a third group.

The following are guidelines related to calculations in queries.

Determine whether calculations are required.

1. **Determine whether calculations are required**. Examine the query or request to see if there are special calculations to be included. Look for words such as "total," "sum," "compute," or "calculate."

2. **Determine a name for the calculated field**. If calculations are required, decide on the name for the field. Assign a name that helps identify the contents of the field. For example, if you are adding the cost of a number of items, the name "Total Cost" would be appropriate. The name, also called an **alias**, becomes the column name when the query is run.

3. **Determine the format for the calculated field**. Determine how the calculated field should appear. If the calculation involves monetary amounts, you would use the currency format. If the calculated value contains decimals, determine how many decimal places to display.

Plan Ahead

To Use a Calculated Field in a Query

If you have determined that you need a calculated field in a query, you enter a name (alias) for the calculated field, a colon, and then the expression in one of the columns in the Field row. Any fields included in the expression must be enclosed in square brackets [ ]. For the total amount, for example, you will type Total Amount:[Amount Paid]+[Current Due] as the expression.

You can type the expression directly into the Field row. You will not be able to see the entire entry, however, because the Field row is not large enough. The preferred way is to select the column in the Field row and then use the Zoom command on its shortcut menu. When Access displays the Zoom dialog box, you can enter the expression.

You are not restricted to addition in calculations. You can use subtraction (-), multiplication (*), or division (/). You also can include parentheses in your calculations to indicate which calculations should be done first.

The steps on the next page use a calculated field to display the number, name, amount paid, current due, and the total amount for all clients.

1

- Create a query with a field list for the Client table.

- Add the Client Number, Client Name, Amount Paid, and Current Due fields to the query.

- Right-click the Field row in the first open column in the design grid to display a shortcut menu (Figure 2–60).

Figure 2–60

2

- Click Zoom on the shortcut menu to display the Zoom dialog box.

- Type `Total Amount:[Amount Paid]+[Current Due]` in the Zoom dialog box (Figure 2–61).

Q&A

Do I always need to put square brackets around field names?

If the field name does not contain spaces, square brackets are technically not necessary, although it is still acceptable to use the brackets. It is a good practice, however, to get in the habit of using the brackets.

Figure 2–61

3

- Click the OK button to enter the expression (Figure 2–62).

Figure 2–62

4

- View the query results (Figure 2–63).

🔎 **Experiment**

- Return to Design view and try other expressions. In at least one case, omit the Total Amount and the colon. In at least one case, intentionally misspell a field name. In each case, view the results to see the effect of your changes. When finished, re-enter the original expression.

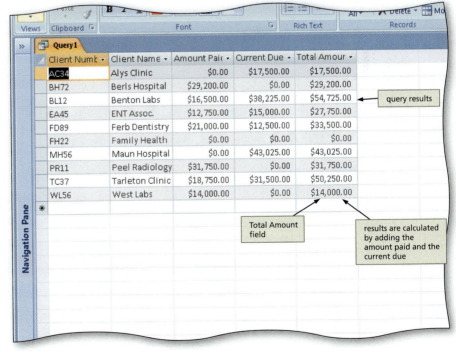

Figure 2–63

Instead of clicking Zoom on the shortcut menu, you can click Build. Access displays the Expression Builder dialog box that provides assistance in creating the expression. If you know the expression you will need, however, it is often easier to enter it using the Zoom command.

To Change a Caption

You can change the way items appear in the results of a query by changing their format. You also can change a query result's heading at the top of a column by changing the caption. Just as when you omitted duplicates, you will make this change by using a property sheet. In the property sheet, you can change the desired property, such as the format, the number of decimal places, or the caption. The following steps change the caption of the Amount Paid field to Paid and the caption of the Current Due field to Due.

- Return to Design view.

- Click Design on the Ribbon to display the Design tab.

- Click the Amount Paid field in the design grid, and then click the Property Sheet button on the Design tab.

- Click the Caption box, and then type Paid as the caption (Figure 2–64).

Q&A

My property sheet looks different. What should I do?

If your sheet looks different, you clicked the wrong place and will have to close the property sheet and repeat this step.

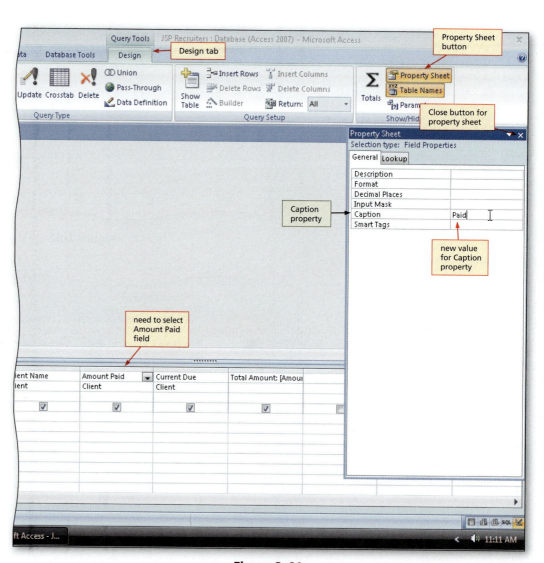

Figure 2–64

2

- Close the property sheet by clicking its Close button.

- Click the Current Due field in the design grid, and then click the Property Sheet button on the Design tab.

- Click the Caption box, and then type Due as the caption.

- Close the Property Sheet by clicking its Close button.

- View the query results (Figure 2–65).

3

- Click the Close 'Query1' button to close the query.

- When asked if you want to save your changes, click the No button.

Q&A

What would happen if I clicked the Yes button instead of the No button?

If you had saved the query, the changes you made to the properties would be saved in the database along with the query.

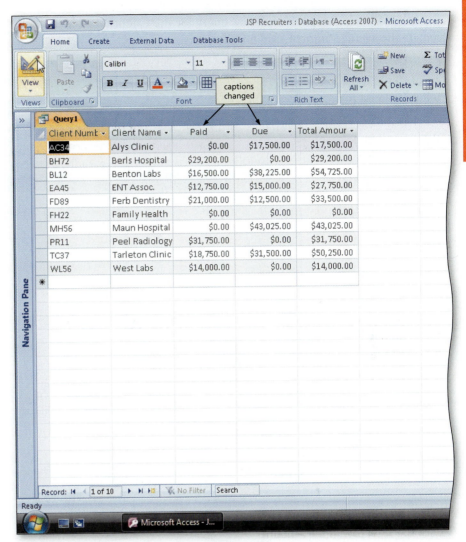

Figure 2–65

Other Ways

1. Right-click field in design grid, click Properties on shortcut menu

Calculating Statistics

For group calculations, Microsoft Access supports several built-in statistics: COUNT (count of the number of records), SUM (total), AVG (average), MAX (largest value), MIN (smallest value), STDEV (standard deviation), VAR (variance), FIRST (first value), and LAST (last value). These statistics are called aggregate functions. An **aggregate function** is a function that performs some mathematical function against a group of records. To use any of these aggregate functions in a query, you include it in the Total row in the design grid. The Total row routinely does not appear in the grid. To include it, click the Totals button on the Design tab.

To Calculate Statistics

The following steps create a new query for the Client table, include the Total row in the design grid, and then calculate the average amount paid for all clients.

- Create a new query with a field list for the Client table.

- If necessary, click Design on the Ribbon to display the Design tab.

- Add the Amount Paid field to the query.

- Click the Totals button on the Design tab to include the Total row in the design grid (Figure 2-66).

Figure 2-66

- Click the Total row in the Amount Paid column to display the Total box arrow.

- Click the Total box arrow to display the Total list (Figure 2-67).

Figure 2-67

3

- Click Avg to indicate that Access is to calculate an average (Figure 2–68).

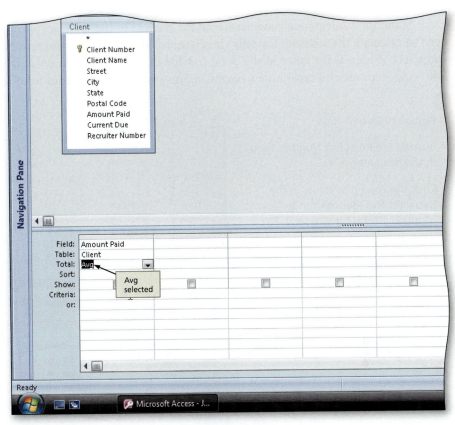

Figure 2–68

4

- View the query results (Figure 2–69).

Experiment

- Return to Design view and try other aggregate functions. In each case, view the results to see the effect of your selection. When finished, select average once again.

Figure 2–69

To Use Criteria in Calculating Statistics

Sometimes calculating statistics for all the records in the table is appropriate. In other cases, however, you will need to calculate the statistics for only those records that satisfy certain criteria. To enter a criterion in a field, first you select Where as the entry in the Total row for the field, and then enter the criterion in the Criteria row. The following steps use this technique to calculate the average amount paid for clients of recruiter 21.

- Return to Design view.

- Include the Recruiter Number field in the design grid.

- Click the Total box arrow in the Recruiter Number column to produce a Total list (Figure 2–70).

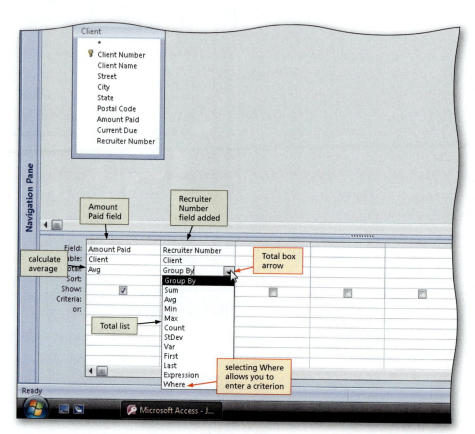

Figure 2–70

- Click Where.

- Type 21 as the criterion for the Recruiter Number field (Figure 2–71).

Figure 2–71

- View the query results
  (Figure 2–72).

Figure 2–72

To Use Grouping

Another way statistics often are used is in combination with grouping; that is, statistics are calculated for groups of records. You may, for example, need to calculate the average amount paid for the clients of each recruiter. You will want the average for the clients of recruiter 21, the average for clients of recruiter 24, and so on.

Grouping means creating groups of records that share some common characteristic. In grouping by Recruiter Number, for example, the clients of recruiter 21 would form one group, the clients of recruiter 24 would form a second, and the clients of recruiter 27 form a third group. The calculations then are made for each group. To indicate grouping in Access, select Group By as the entry in the Total row for the field to be used for grouping.

The following steps calculate the average amount paid for clients of each recruiter.

- Return to Design view and clear the design grid.

- Include the Recruiter Number field in the query.

- Include the Amount Paid field in the query.

- Select Avg as the calculation in the Total row for the Amount Paid field (Figure 2–73).

Q&A

Why didn't I need to change the entry in the Total Row for the Recruiter Number field?

Group By currently is the entry in the Total row for the Recruiter Number field, which is correct; thus, it was not changed.

Figure 2–73

2
- View the query results (Figure 2–74).

3
- Close the query.
- Do not save your changes.

Figure 2–74

Crosstab Queries

Crosstab queries are useful for summarizing data. A crosstab query calculates a statistic (for example, sum, average, or count) for data that is grouped by two different types of information. One of the types will appear down the side of the resulting datasheet, and the other will appear across the top.

For example, if you have determined that a query must summarize the sum of the amounts paid grouped by both city and recruiter number, you could have cities as the row headings, that is, down the side. You could have recruiter numbers as the column headings, that is, across the top. The entries within the data sheet represent the total of the amounts paid. Figure 2–75 shows a crosstab in which the total of amount paid is grouped by both city and recruiter number with cities down the left-hand side and recruiter numbers across the top. For example, the entry in the row labeled Fort Stewart and in the column labeled 21 represents the total of the amount paid by all clients of recruiter 21 who are located in Fort Stewart.

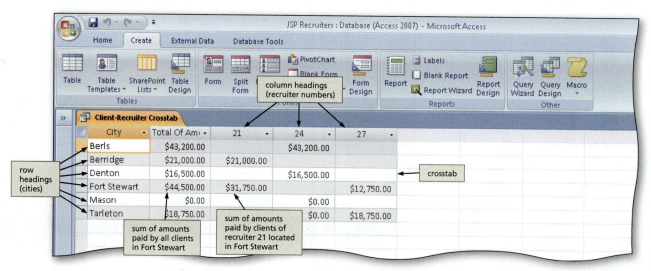

Figure 2–75

To Create a Crosstab Query

The following steps use the Crosstab Query wizard to create a crosstab query.

1

- Click Create on the Ribbon to display the Create tab.

- Click the Query Wizard button to display the New Query dialog box (Figure 2–76).

Figure 2–76

2

- Click Crosstab Query Wizard in the New Query dialog box.

- Click the OK button to display the Crosstab Query Wizard (Figure 2–77).

Figure 2–77

- With the Tables option button selected and the Client table selected, click the Next button to display the next Crosstab Query Wizard screen.

- Click the City field, and then click the Add Field button to select the City field for row headings (Figure 2–78).

Figure 2–78

4

- Click the Next button to display the next Crosstab Query Wizard screen.

- Click the Recruiter Number field to select the Recruiter Number field for column headings (Figure 2–79).

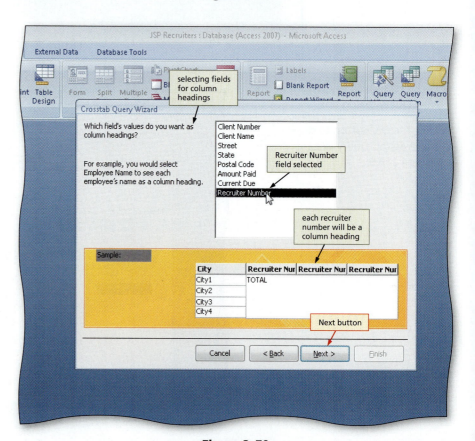

Figure 2–79

5

● Click the Next button to display the next Crosstab Query Wizard screen.

● Click the Amount Paid field to select the Amount Paid field for calculations.

 Experiment

● Click other fields. For each field, examine the list of calculations that are available. When finished, click the Amount Paid field again.

● Click Sum to select Sum as the calculation to be performed (Figure 2–80).

Q&A My list of functions is different. What did I do wrong?

Either you clicked the wrong field, or the Amount Paid field has the wrong data type. If you mistakenly assigned it the Text data type for example, you would not see Sum in the list of available calculations.

Figure 2–80

6

● Click the Next button to display the next Crosstab Query Wizard screen.

● Type `Client-Recruiter Crosstab` as the name of the query (Figure 2–81).

7

● Click the Finish button to produce the crosstab shown in Figure 2–75 on page AC 122.

● Close the query.

Q&A If I want to view the crosstab at some future date, can I just open the query?

Yes.

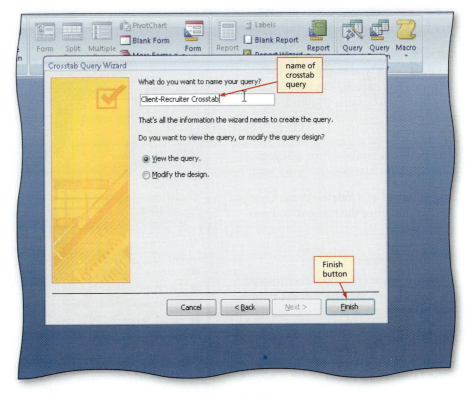

Figure 2–81

To Customize the Navigation Pane

Currently the entries in the Navigation Pane are organized by table. That is, the queries, forms, and reports associated with a particular table appear after the name of the table. In addition, all tables are included. You might want to change the way the information is organized. For example, you might wish to have all the queries appear together, all the forms appear together, and all the reports appear together, regardless of the table on which they are based. The following steps change the organization of the Navigation Pane.

- If necessary, click the Shutter Bar Open/Close Button to show the Navigation Pane.

- Click the Navigation Pane arrow to produce the Navigation Pane menu (Figure 2–82).

Q&A

If the Navigation Pane gets too cluttered, can I hide the objects in a group? For example, if the organization is by table, can I hide the objects (forms, queries, reports) for the table group and only show the table name?

Yes. Click the up arrow on the group bar. The objects under the table group will no longer appear and the up arrow will become a down arrow. To redisplay the objects, click the down arrow.

Figure 2–82

- Click Object Type to organize the Navigation Pane by the type of object rather than by table (Figure 2–83).

- Click the Navigation Pane arrow to produce the Navigation Pane menu.

- Click Tables and Related Views to once again organize the Navigation Pane by table.

 Experiment

- Select different Navigate To Category options to see the effect of the option. With each option you select, select different Filter By Group options to see the effect of the filtering. When you have finished experimenting, select the Tables and Related Views Navigate To Category option and the All Tables Filter By Group option.

Figure 2–83

To Quit Access

You saved all your changes and are ready to quit Access. The following step quits Access.

 Click the Close button on the right side of the Access title bar to quit Access.

BTW

Quick Reference
For a table that lists how to complete the tasks covered in this book using the mouse, Ribbon, shortcut menu, and keyboard, see the Quick Reference Summary at the back of this book, or visit the Access 2007 Quick Reference Web page (scsite.com/ac2007/qr).

Chapter Summary

In this chapter you have learned to create queries, enter fields, enter criteria, use text and numeric data in queries, use wildcards, use compound criteria, create parameter queries, sort data in queries, join tables in queries, perform calculations in queries, create crosstab queries, and customize the Navigation Pane. The following list includes all the new Access skills you have learned in this chapter.

1. Use the Simple Query Wizard to Create a Query (AC 78)
2. Use a Criterion in a Query (AC 81)
3. Print the Results of a Query (AC 83)
4. Create a Query in Design View (AC 83)
5. Add Fields to the Design Grid (AC 85)
6. Use Text Data in a Criterion (AC 86)
7. Use a Wildcard (AC 87)
8. Use Criteria for a Field Not Included in the Results (AC 88)
9. Create a Parameter Query (AC 90)
10. Save a Query (AC 91)
11. Use a Saved Query (AC 92)
12. Use a Number in a Criterion (AC 93)
13. Use a Comparison Operator in a Criterion (AC 94)
14. Use a Compound Criterion Involving AND (AC 95)
15. Use a Compound Criterion Involving OR (AC 96)
16. Clear the Design Grid (AC 98)
17. Sort Data in a Query (AC 98)
18. Omit Duplicates (AC 100)
19. Sort on Multiple Keys (AC 101)
20. Create a Top-Values Query (AC 102)
21. Join Tables (AC 105)
22. Save the Query (AC 107)
23. Change Join Properties (AC 108)
24. Create a Report Involving a Join (AC 109)
25. Print a Report (AC 111)
26. Restrict the Records in a Join (AC 112)
27. Use a Calculated Field in a Query (AC 113)
28. Change a Caption (AC 116)
29. Calculate Statistics (AC 118)
30. Use Criteria in Calculating Statistics (AC 120)
31. Use Grouping (AC 121)
32. Create a Crosstab Query (AC 123)
33. Customize the Navigation Pane (AC 126)

 If you have a SAM user profile, you may have access to hands-on instruction, practice, and assessment. Log in to your SAM account (http://sam2007.course.com) to launch any assigned training activities or exams that relate to the skills covered in this chapter.

Learn It Online

Test your knowledge of chapter content and key terms.

Instructions: To complete the Learn It Online exercises, start your browser, click the Address bar, and then enter the Web address scsite.com/ac2007/learn. When the Access 2007 Learn It Online page is displayed, click the link for the exercise you want to complete and then read the instructions.

Chapter Reinforcement TF, MC, and SA
A series of true/false, multiple choice, and short answer questions that test your knowledge of the chapter content.

Flash Cards
An interactive learning environment where you identify chapter key terms associated with displayed definitions.

Practice Test
A series of multiple choice questions that test your knowledge of chapter content and key terms.

Who Wants To Be a Computer Genius?
An interactive game that challenges your knowledge of chapter content in the style of a television quiz show.

Wheel of Terms
An interactive game that challenges your knowledge of chapter key terms in the style of the television show *Wheel of Fortune*.

Crossword Puzzle Challenge
A crossword puzzle that challenges your knowledge of key terms presented in the chapter.

Apply Your Knowledge

Reinforce the skills and apply the concepts you learned in this chapter.

Using the Query Wizard, Creating a Parameter Query, Joining Tables, and Creating a Report
Instructions: Start Access. Open the The Bike Delivers database that you modified in Apply Your Knowledge in Chapter 1 on page AC 64. (If you did not complete this exercise, see your instructor for a copy of the modified database.)

Perform the following tasks:
1. Use the Simple Query Wizard to create a query for the Customer table. Include the Customer Name, Balance, and Courier Number in the query. Assign the name, Customer Query, to the query.

2. Create a query for the Customer table and add the Customer Number, Customer Name, Courier Number, and Balance fields to the design grid. Sort the records in descending order by Balance. Add a criterion for the Courier Number field that allows the user to enter a different courier each time the query is run. Save the query as Courier Parameter Query.

3. Create a query that joins the Courier and the Customer tables. Add the Courier Number, First Name, and Last Name fields from the Courier table and the Customer Number and Customer Name fields from the Customer table. Sort the records in ascending order by Courier Number and Customer Number. All couriers should appear in the result even if they currently have no customers. Save the query as Courier-Customer Query.

4. Create the report shown in Figure 2–84. The report uses the Courier-Customer Query.

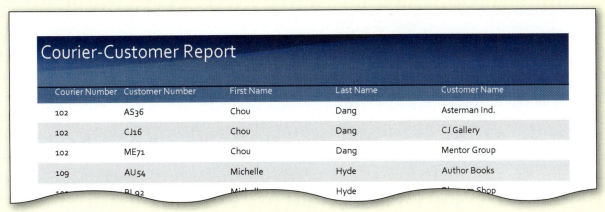

Figure 2–84

5. Submit the revised database in the format specified by your instructor.

Extend Your Knowledge

Extend the skills you learned in this chapter and experiment with new skills. You may need to use Help to complete the assignment.

Creating Crosstab Queries, Creating Queries Using Criteria

Instructions: Start Access. Open the Groom n Fluff database. See the inside back cover of this book for instructions for downloading the Data Files for Students, or see your instructor for information on accessing the files required in this book.

Groom n Fluff is a small pet grooming business. The owner has created an Access database in which to store information about the customers she serves and the pet groomers she employs. You will create the crosstab query shown in Figure 2–85. You also will query the database using specified criteria.

Figure 2–85

Continued >

Extend Your Knowledge *continued*

Perform the following tasks:

1. Create the crosstab query shown in Figure 2–85 on the previous page. The crosstab groups the average of customers' balances by city and groomer number.

2. Create a query to find all customers who do not live in Grant City. Include the Customer Number, Last Name, and Balance fields in the design grid. Save the query as Not Criteria Query.

3. Create a query to find all customers who do not have a telephone number. Include the Customer Number, Last Name, First Name, Street, and City fields in the query results. Save the query as Missing Values Query.

4. Create a query to find all customers whose balance is between $20.00 and $60.00. Include the Customer Number, Last Name, and Balance fields in the design grid. Save the query as Number Range Query.

5. Create a query to find all customers where the groomer number is 203 or 205 and the balance is greater than $40.00. Include the Customer Number, Last Name, First Name, Balance, and Groomer Number fields in the design grid. Save the query as Compound Criteria Query.

6. Change the database properties, as specified by your instructor. Submit the revised database in the format specified by your instructor.

Make It Right

Analyze a database and correct all errors and/or improve the design.

Correcting Errors in the Query Design

Instructions: Start Access. Open the Keep It Green database. See the inside back cover of this book for instructions for downloading the Data Files for Students, or see your instructor for information on accessing the files required in this book.

Keep It Green is a database maintained by a small landscaping business. The queries shown in Figure 2–86 contain a number of errors that need to be corrected before the queries run properly. The sort query shown in Figure 2–86a displays the query results in the proper order (First Name, Last Name, Street, City) but it is sorted incorrectly. The query results should be sorted by last name within city in ascending order. Also the caption for the Street field should be Address. Save the query with your changes.

When you try to run the join query for the Keep It Green database, the message shown in Figure 2–86b appears. The query joins the Worker table and the Customer table. It also calculates the total amount for each customer. The query should be sorted in alphabetical order by worker last name and customer last name. Correct the error that is causing the message shown in Figure 2–86b and sort the records properly. Save the query with your changes.

Change the database properties, as specified by your instructor. Submit the revised database in the format specified by your instructor.

(a) Incorrect Sort Query

(b) Incorrect Join Query

Figure 2–86

In the Lab

Design, create, modify, and/or use a database following the guidelines, concepts, and skills presented in this chapter. Labs are listed in order of increasing difficulty.

Lab 1: Querying the JMS TechWizards Database

Problem: The management of JMS TechWizards has determined a number of questions it wants the database management system to answer. You must obtain answers to the questions posed by management.

Instructions: Use the database created in the In the Lab 1 of Chapter 1 on page AC 67 for this assignment or see your instructor for information on accessing the files required for this book. Perform the following tasks:

1. Open the JMS TechWizards database and create a new query for the Client table that includes the Client Number, Client Name, and Technician Number fields in the design grid for all clients where the technician number is 23. Save the query as Lab 2-1 Step 1 Query.

2. Create a query that includes the Client Number, Client Name, and Paid fields for all clients located in Liberty Corner with a paid amount greater than $500.00. Save the query as Lab2-1 Step 2 Query.

3. Create a query that includes the Client Number, Client Name, Street, and City fields for all clients whose names begin with Gr. Save the query as Lab 2-1 Step 3 Query.

4. Create a query that lists all cities in descending order. Each city should appear only once. Save the query as Lab 2-1 Step 4 Query.

5. Create a query that allows the user to enter the city to search when the query is run. The query results should display the Client Number, Client Name, and Billed. Test the query by searching for those records where the client is located in Anderson. Save the query as Client-City Query.

Continued >

6. Include the Client Number, Client Name, and Billed fields in the design grid. Sort the records in descending order by the Billed field. Display only the top 25 percent of the records in the query result. Save the query as Lab 2-1 Step 6 Query.

7. Join the Technician and the Client table. Include the Technician Number, First Name, and Last Name fields from the Technician table. Include the Client Number, Client Name, and Billed from the Client table. Sort the records in ascending order by technician's last name and client name. All technicians should appear in the result even if they currently have no clients. Save the query as Technician-Client query.

8. Open the Technician-Client query in Design view and remove the Client table. Add the Hourly Rate field to the design grid following the Last Name field. Calculate the number of hours each technician has worked (YTD Earnings/Hourly Rate). Assign the alias Hours Worked to the calculated field. Change the caption for the Hourly Rate field to Rate. Display hours worked as an integer (0 decimal places). Use the Save As command to save the query as Lab 2-1 Step 8 Query.

9. Create a query to display the average billed amount for all clients. Save the query as Lab 2-1 Step 9 Query.

10. Create a query to count the number of clients for technician 23. Save the query as Lab 2-1 Step 10 Query.

11. Create a query to display the average billed amount for each technician. Save the query as Lab 2-1 Step 11 Query.

12. Create the crosstab shown in Figure 2–87. The crosstab groups total of clients' paid amounts by city and technician number. Save the crosstab as City-Technician Crosstab.

13. Submit the revised database in the format specified by your instructor.

Figure 2–87

In the Lab

Lab 2: Querying the Hockey Fan Zone Database

Problem: The management of the Hockey Fan Zone store has determined a number of questions it wants the database management system to answer. You must obtain answers to the questions posed by management.

Instructions: Use the database created in the In the Lab 2 of Chapter 1 on page AC 68 for this assignment, or see your instructor for information on accessing the files required for this book. Perform the following tasks:

1. Open the Hockey Fan Zone database and use the query wizard to create a query that includes the Item Number, Description, On Hand, and Cost fields for all records in the Item table. Name the query Lab 2-2 Step 1 Query.

2. Create a query that includes the Item Number, Description, Cost, and Supplier Code fields for all products where the Supplier Code is LG. Save the query as Lab 2-2 Step 2 Query.

3. Create a query that includes the Item Number and Description fields for all products where the description starts with the letter B. Save the query as Lab 2-2 Step 3 Query.

4. Create a query that includes the Item Number and Description field for all products with a cost less than $5.00. Save the query as Lab 2-2 Step 4 Query.

5. Create a query that includes the Item Number and Description field for all products with a selling price greater than $15.00. Save the query as Lab 2-2 Step 5 Query.

6. Create a query that includes all fields for all products with a selling price greater than $10.00 and where the number on hand is fewer than 10. Save the query as Lab 2-2 Step 6 Query.

7. Create a query that includes all fields for all products that have a selling price greater than $15.00 or a supplier code of AC. Save the query as Lab 2-2 Step 7 Query.

8. Join the Supplier table and the Item table. Include the Supplier Code and Supplier Name fields from the Supplier table and the Item Number, Description, On Hand, and Cost fields from the Item table. Sort the records in ascending order by Supplier Code and Item Number. Save the query as Supplier-Item Query. Note that the Report Wizard limits the size of the On Hand column header because it is a number field.

9. Create the report shown in Figure 2–88. The report uses the Supplier-Item query and the Module style.

Supplier-Item Report

Supplier Code	Item Number	Supplier Name	Description	Hand	Cost
AC	5923	Ace Clothes	Jersey	12	$21.45
AC	7810	Ace Clothes	Tee Shirt	32	$9.50
LG	3663	Logo Goods	Ball Cap	30	$11.15
LG	4563	Logo Goods	Earrings	10	$4.50
LG	4593	Logo Goods	Foam Finger	25	$2.95
LG	7930	Logo Goods	Visor	9	$11.95
MN	3683	Mary's Novelties	Bumper Sticker	50	$0.95
MN	6189	Mary's Novelties	Koozies	35	$2.00
MN	6343	Mary's Novelties	Note Cube	7	$5.75

Figure 2–88

10. Create a query that includes the Item Number, Description, On Hand, and Cost fields. Calculate the inventory value (on hand * cost) for all records in the table. Change the caption for the On Hand column to In Stock. Format inventory value as currency with two decimal places. Sort the records in descending order by inventory value. Save the query as Lab 2-2 Step 10 Query.

11. Create a query that calculates and displays the average cost of all items. Save the query as Lab 2-2 Step 11 Query.

12. Create a query that calculates and displays the average cost of items grouped by supplier code. Save the query as Lab 2-2 Step 12 Query.

13. Submit the revised database in the format specified by your instructor.

In the Lab

Lab 3: Querying the Ada Beauty Supply Database

Problem: The management of Ada Beauty Supply has determined a number of questions it wants the database management system to answer. You must obtain answers to the questions posed by management.

Instructions: Use the database created in the In the Lab 3 of Chapter 1 on page AC 69 for this assignment, or see your instructor for information on accessing the files required for this book. For Part 1 and Part 3, save each query using a format similar to the following: Lab 2-3 Part 1a Query, Lab 2-3 Part 3a Query, and so on. Submit the revised database in the format specified by your instructor.

Instructions Part 1: Create a new query for the Customer table and include the Customer Number, Customer Name, Balance, and Amount Paid fields in the design grid. Answer the following questions: (a) Which customers' names begin with C? (b) Which customers are located on Devon? (c) Which customers have a balance of $0.00? (d) Which customers have a balance greater than $200.00 and have an amount paid less than $800.00? (e) Which two customers have the highest balances? (f) For each customer, what is the total of the balance and amount paid amounts?

Instructions Part 2: Join the Sales Rep and the Customer table. Include the Sales Rep Number, First Name, and Last Name from the Sales Rep table and the Customer Number, Customer Name, and Amount Paid from the Customer table in the design grid. Sort the records in ascending order by Sales Rep Number and Customer Number. All sales reps should appear in the result even if they currently have no customers. Save the query as Sales Rep-Customer Query.

Instructions Part 3: Calculate the following statistics: (a) What is the average balance for customers assigned to sales rep 44? (b) What is the total balance for all customers? (c) What is the total amount paid for each sales rep?

Cases and Places

Apply your creative thinking and problem solving skills to design and implement a solution.

• EASIER   •• MORE DIFFICULT

• 1: Querying the Second Hand Goods Database

Use the Second Hand Goods database you created in Cases and Places 1 in Chapter 1 on page AC 71 for this assignment, or see your instructor for information on accessing the files required for this book. Create queries for the following:

a. Find the number and description of all items that contain the word Table.

b. Find the item number, description, and condition of the item that has the earliest posting date.

c. Find the total price of each item available for sale. Show the item description and total price.

d. Find the seller of each item. Show the seller's first name and last name as well as the item description, price, quantity, and date posted. Sort the results by item description within seller last name.

e. Create a parameter query that will allow the user to enter an item description when the query is run. The user should see all fields in the query result.

f. Find all items posted between April 1, 2008 and April 4, 2008. The user should see all fields in the query result.

Submit the revised database in the format specified by your instructor.

• 2: Querying the BeachCondo Rentals Database

Use the BeachCondo Rentals database you created in Cases and Places 2 in Chapter 1 on page AC 71 for this assignment, or see your instructor for information on accessing the files required for this book. Create queries for the following:

a. Find all units that rent for less than $1,000 per week and have at least two bedrooms. The user should see all fields in the query result.

b. Find all units that are on the fourth floor. (Hint: The first digit of the Unit Number field indicates the floor.) Include the Unit Number and the Weekly Rate fields in the query result.

c. Find all units that have more than one bedroom and more than one bathroom and provide linens. Include the Unit Number, Bedrooms, and Weekly Rate fields in the query result.

d. Owner BE20 offers a 15 percent discount on the weekly rate if renters rent for more than one week. What is the discounted weekly rental rate for his units? Your result should include the unit number, bedrooms, bathrooms, sleeps, and discounted weekly rate in your result. Be sure the discounted rate appears as currency.

e. List the owner's first and last name as well as telephone number. Also include the unit number and the weekly rate. All owners should appear in the result even if they currently have no rental units.

f. Find the highest and lowest weekly rate.

Submit the revised database in the format specified by your instructor.

•• 3: Querying the Restaurant Database

Use the restaurant database you created in Cases and Places 3 in Chapter 1 on page AC 71 for this assignment, or see your instructor for information on accessing the files required for this book. Using the Plan Ahead guidelines presented in this chapter, determine at least five questions the conference director might want to ask the database. Using a word processing program, such as Microsoft Word, write the questions in your own words. Then, design the queries for Access. Run and save each query. Submit the Word document and the revised database in the format specified by your instructor.

Continued >

Cases and Places *continued*

•• 4: Designing Queries to Help in Your Job Search

Make It Personal

Use the contacts database you created in Cases and Places 4 in Chapter 1 on page AC 71 for this assignment, or see your instructor for information on accessing the files required for this book. Consider your own personal job situation. What questions would you want to ask this database? Using a word processing program, such as Microsoft Word, write the questions in your own words. Can your database answer the questions that you listed? If it can, design the queries for Access. Run and save each query. In your Word document, identify which questions were posed to Access and which questions could not be answered. For questions that could not be answered, explain why your database cannot answer the question. Submit the Word document and the revised database in the format specified by your instructor.

•• 5: Creating Queries to Analyze Data

Working Together

Obtain a copy of the weather page of your local newspaper. As a team, choose 30 cities of interest. Create a database that contains one table and has five fields (City, State or Province, High Temp, Low Temp, Sky). Use the newspaper's abbreviations for Sky; for example, c for cloudy, r for rain and so on. Create queries that do the following:

a. Display the five cities with the highest high temperatures.

b. Calculate the difference between the high and low temperatures for each city.

c. Display the average high and low temperature for all cities.

d. List the states or provinces in your table. Each state or province should appear only once.

Write a one-page paper that explains what the team learned from querying the database and any conclusions you can draw about the data — for example, describe the Sky conditions for the cities with the least difference in high and low temperature. Submit the assignment in the format specified by your instructor.

3 Maintaining a Database

Objectives

You will have mastered the material in this chapter when you can:

- Add, change, and delete records
- Search for records
- Filter records
- Update a table design
- Format a datasheet
- Use action queries to update records

- Specify validation rules, default values, and formats
- Create and use single-valued and multivalued Lookup fields
- Specify referential integrity
- Use a subdatasheet
- Sort records

3 | Maintaining a Database

Introduction

Once a database has been created and loaded with data, it must be maintained. **Maintaining the database** means modifying the data to keep it up-to-date, such as adding new records, changing the data for existing records, and deleting records. Updating can include mass updates or mass deletions; that is, updates to, or deletions of, many records at the same time.

Maintenance of a database can also involve the need to **restructure the database** periodically; that is, to change the database structure. Restructuring can include adding new fields — including both Lookup and multivalued fields — to a table, changing the characteristics of existing fields, and removing existing fields. It also includes the creation of validation rules and referential integrity. Validation rules ensure validity of the data in the database, while referential integrity ensures the validity of the relationships.

Maintaining a database also can include filtering records, a process that ensures that only the records that satisfy some criterion appear when viewing and updating the data in a table. Changing the appearance of a datasheet is a maintenance activity. Finally, backing up the database as well as compacting and repairing a database are database maintenance tasks as well.

Project — Maintaining a Database

JSP Recruiters faces the task of keeping its database up-to-date. As the agency takes on new clients and recruiters, it will need to add new records, make changes to existing records, and delete records. JSP managers have found they must change the structure of the database to categorize the clients by type. They will do this by adding a Client Type field to the Client table. They also want to track the specialties that are of interest to clients. They will do so by adding a Specialties Needed field to the Client table. Because clients may need more than one specialty, this field will be a multivalued field. Along with these changes, JSP staff want to change the appearance of a datasheet when displaying data.

JSP would like the ability to make mass updates, that is, to update or delete many records in a single operation. They want rules that make sure users can enter only valid data into the database, and they want to ensure that it is not possible for the database to contain a client who is not associated with a specific recruiter. Finally, they want to improve the efficiency of certain types of processing, specifically sorting and retrieving data.

Figure 3–1 summarizes some of the various types of activities involved in maintaining the JSP Recruiters database.

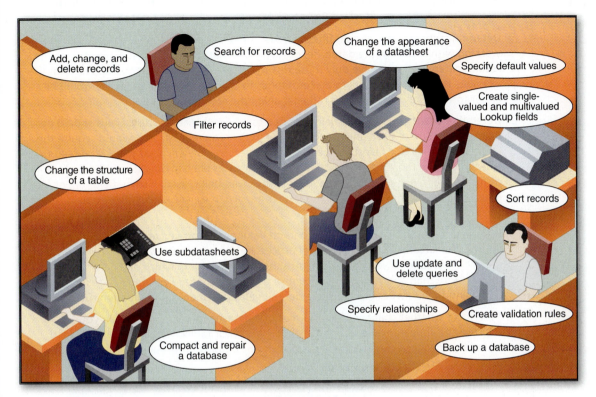

Figure 3–1

Overview

As you read through this chapter, you will learn how to maintain a database by performing these general tasks:

- Add, change, and delete records.
- Filter records so that only those records that satisfy some criterion appear in a datasheet or form.
- Change the structure of a table.
- Make mass changes to a table.
- Create validation rules to ensure that the database contains only valid data.
- Change the appearance of a datasheet.
- Enforce relationships by creating referential integrity.
- Order records.
- Perform special database operations such as backing up a database and compacting a database.

Plan Ahead

Database Maintenance Guidelines

1. **Determine when it is necessary to add, change, or delete records in a database.** Decide when updates are necessary. Also determine whether the updates are to be made to individual records or whether mass updates would be more efficient. For example, if a state changes an area code, a mass update would be more efficient.

2. **Determine whether you should filter records.** For each situation where a user will be working with a table in the database, examine whether it might be desirable to have the records filtered, that is, have only those records that satisfy some criterion appear. For example, if a user only wants to make changes to clients in a particular city, it would be easier to view only those records rather than all the records in the table.

3. **Determine whether additional fields are necessary or whether existing fields should be deleted.** Have there been any changes to the initial requirements that would require the addition of a field (or fields) to one of the tables? If so, you will need to add the field to the appropriate table. Also, now that the database has been in operation for a period of time, determine whether all the fields actually are being used. If some fields are not in use, verify that they are, in fact, no longer needed. If so, you can delete the field from the table.

4. **Determine whether validation rules, default values, and formats are necessary.** Can you improve the accuracy of the data entry process by enforcing data validation? What values are allowed for a particular field? Are there some fields in which one particular value is used more than another? You can control the values that are entered in a field by modifying the table design to include default values, formats, and validation rules.

5. **Determine whether changes to the format of a datasheet are desirable.** Can you improve the appearance of the Datasheet view of your tables? Once you have decided on a particular appearance, it is a good idea to be consistent throughout all your tables except in special circumstances.

6. **Identify related tables in order to implement relationships between the tables.** Examine the database design you created earlier to identify related tables. For each pair of related tables, you will need to make decisions about the implementation of the relationship between the tables.

When necessary, more specific details concerning the above decisions and/or actions are presented at appropriate points in the chapter. The chapter also will identify the use of these guidelines in database maintenance tasks such as those shown in Figure 3–1 on the previous page.

Starting Access

If you are using a computer to step through the project in this chapter and you want your screen to match the figures in this book, you should change your screen's resolution to 1024 × 768. For information about how to change a computer's resolution, read Appendix E.

To Start Access

The following steps, which assume Windows Vista is running, start Access.

1 Click the Start button on the Windows Vista taskbar to display the Start menu.

2 Click All Programs at the bottom of the left Pane on the Start menu to display the All Programs list and then click Microsoft Office in the All Programs list to display the Microsoft Office list.

3 Click Microsoft Office Access 2007 on the Microsoft Office list to start Access and display the Getting Started with Microsoft Office Access window.

4 If the Access window is not maximized, click the Maximize button on its title bar to maximize the window.

> **Note:** If you are using Windows XP, see Appendix F for alternate steps.

To Open a Database

In Chapter 1, you created your database on a USB flash drive using the file name, JSP Recruiters. There are two ways to open the file containing your database. If the file you created appears in the Recent Documents list, you can click it to open the file. If not, you can use the More button to open the file. The following steps use the More button to open the JSP Recruiters database from the USB flash drive.

> **Note:** If you are using Windows XP, see Appendix F for alternate steps.

1 With your USB flash drive connected to one of the computer's USB ports, click the More button to display the Open dialog box.

2 If the Folders list is displayed below the Folders button, click the Folders button to remove the Folders list.

3 If necessary, click Computer in the Favorite Links section and then double-click UDISK 2.0 (E:) to select the USB flash drive, as the new open location. (Your drive letter might be different.)

4 Click JSP Recruiters to select the file name.

5 Click the Open button to open the database.

6 If a Security Warning appears, click the Options button to display the Microsoft Office Security Options dialog box.

7 Click the Enable this content option button.

8 Click the OK button to enable the content.

Updating Records

Keeping the data in a database up-to-date requires updating records in three ways: adding new records, changing the data in existing records, and deleting existing records.

Adding Records

In Chapter 1, you added records to a database using Datasheet view; that is, as you added records, the records appeared on the screen in a datasheet. The data looked like a table. When you need to add additional records, you can use the same techniques.

In Chapter 1, you used a split form to view records. The split form contained both a form and a datasheet. You can use either portion to add records. You also can use a simple form, that is, a form that does not contain a datasheet. Whether you use a simple form or the form portion of a split form, you can use the form to update the table. To add new records, change existing records, or delete records, you use the same techniques you used in Datasheet view. The following steps create a simple form and then add a record to the Client table using the form.

To Create a Simple Form

Rather than using a split form, you may wish just to view the data in a form without also having a datasheet on the screen. If you already have created such a form, you can open it. If not, you can create a simple form to use. The following steps create a simple form.

- Show the Navigation Pane if it is currently hidden.

- If necessary, click the Client table in the Navigation Pane to select it.

- Click Create on the Ribbon to display the Create tab (Figure 3–2).

Figure 3–2

2

• Click the Form button on the Create tab to create a simple form (Figure 3–3).

Q&A How can I tell which view of the form is currently on the screen?

Point to the button that is highlighted in the lower-right corner of the screen. The ScreenTip indicates the current view. At the present time, the form appears in Layout view.

Q&A Which view should I use if I want to enter records?

Form view.

Figure 3–3

3

• Click the Form View button to display the form in Form view (Figure 3–4).

Q&A Could I use the View button to display the form in Form view?

Yes. Click the arrow at the bottom of the button and then click Form View.

Experiment

• Click the various navigation buttons (First record, Next record, Previous record, and Last record) to see each button's effect. Click the Current Record box, change the record number, and press the ENTER key to see how to move to a specific record.

Figure 3–4

To Use a Form to Add Records

Once a form is open in Form view you can add records using the same techniques you used to add records in Datasheet view. The following steps use the form just created to add records.

- Click the New (blank) record button on the Navigation bar to enter a new record, and then type the data for the new record as shown in Figure 3–5. Press the TAB key after typing the data in each field, except after typing the data for the final field (Recruiter Number).

- Press the TAB key to complete the entry of the record.

- Click the Close 'Client' button to close the Client form.

- Click the No button when asked if you want to save your changes.

Q&A | Why not save the form?

If you wish to use this form frequently in the future, you would probably save it. It is very easy to re-create the form whenever you need it, however.

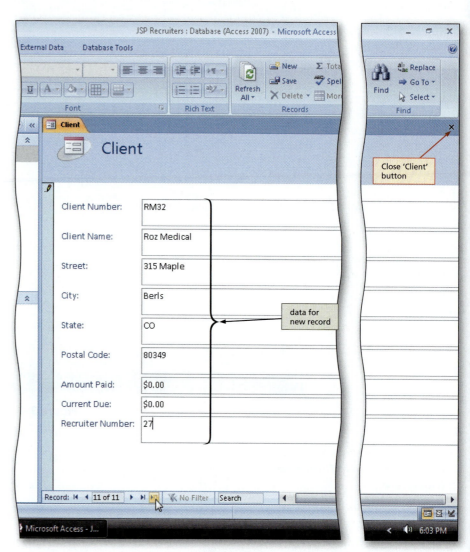

Figure 3–5

Other Ways

1. Click New button on Ribbon
2. Press CTRL+PLUS SIGN (+)

To Search for a Record

In the database environment, **searching** means looking for records that satisfy some criteria. Looking for the client whose number is MH56 is an example of searching. The queries in Chapter 2 also were examples of searching. Access had to locate those records that satisfied the criteria.

A need for searching also exists when using Form view or Datasheet view. To update client MH56, for example, first you need to find the client.

The following steps show how to search for the client whose number is MH56.

1

- Right-click Client Form in the Navigation Pane and click Open on the shortcut menu to open the form in Form view.

- Hide the Navigation Pane (Figure 3–6).

Q&A Which command on the shortcut menu gives me Form view? I see both Layout view and Design view, but no option for Form view.

The Open command opens the form in Form view.

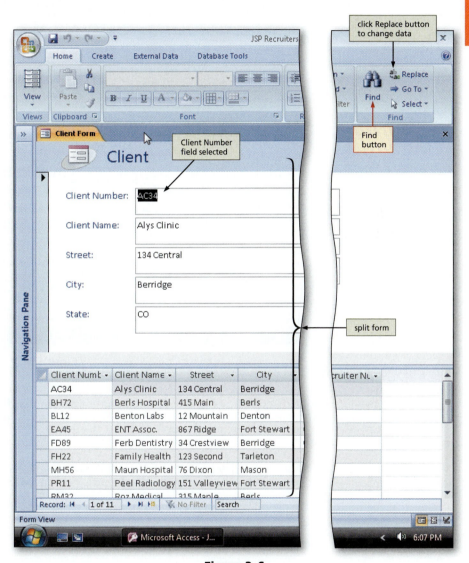

Figure 3–6

2

- Click the Find button on the Home tab to display the Find and Replace dialog box.

- Type MH56 in the Find What text box.

- Click the Find Next button in the Find and Replace dialog box to find client MH56 (Figure 3–7).

Q&A

Can I also find records in Datasheet view or in Form view?

Yes. You use the same process to find records whether you are viewing the data with split form, in Datasheet view, or in Form view.

🔍 **Experiment**

- Find records using other client numbers. Try to find a record using a client number that does not exist. Click in a different field and try to find records based on the value in that field. Try to use wildcards just as you did in queries. When done, once again locate client MH56.

Figure 3–7

exist. Click in a different field and try to find records based on the value in that field. Try to use wildcards just as you did in queries. When done, once again locate client MH56.

3

- Click the Cancel button in the Find and Replace dialog box to remove the dialog box from the screen.

Q&A

Why does the button in the dialog box read Find Next rather than simply Find?

In some cases, after locating a record that satisfies a criterion, you might need to find the next record that satisfies the same criterion. For example, if you just found the first client whose recruiter number is 24, you then may want to find the second such client, then the third, and so on. To do so, click the Find Next button. You will not need to retype the value each time.

Q&A

Can I replace one value with another using this dialog box?

Yes. Either click the Replace button on the Ribbon or the Replace tab in the Find and Replace dialog box. You then can enter both the value to find and the replacement value.

Other Ways
1. Press CTRL+F

To Update the Contents of a Record

After locating the record to be changed, select the field to be changed by clicking the field. You also can press the TAB key repeatedly. Then make the appropriate changes. (Clicking the field automatically produces an insertion point. If you use the TAB key, you will need to press F2 to produce an insertion point.)

The following step uses Form view to change the name of client MH56 from Maun Hospital to Munn Hospital by deleting the letters au and then inserting the letters un after the letter M.

1

- Click in the Client Name field in the datasheet for client MH56 after the letter M to select the field.

- Press the DELETE key twice to delete the letters au.

- Type the letters un after the letter M.

- Press the TAB key to complete the change and move to the next field (Figure 3–8).

Q&A Could I have changed the contents of the field in the form?

Yes. You first will need to ensure the record to be changed appears in the form. You can then change the value just as in the datasheet.

Q&A Do I need to save my change?

No. Once you move to another record or close this table, the change to the name will become permanent.

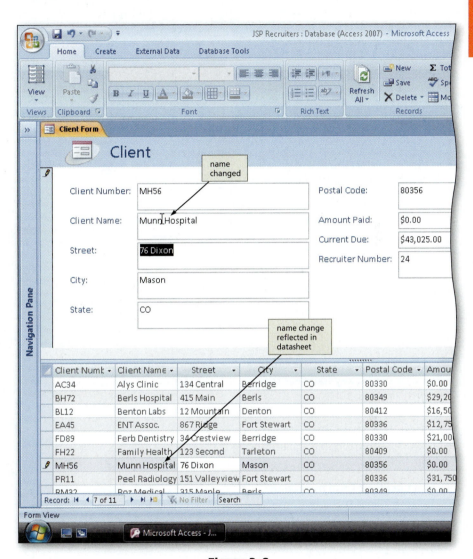

Figure 3–8

To Delete a Record

When records no longer are needed, **delete the records** (remove them) from the table. If client EA45 no longer is served by JSP Recruiters and its final payment is made, the record can be deleted. The following steps delete client EA45.

- With the Client Form open, click the record selector in the datasheet (the small box that appears to the left of the first field) of the record on which the client number is EA45 (Figure 3–9).

Q&A

That technique works in the datasheet portion. How do I select the record in the form portion?

With the desired record appearing in the form, click the record selector (the triangle in front of the record) to select the entire record.

Figure 3–9

- Press the DELETE key to delete the record (Figure 3–10).

3

- Click the Yes button to complete the deletion.

- Close the Client Form by clicking the Close 'Client Form' button.

Figure 3–10

Other Ways

1. Click Delete button on Ribbon

Filtering Records

You can use the Find button in either Datasheet view or Form view to locate a record quickly that satisfies some criterion (for example, the client number is MH56). All records appear, however, not just the record or records that satisfy the criterion. To have only the record or records that satisfy the criterion appear, use a **filter**. Four types of filters are available: Filter By Selection, Common Filters, Filter By Form, and Advanced Filter/Sort. You can use a filter in either Datasheet view or Form view.

**Plan
Ahead**

Determine whether you should filter records.
If you determine that it is desirable to have only those records that satisfy some criterion appear, you have two choices. You can create a query or create a filter. The following guidelines apply to this decision.

1. If you think that you frequently will want to display records that satisfy precisely this same criterion, you should consider creating a query whose results only contain the records that satisfy the criterion. To display those records in the future, simply open the query.

2. If you are viewing data in a datasheet or form and decide you want to restrict the records to be included, it is easier to create a filter than create a query. You can create and use the filter while you are viewing the data.

3. If you have created a filter that you would like to be able to use again in the future, you can save the filter as a query.

   If you have decided that it is appropriate to use a filter, you need to decide which type of filter to use.

1. If your criterion for filtering is that the value in a particular field matches or does not match a certain specific value, you can use Filter By Selection.

2. If your criterion only involves a single field but is more complex, for example, that the value in the field begins with a certain collection of letters, you can use a Common Filter.

3. If your criterion involves more than one field, use Filter By Form.

4. If your criterion involves more than a single And or Or, or if it involves sorting, you will probably find it simpler to use Advanced Filter/Sort.

To Use Filter By Selection

The simplest type of filter is called **Filter By Selection**. To use Filter By Selection, you give Access an example of the data you want by selecting the data within the table. You then choose the option you want on the Selection menu. If you have determined that you only want to display those clients located in Berridge, Filter By Selection is appropriate. The following steps use Filter By Selection in Datasheet view to display only the records for clients in Berridge.

- Open the Client Form and hide the Navigation Pane.

- Click the City field on the first record in the datasheet portion of the form to select Berridge as the city (Figure 3–11).

Q&A

Could I have selected the City field on the fourth record, which is also Berridge?

Yes. It does not matter which record you select as long as the city is Berridge.

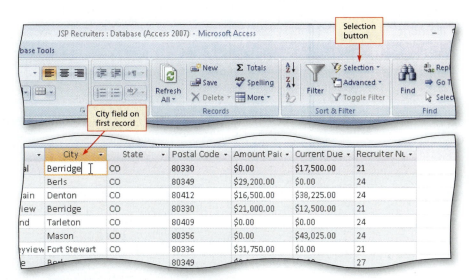

Figure 3–11

2

● Click the Selection button on the Home tab to display the Selection menu (Figure 3–12).

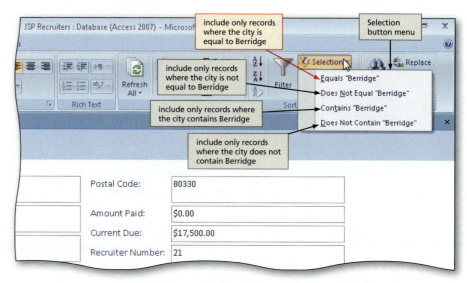

Figure 3–12

3

● Click Equals "Berridge" to select only those clients whose city is Berridge (Figure 3–13).

Q&A

Can I also filter in Datasheet view or in Form view?

Yes. Filtering works the same whether you are viewing the data with split form, in Datasheet view, or in Form view.

Experiment

● Try each of the other values in the Selection menu to see their effect. When done, once again select those clients whose city is Berridge.

Figure 3–13

To Toggle a Filter

The following step toggles the filter to redisplay all records.

1

• Click the Toggle Filter button on the Home tab to toggle the filter and redisplay all records (Figure 3–14).

Does that action clear the filter?

No. The filter is still in place. If you click the Toggle Filter button a second time, you again will see only the filtered records.

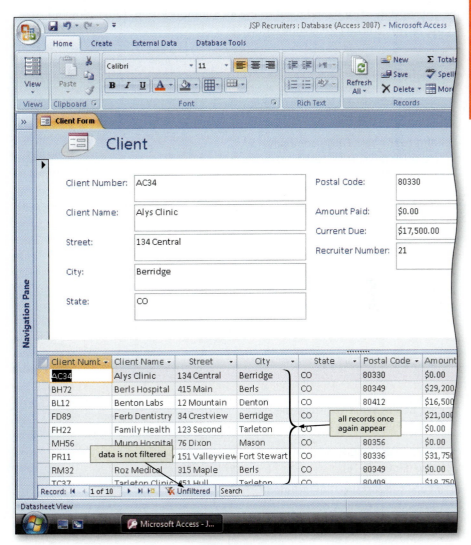

Figure 3–14

TO CLEAR A FILTER

Once you have finished using a filter, you can clear the filter. After doing so, you no longer will be able to use the filter by pressing the Toggle Filter button. To clear a filter, you use the following steps.

1. Click the Advanced button on the Home tab.

2. Click Clear All Filters on the Advanced menu.

Using Wildcards in Filters

Both the question mark (?) and the asterisk (*) wildcards can be used in filters created using Advanced Filter/Sort.

To Use a Common Filter

You can filter individual fields by clicking the arrow to the right of the field name and using a Common Filter. If you have determined you want to include those clients whose city begins with Ber, Filter By Selection would not be appropriate. You would need to use a Common Filter. The following steps use a common filter to include only those clients whose city begins with Ber.

• Be sure the Home tab is selected.

• Click the City arrow to display the common filter menu.

• Point to the Text Filters command to display the custom text filters (Figure 3–15).

Q&A

I selected the City field and then clicked the Filter button on the Home tab. My screen looks the same. Is this right?

Yes. That is another legitimate way to display the common filter menu.

Figure 3–15

• Click Begins With to display the Custom Filter dialog box.

• Type Ber as the City begins with value (Figure 3–16).

Q&A

If I wanted certain cities included, could I use the check boxes?

Yes. Be sure the cities you want are the only ones checked. One way to do this is to click the Select All check box to remove all the check marks and then click the check boxes for the cities you want to include. Another way is to clear the check boxes for the cities you don't want. Use whichever technique you find more convenient.

Experiment

• Try other options in the Common Filter menu to see their effect. When done, once again select those clients whose city begins with Ber.

Figure 3–16

3

● Click the OK button to filter the records (Figure 3–17). (Your order may be different.)

Q&A

Can I use the same technique in Form view?

In Form view, you would need to click the field and then click the Filter button to display the Common Filter menu. The rest of the process would be the same.

4

● Click the Toggle Filter button on the Home tab to toggle the filter and redisplay all records.

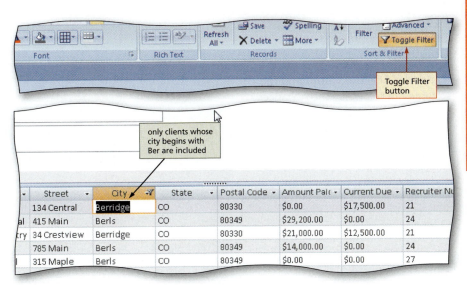

Figure 3–17

To Use Filter By Form

Filter By Selection is a quick and easy way to filter by the value in a single field. For more complex criteria, however, it is not appropriate. For example, if you determined you only wanted those clients whose postal code is 80330 and whose amount paid is 0, you could not use either the Filter by Selection or the Common Filter processes. Rather, you would use **Filter By Form**. The following steps use Filter By Form to restrict the records that appear.

1

● Click the Advanced button on the Home tab to display the Advanced menu (Figure 3–18).

Figure 3–18

2

- Click Clear All Filters on the Advanced menu to clear the existing filter.

- Click the Advanced button on the Home tab to display the Advanced menu a second time.

- Click Filter By Form on the Advanced menu.

- Click the Postal Code field, click the arrow that appears, and then click 80330.

- Click the Amount Paid field, click the arrow that appears, and then click 0 (Figure 3–19).

Q&A

Is there any difference in the process if I am viewing a table in Datasheet view rather than in Form view or in a split form?

In Datasheet view, you will make your entries in a datasheet rather than a form. Otherwise, the process is the same.

- Click the Toggle Filter button on the Home tab to apply the filter (Figure 3–20).

Experiment

- Select Filter By Form again and enter different criteria. In each case, toggle the filter to see the effect of your selection. When done, once again select those clients whose postal code is 80330 and whose amount paid is 0.

Figure 3–19

Figure 3–20

To Use Advanced Filter/Sort

In some cases, your criteria may be too complex even for Filter By Form. You might decide you want to include any client for which the postal code is 80330 and the amount paid is $0. You also may want to include any client whose amount paid is greater than $20,000, no matter where the client is located. Further, you might want to have the results sorted by name. To filter records using complex criteria, you need to use Advanced Filter/Sort as in the following steps.

1

- Click the Advanced button on the Home tab to display the Advanced menu, and then click Clear All Filters on the Advanced menu to clear the existing filter.

- Click the Advanced button on the Home tab to display the Advanced menu a second time.

- Click Advanced Filter/Sort on the Advanced menu.

- Expand the size of the field list so all the fields in the Client Table appear.

- Include the Client Number field and select Ascending as the sort order.

- Include the Postal Code field and enter 80330 as the criterion.

- Include the Amount Paid field and enter 0 as the criterion in the Criteria row and >20000 as the criterion in the Or row (Figure 3–21).

Figure 3–21

2
- Click the Toggle Filter button on the Home tab to toggle the filter and view the results. Click the Client Form tab to view the Client table (Figure 3–22).

Experiment

- Select Advanced Filter/Sort again and enter different sorting options and criteria. In each case, toggle the filter to see the effect of your selection. When done, change back to the sorting options and criteria you entered in Step 1.

3
- Click Clear All Filters on the Advanced menu.

- Close the Client Form.

Figure 3–22

Filters and Queries

Filters and queries are related in three ways.

1. You can apply a filter to the results of a query just as you can apply a filter to a table.

2. When you have created a filter using either Filter By Form or Advanced Filter/ Sort, you can save the filter settings as a query by using the Save As Query command on the Advanced menu.

3. You can restore filter settings that you previously saved in a query by using the Load From Query command on the Advanced menu.

BTW

Moving a Field in a Table Structure
If you add a field to a table and later realize the field is in the wrong location, you can move the field. To do so, click the row selector for the field and then drag the field to the new location.

Changing the Database Structure

When you initially create a database, you define its **structure**; that is, you assign names and types to all the fields. In many cases, the structure you first define will not continue to be appropriate as you use the database.

Perhaps a field currently in the table no longer is necessary. If no one ever uses a particular field, it is not needed in the table. Because it is occupying space and serving no useful purpose, you should remove it from the table. You also would need to delete the field from any forms, reports, or queries that include it.

More commonly, an organization will find that it needs to maintain additional information that was not anticipated at the time the database was first designed. The organization's own requirements may have changed. In addition, outside regulations that the organization must satisfy may change as well. In either case, the organization must add additional fields to an existing table.

To make any of these changes, you first must open the table in Design view.

To DELETE A FIELD

If a field in one of your tables no longer is needed; for example, it serves no useful purpose or it may have been included by mistake, you should delete the field. To delete a field you would use the following steps.

1. Open the table in Design view.
2. Click the row selector for the field to be deleted.
3. Press the DELETE key.
4. When Access displays the dialog box requesting confirmation that you want to delete the field, click the Yes button.

To Add a New Field

You can add fields to a table in a database. JSP Recruiters has decided that it needs to categorize its clients. To do so requires an additional field, Client Type. The possible values for Client Type are MED (which indicates the client is a medical institution), DNT (which indicates the client is a dental organization), or LAB (which indicates the client is a lab). The following steps add the Client Type to the Client table immediately after the Postal Code field.

1

- Show the Navigation Pane, and then right-click the Client table to display a shortcut menu.

- Click Design View on the shortcut menu to open the Client table in Design view.

- Click the row selector for the Amount Paid field, and then press the INSERT key to insert a blank row above the Amount Paid row (Figure 3–23).

2

- Click the Field Name column for the new field. If necessary, erase any text that appears.

- Type `Client Type` as the field name and then press the TAB key.

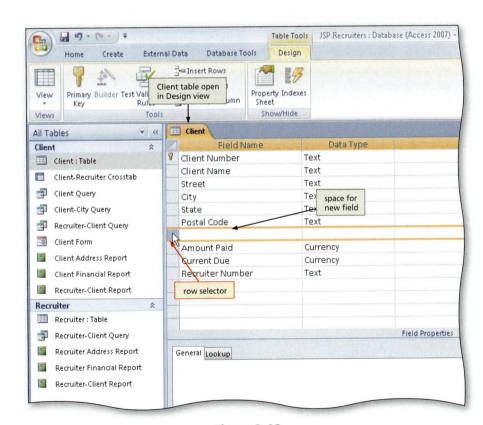

Figure 3–23

Other Ways
1. Click Insert Rows button on Ribbon

To Create a Lookup Field

Because there are only three possible values for the Client Type field, you should make it easy for users to enter the appropriate value. A **Lookup field** allows the user to select from a list of values.

The following steps make the Client Type field a Lookup field.

• If necessary, click the Data Type column for the Client Type field, and then click the arrow to display the menu of available data types (Figure 3–24).

Figure 3–24

• Click Lookup Wizard, and then click the 'I will type in the values that I want.' option button to indicate that you will type in the values (Figure 3–25).

Q&A When would I use the other option button?

You would use the other option button if the data to be entered in this field is found in another table or query.

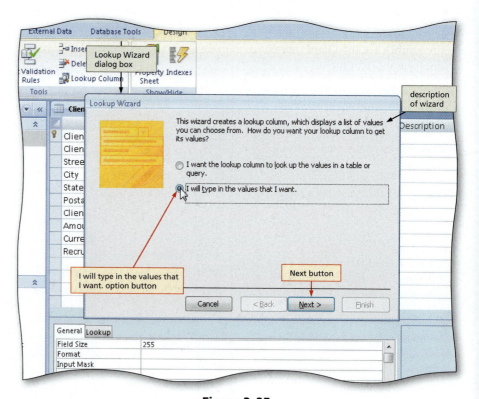

Figure 3–25

3
- Click the Next button to display the next Lookup Wizard screen (Figure 3–26).

Figure 3–26

4
- Click the first row of the table (below Col1), and then type MED as the value in the first row.

- Press the DOWN ARROW key, and then type DNT as the value in the second row.

- Press the DOWN ARROW key, and then type LAB as the value in the third row (Figure 3–27).

Figure 3–27

Click the Next button to display the next Lookup Wizard screen.

Ensure Client Type is entered as the label for the lookup column and that the Allow Multiple Values check box is NOT checked (Figure 3–28).

Figure 3–28

Click the Finish button to complete the definition of the Lookup Wizard field.

Q&A

Why does the data type for the Client Type field still show Text?

The data type is still Text because the values entered in the wizard were entered as text.

To Add a Multivalued Field

BTW

Multivalued Fields
If you plan to move your data to SQL Server at a later date, do not use multivalued fields. When you upsize a database containing multivalued fields to SQL Server, the field is converted to a memo field that contains the delimited set of values. This may mean that you need to do some redesign of your database.

Normally, fields contain only a single value. In Access 2007 it is possible to have **multivalued fields**, that is, fields that can contain more than one value. JSP Recruiters wants to use such a field to store the abbreviations of all the specialties their clients need (see Table 3–1 for the specialty abbreviations and descriptions). Unlike the Client Type, where each client only had one type, clients can require multiple specialty descriptions.

Table 3–1 Specialty Abbreviations and Descriptions	
Specialty Abbreviation	**Description**
CLS	Clinical Laboratory Specialist
CNA	Certified Nursing Assistant
CRNA	Certified Registered Nurse Anesthetist
DH	Dental Hygienist
Dnt	Dentist
EMT	Emergency Medical Technician
NP	Nurse Practitioner
OT	Occupational Therapist
PA	Physician Assistant
Phy	Physician
PT	Physical Therapist
RN	Registered Nurse
RT	Respiratory Therapist

One client might need CNA, PA, Phy, and RN employees (Certified Nursing Assistants, Physician Assistants, Physicians, and Registered Nurses). Another client might only need RTs (Respiratory Therapists).

To create a multivalued field, create a Lookup field being sure to check the Allow Multiple Values check box. The following steps create a multivalued field.

1 Click the row selector for the Amount Paid field, and then press the INSERT key to insert a blank row.

2 Click the Field Name column for the new field, type `Specialties Needed` as the field name, and then press the DOWN ARROW key.

3 Click the Data Type column for the Specialties Needed field, and then click Lookup Wizard in the menu of available data types to start the Lookup Wizard.

4 Click the 'I will type in the values that I want.' option button to indicate that you will type in the values.

5 Click the Next button to display the next Lookup Wizard screen.

6 Click the first row of the table (below Col1), and then type `CLS` as the value in the first row.

7 Enter the remaining values from the first column in Table 3–1. Before typing each value, press the TAB key to move to a new row.

8 Click the Next button to display the next Lookup Wizard screen.

9 Ensure Specialties Needed is entered as the label for the lookup column.

10 Click the Allow Multiple Values check box to allow multiple values.

11 Click the Finish button to complete the definition of the Lookup Wizard field.

To Save the Changes and Close the Table

The following steps save the changes; that is, it saves the addition of the two new fields and closes the table.

1 Click the Save button on the Quick Access Toolbar to save the changes.

2 Click the Close 'Client' button.

TO MODIFY SINGLE OR MULTIVALUED LOOKUP FIELDS

You may find that you later want to change the list of choices in a Lookup field. If you find you need to modify a single or multivalued Lookup field you have created, you can use the following steps.

1. Open the table in Design view and select the field to be modified.
2. Click the Lookup Tab in the field properties.
3. Change the list in the Row Source property to change the desired list of values.

BTW

Modifying Table Properties
You can change the properties of a table by opening the table in Design view and then clicking the Property Sheet button on the Table Tools tab. Access will display the property sheet for the table. To display the records in a table in an order other than primary key order (the default sort order), use the Order By property. For example, to display the Client table automatically in Client Name order, click the Order By property box, type `Client.Client Name` in the property box, close the property sheet, and save the change to the table design. When you open the Client table in Datasheet view, the records will be sorted in Client Name order.

Mass Changes

In some cases, rather than making individual changes to records, you will want to make mass changes. That is, you will want to add, change, or delete many records in a single operation. You can do this with action queries. An **action query** adds, deletes, or changes data in a table. An **update query** allows you to make the same change to all records satisfying some criterion. If you omit the criterion, you will make the same changes to all records in the table. A **delete query** allows you to delete all the records satisfying some criterion. You can add the results of a query to an existing table by using an **append query**. You also can add the results to a new table by using a **make-table query**.

To Use an Update Query

The Client Type field is blank on every record. One approach to entering the information for the field would be to step through the entire table, assigning each record its appropriate value. If most of the clients have the same type, a simpler approach is available.

In the JSP Recruiters database, for example, most clients are type MED. Initially, you can set all the values to MED. To accomplish this quickly and easily, you can use an update query, which is a query that makes the same change to all the records satisfying a criterion. Later, you can change the type for dental organizations and labs.

The following steps use an update query to change the value in the Client Type field to MED for all the records. Because all records are to be updated, criteria are not required.

1

- Create a new query for the Client table.

- Click the Update button on the Design tab, double-click the Client Type field to select the field, click the Update To row in the first column of the design grid, and then type MED as the new value (Figure 3–29).

Q&A

Don't I have to enter a criterion?

If you only want the change to be made on some of the records, you would need to enter a criterion to identify those records. Without a criterion, the change will be made on all records, which is what you want in this update.

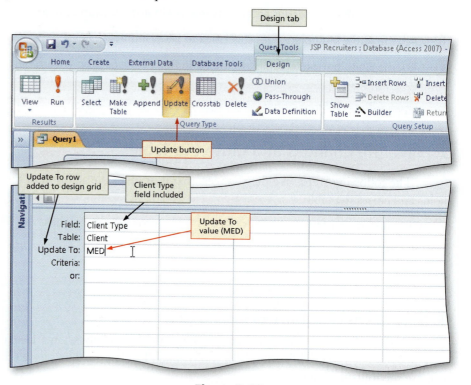

Figure 3–29

2
• Click the Run button on the Design tab to run the query and update the records (Figure 3–30).

Q&A Why don't I click the View button to update the records?

The purpose of the View button is to simply view results. The Run button causes the updates specified by the query to take place.

Q&A Why doesn't the dialog box appear on my screen when I click the Run button?

If the dialog box does not appear, it means that you did not choose the Enable this content option button when you first opened the database. Close the database, open it again, and enable the content in the Microsoft Office Security Options dialog box. Then, create and run the query again.

 Experiment

• Create an Update query to change the client type to DNT. Enter a criterion to restrict the records to be updated, and then run the query. Open the table to view your changes. When finished, create and run an Update query to change the client type to MED on all records.

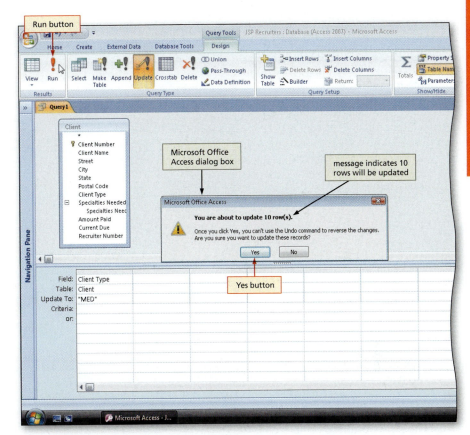

Figure 3–30

3
• Click the Yes button to make the changes.

Other Ways	
1. Right-click any open area in upper Pane, point to Query Type on shortcut menu,	click Update Query on Query Type submenu

To Use a Delete Query

In some cases, you may need to delete several records at a time. If, for example, all clients in a particular postal code are to be serviced by another firm, the clients with this postal code can be deleted from the JSP Recruiters database. Instead of deleting these clients individually, which could be very time-consuming in a large database, you can delete them in one operation by using a **delete query**, which is a query that will delete all the records satisfying the criteria entered in the query.

You can preview the data to be deleted in a delete query before actually performing the deletion. To do so, click the View button after you create the query, but before you run it. The records to be deleted then would appear in Datasheet view. To delete the records, click the View button again to change to Design view. Click the Run button, and then click the Yes button in the Microsoft Office Access dialog box when asked if you want to delete the records.

The following steps use a delete query to delete any client whose postal code is 80412 without first previewing the data to be deleted. (Only one such client currently exists in the database.)

- Clear the grid.

- Click the Delete button on the Design tab to make the query a Delete query (Figure 3–31).

- Double-click the Postal Code field to select the field.

- Click the Criteria row for the Postal Code field and type 80412 as the criterion.

Figure 3–31

- Run the query by clicking the Run button (Figure 3–32).

- Click the Yes button to complete the deletion.

- Close the Query window. Do not save the query.

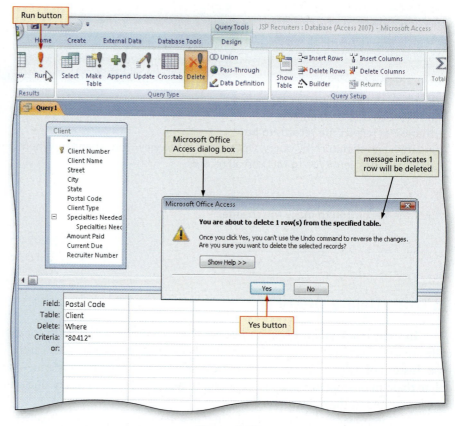

Figure 3–32

Other Ways

1. Right-click any open area in upper Pane, point to Query Type on shortcut menu, click Delete Query on Query Type submenu

To Use an Append Query

An append query adds a group of records from one table to the end of another table. For example, suppose that JSP Recruiters acquires some new clients and a database containing a table with those clients. To avoid entering all this information manually, you can append it to the Client table in the JSP Recruiters database using the append query. To create an append query, you would use the following steps.

1. Create a query for the table containing the records to append.
2. In Design view, indicate the fields to include, and then enter any necessary criteria.
3. View the query results to be sure you have specified the correct data, and then return to Design view.
4. Click the Append button on the Design tab.
5. When Access displays the Append dialog box, specify the name of the table to receive the new records and its location. Run the query by clicking the Run button on the Design tab.
6. When Access indicates the number of records to be appended, click the Yes button.

To Use a Make-Table Query

In some cases, you might want to add the records from an existing table to a new table, that is, a table that has not yet been created. If so, use a make-table query to add the records to a new table. Access will create this table as part of the process and add the records to it. To create a make-table query, you would use the following steps.

1. Create a query for the table containing the records to add.
2. In Design view, indicate the fields to include, and then enter any necessary criteria.
3. View the query results to be sure you have specified the correct data, and then return to Design view.
4. Click the Make Table button on the Design tab.
5. When Access displays the Make Table dialog box, specify the name of the table to receive the new records and its location. Run the query by clicking the Run button on the Design tab.
6. When Access indicates the number of records to be inserted, click the Yes button.

Validation Rules

You now have created, loaded, queried, and updated a database. Nothing you have done so far, however, makes sure that users enter only valid data. To ensure the entry of valid data, you create **validation rules**; that is, rules that a user must follow when entering the data. As you will see, Access will prevent users from entering data that does not follow the rules. The steps also specify **validation text**, which is the message that will appear if a user violates the validation rule.

Validation rules can indicate a **required field**, a field in which the user actually must enter data. For example, by making the Client Name field a required field, a user actually must enter a name (that is, the field cannot be blank). Validation rules can make sure a user's entry lies within a certain **range of values**; for example, that the values in the Amount Paid field are between $0.00 and $100,000.00. They can specify a **default value**; that is, a value that Access will display on the screen in a particular field before the user begins adding a record. To make data entry of client numbers more convenient, you also can have lowercase letters appear automatically as uppercase letters. Finally, validation rules can specify a collection of acceptable values; for example, that the only legitimate entries for the Client Type field are MED, DNT, and LAB.

BTW

Using Wildcards in Validation Rules
You can include wildcards in validation rules. For example, if you enter the expression, like C?, in the Validation Rule box for the State field, the only valid entries for the field will be CA, CO, and CT.

To Specify a Required Field

To specify that a field is to be required, change the value for the Required property from No to Yes. The following steps specify that the Client Name field is to be a required field.

- Show the Navigation Pane, and then open the Client table in Design view.

- Select the Client Name field by clicking its row selector.

- Click the Required property box in the Field Properties Pane, and then click the down arrow that appears.

- Click Yes in the list (Figure 3–33).

Q&A What is the effect of this change?

Users cannot leave the Client Name field blank when entering or editing records.

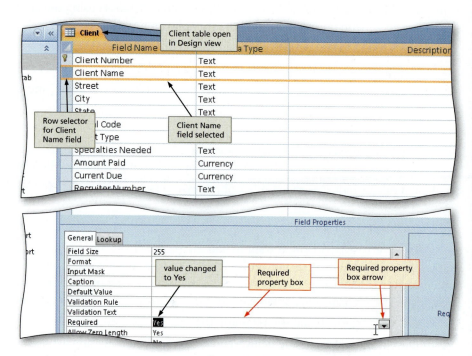

Figure 3–33

To Specify a Range

The following step specifies that entries in the Amount Paid field must be between $0.00 and $100,000.00. To indicate this range, the criterion specifies that the amount paid value must be both >= 0 (greater than or equal to 0) and <= 100000 (less than or equal to 100000).

- Select the Amount Paid field by clicking its row selector, click the Validation Rule property box to produce an insertion point, and then type >=0 and <=100000 as the rule.

- Click the Validation Text property box to produce an insertion point, and then type Must be at least $0.00 and at most $100,000 as the text (Figure 3–34).

Q&A What is the effect of this change?

Users now will be prohibited from entering an amount paid value that either is less than $0.00 or greater than $100,000.00 when they add records or change the value in the Amount Paid field.

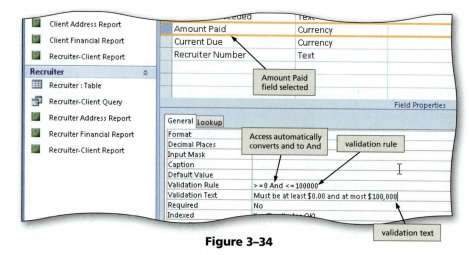

Figure 3–34

To Specify a Default Value

To specify a default value, enter the value in the Default Value property box. The following step specifies MED as the default value for the Client Type field. This simply means that if users do not enter a client type, the type will be MED.

1

- Select the Client Type field. Click the Default Value property box to produce an insertion point, and then type =MED as the value (Figure 3–35).

Figure 3–35

To Specify a Collection of Allowable Values

The only allowable values for the Client Type field are MED, DNT, and LAB. An appropriate validation rule for this field prevents Access from accepting any entry other than these three possibilities. The following step specifies the legal values for the Client Type field.

1

- Make sure the Client Type field is selected.

- Click the Validation Rule property box to produce an insertion point and then type =MED Or =DNT Or =LAB as the validation rule.

- Click the Validation Text property box and then type Must be MED, DNT, or LAB as the validation text (Figure 3–36).

Q&A

What is the effect of this change?

Users now will be allowed to enter only MED, DNT, or LAB in the Client Type field when they add records or make changes to this field.

Figure 3–36

To Specify a Format

To affect the way data appears in a field, you can use a **format**. To use a format with a Text field, you enter a special symbol, called a **format symbol**, in the field's Format property box. The Format property uses different settings for different data types. The following step specifies a format for the Client Number field in the Client table and illustrates the way you enter a format. The format symbol used in the example is >, which causes Access to display lowercase letters automatically as uppercase letters. The format symbol < causes Access to display uppercase letters automatically as lowercase letters.

1

- Select the Client Number field.

- Click the Format property box and then type > (Figure 3–37).

Q&A

What is the effect of this change?

From this point on, any lowercase letters will appear automatically as uppercase when users add records or change the value in the Client Number field.

Q&A

Client numbers are supposed to be four characters long. Is there a way to ensure users don't type more than four characters?

Yes. The Field Size property dictates how many characters the users can type, so if you wanted to ensure that a maximum of four characters be allowed, you could change the field size from 255 to 4.

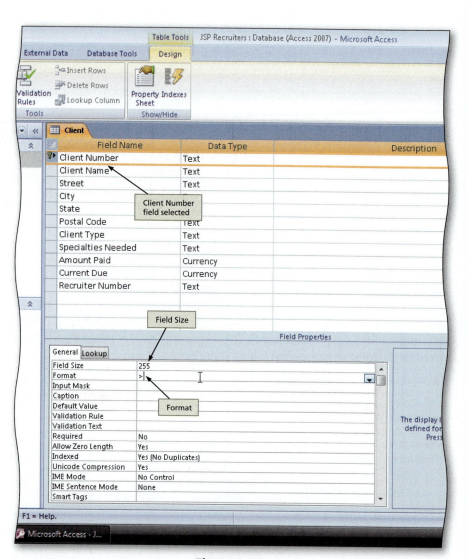

Figure 3–37

To Save the Validation Rules, Default Values, and Formats

The following steps save the validation rules, default values, and formats.

1
- Click the Save button on the Quick Access Toolbar to save the changes (Figure 3–38).

2
- Click the No button to save the changes without testing current data.

- Close the Client table.

Q&A

Should I always click the No button when saving validation rules?

If this were a database used to run a business or to solve some other critical need, you would click Yes. You would want to be sure that the data already in the database does not violate the rules.

Figure 3–38

BTW

Changing Data Types
It is possible to change the data type for a field that already contains data. Before you change a data type, however, you should consider what effect the change will have on other database objects, such as forms, queries, and reports. For example, you could convert a Text field to a Memo field if you find that you do not have enough space to store the data that you need. You also could convert a Number field to a Currency field or vice versa.

Updating a Table that Contains Validation Rules

When updating a table that contains validation rules, Access provides assistance in making sure the data entered is valid. It helps in making sure that data is formatted correctly. Access also will not accept invalid data. Entering a number that is out of the required range, for example, or entering a value that is not one of the possible choices, will produce an error message in the form of a dialog box. The database will not be updated until the error is corrected.

If the client number entered contains lowercase letters, such am49 (Figure 3–39), Access will display the data automatically as AM49 (Figure 3–40).

Figure 3–39

Figure 3–40

If the client type is not valid, such as xxx, Access will display the text message you specified (Figure 3–41) and not allow the data to enter the database.

Figure 3–41

If the amount paid value is not valid, such as 125000, which is too large, Access also displays the appropriate message (Figure 3–42) and refuses to accept the data.

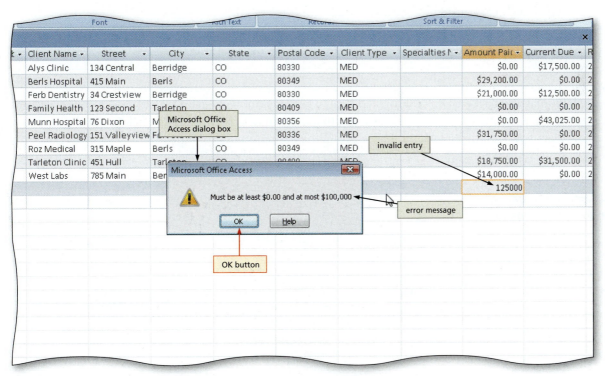

Figure 3–42

If a required field contains no data, Access indicates this by displaying an error message as soon as you attempt to leave the record (Figure 3–43). The field must contain a valid entry before Access will move to a different record.

Figure 3–43

When entering data into a field with a validation rule, you may find that Access displays the error message and you are unable to make the necessary correction. It may be that you cannot remember the validation rule you created or it was created incorrectly. In such a case, you neither can leave the field nor close the table because you have entered data into a field that violates the validation rule.

If this happens, first try again to type an acceptable entry. If this does not work, repeatedly press the BACKSPACE key to erase the contents of the field and then try to leave the field. If you are unsuccessful using this procedure, press the ESC key until the record is removed from the screen. The record will not be added to the database.

Should the need arise to take this drastic action, you probably have a faulty validation rule. Use the techniques of the previous sections to correct the existing validation rules for the field.

To Use a Lookup Field

Earlier, you changed all the entries in the Client Type field to MED. Thus, you have created a rule that will ensure that only legitimate values (MED, DNT, or LAB) can be entered in the field. You also made Client Type a Lookup field using a mass change. You can make changes to a Lookup field by clicking the field to be changed, clicking the arrow that appears in the field, and then selecting the desired value from the list.

The following steps change the Client Type value on the third record to DNT and on the ninth record to LAB.

- Open the Client table in Datasheet view and ensure the Navigation Pane is hidden.

- Click in the Client Type field on the third record to display the arrow (Figure 3–44).

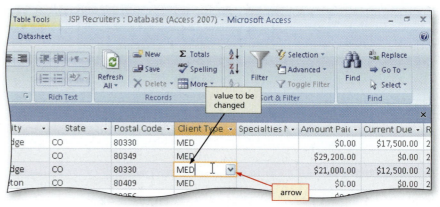

Figure 3–44

2

- Click the down arrow to display the drop-down list of available choices for the Client Type field (Figure 3–45).

Q&A

Could I type the value instead of selecting it from the list?

Yes. Once you have either deleted the previous value or selected the entire previous value, you can begin typing. You do not have to type the full entry. When you begin with the letter, D, for example, Access will automatically add the NT.

erls	CO	80349	MED		$29,200.00	$0.00	2
erridge	CO	80330	MED		$21,000.00	$12,500.00	2
Tarleton	CO	80409	MED		$0.00	$0.00	2
Mason	CO	80356	DNT		$0.00	$43,025.00	2
ort Stewart	CO	80336	LAB		$31,750.00	$0.00	2
erls	CO	80349	MED		$0.00	$0.00	2
arleton	CO	80409	MED		$18,750.00	$31,500.00	2
Berls	CO	80349	MED		$14,000.00	$0.00	2
			MED				

value to select (DNT)

list of available values

Figure 3–45

🔎 **Experiment**

- Select the Client Type field on the first record. Try to change the client type by typing various values. Try to type an invalid Client Type (like SPT). When finished, change the value on the record to MED.

3

- Click DNT to change the value.

- In a similar fashion, change MED on the ninth record to LAB (Figure 3–46).

erls	CO	80349	MED		$29,200.00	$0.00	2
erridge	CO	80330	DNT		$21,000.00	$12,500.00	2
rleton	CO	80409	MED		$0.00	$0.00	2
Mason	CO	80356	MED		$0.00	$43,025.00	2
ort Stewart	CO	80336	MED		$31,750.00	$0.00	2
Berls	CO	80349	MED		$0.00	$0.00	2
Tarleton	CO	80409	MED		$18,750.00	$31,500.00	2
erls	CO	80349	LAB		$14,000.00	$0.00	2
			MED				

values changed

Figure 3–46

To Use a Multivalued Lookup Field

Using a multivalued Lookup field is similar to using a regular Lookup field. The difference is that when you drop down the list, the entries all will be preceded by check boxes. You then can check all the entries that you want. The appropriate entries are shown in Figure 3–47. As indicated in the figure, the specialties needed for client AC34 are CNA, PA, Phy, and RN.

Client Number	Client Name	Specialties Needed
AC34	Alys Clinic	CNA, PA, Phy, RN
BH72	Berls Hospital	CLS, OT, PA, Phy, PT, RN
FD89	Ferb Dentistry	DH, Dnt
FH22	Family Health	NP, Phy, RN
MH56	Munn Hospital	CRNA, OT, Phy, PT, RN
PR11	Peel Radiology	RT
RM32	Roz Medical	CNA, NP, PA, Phy, RN
TC37	Tarleton Clinic	NP, PA, Phy, RN
WL56	West Labs	CLS

Figure 3–47

The following steps make the appropriate entries for the Specialties Needed field.

1

• Click the Specialties Needed field on the first record to display the arrow.

• Click the arrow to display the list of available specialties (Figure 3–48).

Q&A

All the specialties currently appear in the box. What if there were too many specialties to fit?

Access would automatically include a scroll bar that you could use to scroll through all the choices.

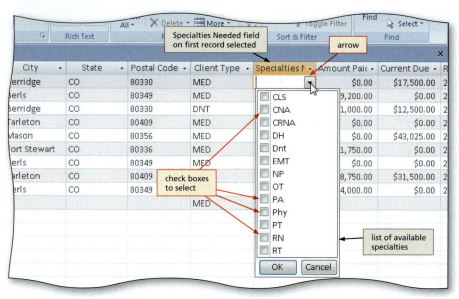

Figure 3–48

2

• Click the CNA, PA, Phy, and RN check boxes to select the specialties for the first client (Figure 3–49).

Figure 3–49

3

• Click the OK button to complete the selection.

• Using the same technique, enter the specialties given in Figure 3–47 on the previous page for the remaining clients (Figure 3–50).

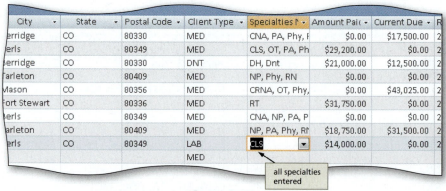

Figure 3–50

To Resize a Column in a Datasheet

The Access default column sizes do not always allow all the data in the field to appear. In some cases, the data may appear, but not the entire field name. You can correct this problem by **resizing** the column (changing its size) in the datasheet. In some instances, you may want to reduce the size of a column. The State field, for example, is short enough that it does not require all the space on the screen that is allotted to it. Changing a column width changes the **layout**, or design, of a table.

The following steps resize the columns in the Client table and save the changes to the layout.

1

- Point to the right boundary of the field selector for the Specialties Needed field (Figure 3–51) so that the mouse pointer becomes a doubled-ended arrow.

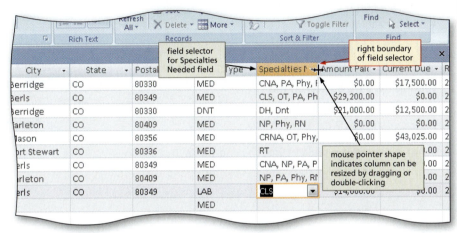

Figure 3–51

2

- Double-click the right boundary of the field selector for the Specialties Needed field to resize the field so that it best fits the data (Figure 3–52).

Figure 3–52

- Use the same technique to resize all the other fields to best fit the data. To resize the Amount Paid, Current Due, and Recruiter Number fields, you will need to scroll the fields by clicking the right scroll arrow shown in Figure 3–52 on the previous page (Figure 3-53).

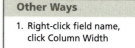

ype ▾	Specialties Needed ▾	Amount Paid ▾	Current Due ▾	Recruiter Number ▾	Add New Field
	CNA, PA, Phy, RN	$0.00	$17,500.00	21	
	CLS, OT, PA, Phy, PT, RN	$29,200.00	$0.00	24	
	DH, Dnt	$21,000.00	$12,500.00	21	
	NP, Phy, RN	$0.00	$0.00	24	
	CRNA, OT, Phy, PT, RN	$0.00	$43,025.00	24	
	RT	$31,750.00	$0.00	21	
	CNA, NP, PA, Phy, RN	$0.00	$0.00	27	
	NP, PA, Phy, RN	$18,750.00	$31,500.00	27	
	CLS	$14,000.00	$0.00	24	

- Save the changes to the layout by clicking the Save button on the Quick Access Toolbar.

- Close the Client table.

Figure 3–53

Q&A What if I closed the table without saving the layout changes?

You would be asked if you want to save the changes.

Other Ways

1. Right-click field name, click Column Width

To Include Totals in a Datasheet

It is possible to include totals and other statistics at the bottom of a datasheet in a special row called the Total row. The following steps display the total of the commissions and the average of the rates for recruiters in the Total row.

- Open the Recruiter table in Datasheet view and hide the Navigation Pane.

- Click the Totals button on the Home tab to include the Total row in the datasheet (Figure 3–54).

Figure 3–54

2
- Click the Total row in the Commission column to display an arrow.
- Click the arrow to display a menu of available computations (Figure 3–55).

Q&A

Will I always get the same list?

No. You only will get the items that make sense for the type of data in the column. You cannot calculate the sum of text data, for example.

3
- Click Sum to calculate the sum of the commissions.

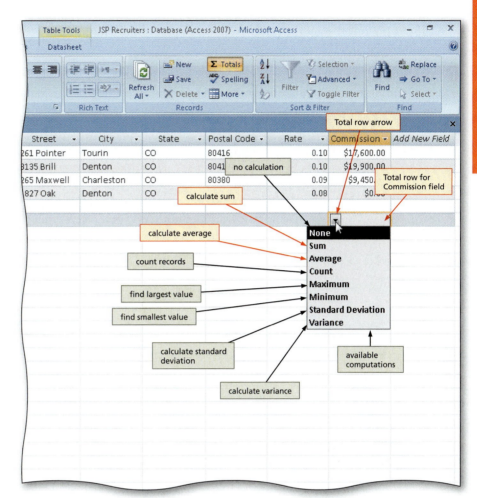

Figure 3–55

4
- Click the Total row in the Rate column to display an arrow.
- Click the arrow to display a menu of available computations.
- Click Average to calculate the average of the rates (Figure 3–56).

Experiment
- Experiment with other statistics. When finished, once again select the sum of the commissions and the average of the rates.

Figure 3–56

To Remove Totals from a Datasheet

If you no longer want the totals to appear as part of the datasheet, you can remove the Total row. The following step removes the Total row.

• Click the Totals button on the Home tab to remove the Total row from the datasheet.

Changing the Appearance of a Datasheet

In addition to resizing columns and displaying totals, you can change the appearance of a datasheet in a variety of other ways. For example, you can change the appearance of gridlines or change the text colors and font. Figure 3–57 shows the various buttons, found on the Home tab, that are available to change the Datasheet appearance.

Figure 3–57

The changes to the datasheet will be reflected not only on the screen, but also when you print or preview the datasheet.

Plan Ahead

Determine whether changes to the format of a datasheet are desirable.
You need to decide if changes to the format of a datasheet would improve its appearance and/or its usefulness. The following are the decisions you would make.

1. Would totals or other calculations be useful in the datasheet? If so, include the Total row and select the appropriate computations.

2. Would different gridlines make the datasheet more useful? If so, change to the desired gridlines.

3. Would alternating colors in the rows make them easier to read? If so, change the alternate fill color.

4. Would a different font and/or font color make the text stand out better? If so, change the font color and/or the font.

5. Is the font size appropriate? Can you see enough data at one time on the screen and yet have the data be readable? If not, change the font size to an appropriate value.

6. Is the column spacing appropriate? Are some columns wider than they need to be? Are there some columns where not all the data is visible? If so, change the column size.

As a general guideline, once you have decided on a particular look for a datasheet, all your datasheets should have the same look, unless there is a compelling reason for one of your datasheets to differ.

To Change Gridlines in a Datasheet

One of the changes you can make to a datasheet is which gridlines appear. You may feel that the appearance would be improved by having only horizontal gridlines. The following steps change the datasheet so that only horizontal gridlines are included.

- Open the Recruiter table in Datasheet view, if it is not already open.
- Click the box in the upper-left corner of the Datasheet selector to select the entire datasheet (Figure 3–58).

Figure 3–58

- Click the Gridlines button on the Home tab to display the Gridlines gallery (Figure 3–59).

Q&A

Does it matter whether I click the button or the arrow?

In this case, it does not matter. Either one will produce the same result.

- Click the Gridlines: Horizontal command in the Gridlines gallery to include only horizontal gridlines.

Experiment

- Experiment with other gridline options. When finished, once again select horizontal gridlines.

Figure 3–59

To Change the Colors and Font in a Datasheet

You also may decide that you can improve the datasheet by changing the colors and the font. The following steps change the Alternate Fill color, a color that appears on every other row in the datasheet. They also change the font color, the font, and the font size.

1

• With the datasheet for the Recruiter table selected, click the Alternate Fill/Back Color button arrow to display the color palette (Figure 3–60).

Q&A Does it matter whether I click the button or the arrow?

Yes. Clicking the arrow produces a color palette. Clicking the button applies the currently selected color. When in doubt, you should click the arrow.

Figure 3–60

2

• Click Aqua Blue (the second from the right color in the standard colors) to select aqua blue as the alternate color.

• Click the Font Color arrow, and then click Red (the second color in the bottom row) in the lower-left corner of standard colors to select Red as the font color.

• Click the Font box arrow, and then select Bodoni MT as the font. (If it is not available, select any font of your choice.)

• Click the Font Size box arrow, and select 10 as the font size (Figure 3–61).

Figure 3–61

Q&A Does the order in which I make these selections make a difference?

No. You could have made these selections in any order.

Experiment

• Experiment with other colors, fonts, and font sizes. When finished, return to the options selected in this step.

Using the Datasheet Formatting Dialog Box

As an alternative to using the individual buttons, you can click the Datasheet Formatting Dialog Box Launcher, shown in Figure 3–61, to display the Datasheet Formatting dialog box (Figure 3–62). You can use the various options in the dialog box to make changes to the datasheet format. Once you are finished, click the OK button to apply your changes.

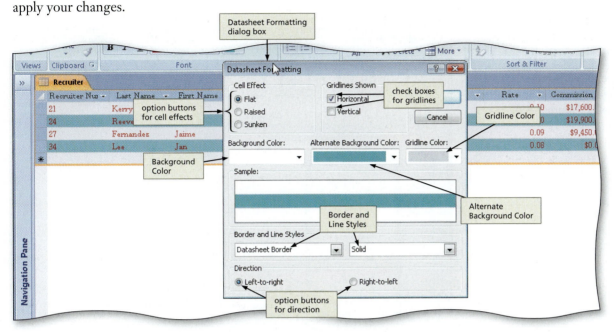

Figure 3–62

To Close the Datasheet Without Saving the Format Changes

The following steps show how to close the datasheet without saving the changes to the format. Because the changes are not saved, the next time you open the Recruiter table it will appear in the original format. If you had saved the changes, the changes would be reflected in its appearance.

1. Click the Close 'Recruiter' button to close the Recruiter table.

2. Click the No button in the Microsoft Office Access dialog box when asked if you want to save your changes.

Multivalued Field in Queries

You can use multivalued fields in queries just as you can use other fields. You have a choice concerning how the multiple values appear. You can choose to have them on a single row or on multiple rows.

To Query a Multivalued Field Showing Multiple Values on a Single Row

To include a multivalued field in the results of a query, place the field in the design grid just like any other field. The results will list all of the values for the multivalued field on a single row, just as in a datasheet. The following steps create a query to display the client number, client name, client type, and specialties needed for all clients.

- Create a query for the Client table and hide the Navigation Pane.

- Include the Client Number, Client Name, Client Type, and Specialties Needed fields (Figure 3–63).

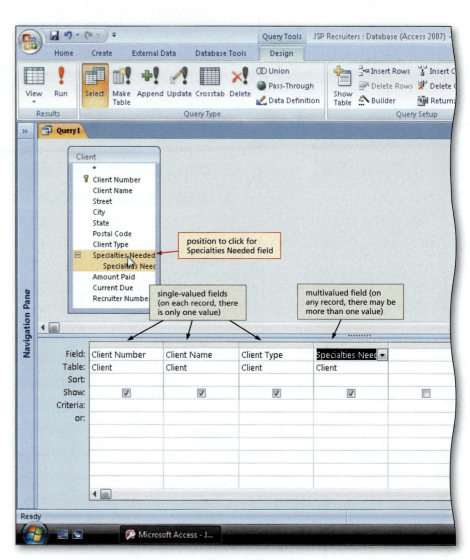

Figure 3–63

2

• View the results (Figure 3–64).

Q&A

Can I include criteria for the multi-valued field?

You can include criteria for the multivalued field when all the entries are displayed on a single row.

Experiment

• Return to Design view and enter various criteria in the Specialties Needed field. Run the queries. When finished, return to the options selected in this step.

Figure 3–64

To Query a Multivalued Field Showing Multiple Values on Multiple Rows

You may be interested in those clients requiring a particular specialty, for example, those clients needing an RN. Unfortunately, you cannot simply put the desired specialty in the Criteria row just as you would with other fields. Instead you need to change the query so that each specialty occurs on a different row by using the Value property. Once you have done so, you can enter criteria just as you would in any other query.

The following steps use the Value property to display each specialty on a separate row.

1

- Return to Design view and ensure the Client Number, Client Name, Client Type, and Specialties Needed fields are selected.

- Click the Specialties Needed field to produce an insertion point, and then type a period and the word `Value` after the word, Needed, to use the Value property (Figure 3–65).

 Q&A I don't see the word, Specialties. Did I do something wrong?

No. There is not enough room to display the entire name. If you wanted to see it, you could point to the right boundary of the column selector and then either drag or double-click.

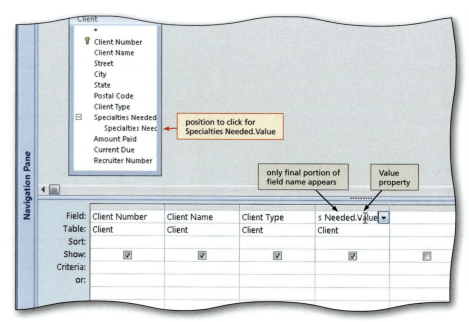

Figure 3–65

Q&A Do I need to type the word Value?

No. You also can double-click the second Specialties Needed entry in the field list.

2

- View the results (Figure 3–66).

Q&A Can I now include criteria for the multivalued field?

Yes. This is now just like any other query. There are no multiple values on any row.

3

- Close the query by clicking the Close 'Query1' button.

- When asked if you want to save the query, click the No button.

Figure 3–66

Referential Integrity

The property that ensures that the value in a foreign key must match that of another table's primary key is called **referential integrity**. A **foreign key** is a field in one table whose values are required to match the *primary key* of another table. In the Client table, the Recruiter Number field is a foreign key that must match the primary key of the Recruiter table; that is, the Recruiter number for any client must be a recruiter currently in the Recruiter table. A client whose Recruiter number is 92, for example, should not be stored because no such recruiter exists.

In Access, to specify referential integrity, you must define a relationship between the tables by using the Relationships command. Access then prohibits any updates to the database that would violate the referential integrity.

The type of relationship between two tables specified by the Relationships command is referred to as a **one-to-many relationship**. This means that *one* record in the first table is related to (matches) *many* records in the second table, but each record in the second table is related to only *one* record in the first. In the JSP Recruiters database, for example, a one-to-many relationship exists between the Recruiter table and the Client table. *One* recruiter is associated with *many* clients, but each client is associated with only a single recruiter. In general, the table containing the foreign key will be the *many* part of the relationship.

BTW

Relationships
You also can use the Relationships command to specify a one-to-one relationship. In a one-to-one relationship, one record in the first record is related to (matches) one record in the second table. In a one-to-one relationship, the matching fields are both primary keys. For example, if JSP Recruiters maintained a company car for each recruiter, the data concerning the cars might be kept in a Car table, in which the primary key is Recruiter Number—the same primary key as the Recruiter table. Thus, there would be a one-to-one relationship between recruiters and cars. Each recruiter is assigned one car and each car is assigned to one recruiter.

Plan Ahead

Identify related tables in order to implement relationships between the tables.
When specifying referential integrity, you need to decide how to handle deletions. In the relationship between clients and recruiters, for example, deletion of a recruiter for whom clients exist, such as recruiter number 21, would violate referential integrity. Any clients for recruiter 21 no longer would relate to any recruiter in the database. You can handle this in two ways. For each relationship, you need to decide which of the approaches is appropriate.

1. The normal way to avoid this problem is to prohibit such a deletion.

2. The other option is to **cascade the delete.** This means that Access would allow the deletion but then delete all related records. For example, it would allow the deletion of the recruiter but then automatically delete any clients related to the deleted recruiter.

You also need to decide how to handle the update of the primary key. In the relationship between recruiters and clients, for example, changing the recruiter number for recruiter 21 to 12 in the Recruiter table would cause a problem. Clients are in the Client table on which the recruiter number is 21. These clients no longer would relate to any recruiter. You can handle this in two ways. For each relationship, you need to decide which of the approaches is appropriate.

1. The normal way of avoiding the problem is to prohibit this type of update.

2. The other option is to **cascade the update.** This means to allow the change, but make the corresponding change in the foreign key on all related records. In the relationship between clients and recruiters, for example, Access would allow the update but then automatically make the corresponding change for any client whose recruiter number was 21. It now will be 12.

To Specify Referential Integrity

The following steps use the Relationships command to specify referential integrity by specifying a relationship between the Recruiter and Client tables. The steps also ensure that update will cascade, but that delete will not.

1

• Click Database Tools on the Ribbon to display the Database Tools tab (Figure 3–67).

Figure 3–67

2

• Click the Relationships button on the Database Tools tab to open the Relationships window and display the Show Table dialog box (Figure 3–68).

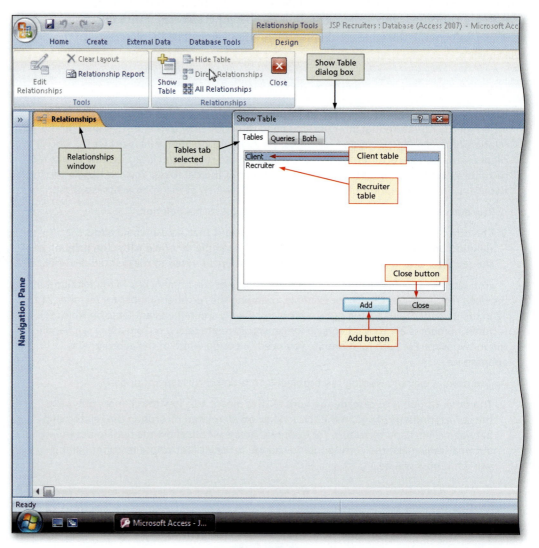

Figure 3–68

3

- Click the Recruiter table and then click the Add button to add the Recruiter table.

- Click the Client table and then click the Add button to add the Client table.

- Click the Close button in the Show Table dialog box to close the dialog box.

- Resize the field lists that appear so all fields are visible (Figure 3–69).

Q&A Do I need to resize the field lists?

No. You can use the scroll bars. Before completing the next step, however, you would need to make sure the Recruiter Number fields in both tables appear on the screen.

4

- Drag the Recruiter Number field in the Recruiter table field list to the Recruiter Number field in the Client table field list to open the Edit Relationships dialog box to create a relationship.

Q&A Do I actually move the field from the Recruiter table to the Client table?

No. The mouse pointer will change shape to indicate you are in the process of dragging, but the field does not move.

- Click the Enforce Referential Integrity check box.

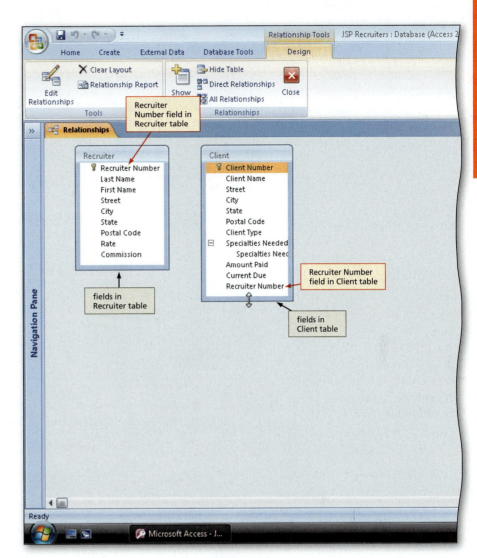

Figure 3–69

- Click the Cascade Update Related Fields check box (Figure 3–70).

Q&A The Cascade check boxes were dim until I clicked the Enforce Referential Integrity check box. Is that correct?

Yes. Until you have chosen to enforce referential integrity, the cascade options have no meaning.

Q&A Can I change the join type like I can in queries?

Yes. Click the Join Type button in the Edit Relationships dialog box. Just as with queries, option button 1 creates an INNER join, option button 2 creates a LEFT join, and option button 3 creates a RIGHT join.

Figure 3–70

5

- Click the Create button to complete the creation of the relationship (Figure 3–71).

Q&A What is the symbol at the lower end of the join line?

It is the mathematical symbol for infinity. It is used here to denote the "many" end of the relationship.

Q&A Can I print a copy of the relationship?

Yes. Click the Relationship Report button on the Design tab to produce a report of the relationship. You can print the report. You also can save it as a report in the database for future use. If you do not want to save it, close the report after you have printed it and do not save the changes.

Figure 3–71

6

- Click the Save button on the Quick Access Toolbar to save the relationship you created.

- Close the Relationships window by clicking the Close 'Relationships' button.

Q&A

Can I later modify the relationship if I want to change it in some way?

Yes. Click the Relationships button on the Database Tools tab. To add another table, click the Show Table button on the Design tab. To remove a table, click the Hide table button. To edit a relationship, select the relationship and click the Edit Relationships button.

Effect of Referential Integrity

Referential integrity now exists between the Recruiter and Client tables. Access now will reject any number in the Recruiter Number field in the Client table that does not match a Recruiter number in the Recruiter table. Attempting to change the recruiter number for a client to one that does not match any recruiter in the Recruiter table would result in the error message shown in Figure 3–72. Similarly, attempting to add a client whose recruiter number does not match would lead to the same error message.

Figure 3–72

Access also will reject the deletion of a recruiter for whom related clients exist. Attempting to delete recruiter 21 from the Recruiter table, for example, would result in the message shown in Figure 3–73.

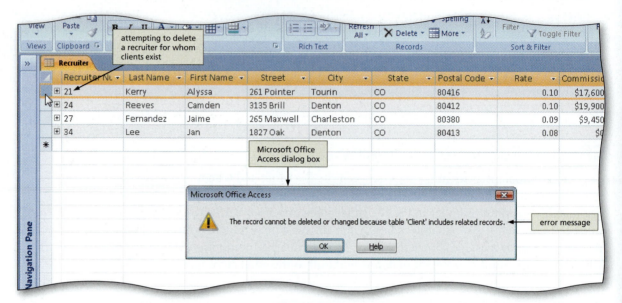

Figure 3–73

Access would, however, allow the change of a recruiter number in the Recruiter table. Then it automatically makes the corresponding change to the recruiter number for all the recruiter's clients. For example, if you changed the recruiter number of recruiter 21 to 12, the same 12 would appear in the recruiter number field for clients.

To Use a Subdatasheet

Now that the Recruiter table is related to the Client table, it is possible to view the clients of a given recruiter when you are viewing the datasheet for the Recruiter table. The clients for the recruiter will appear below the recruiter in a **subdatasheet**. The availability of such a subdatasheet is indicated by a plus sign that appears in front of the rows in the Recruiter table. The following steps display the subdatasheet for recruiter 24.

• Open the Recruiter table and hide the Navigation Pane (Figure 3–74).

Figure 3–74

2

- Click the plus sign in front of the row for Recruiter 24 to display the subdatasheet (Figure 3–75).

Q&A

How do I hide the subdatasheet when I no longer want it to appear?

When you clicked the plus sign, it changed to a minus sign. Click the minus sign.

 Experiment

- Display subdatasheets for other recruiters. Display more than one subdatasheet at a time. Remove the subdatasheets from the screen.

Figure 3–75

3

- Close the datasheet for the Recruiter table.

To Find Duplicate Records

One reason to include a primary key for a table is to eliminate duplicate records. A possibility still exists, however, that duplicate records can get into your database. Perhaps the same client was inadvertently added to the database with a new client number. You can detect this type of redundancy by searching to see if any client's names are duplicated. The **Find Duplicates Query Wizard** allows you to find duplicate records. The following steps illustrate how to use the Find Duplicates Query Wizard to find duplicate records.

1. Click Create on the Ribbon, and then click the Query Wizard button on the Create tab.
2. When Access displays the New Query dialog box, click the Find Duplicates Query Wizard and then click the OK button.
3. Identify the table and field or fields that might contain duplicate information.
4. Indicate any other fields you want displayed.
5. Finish the wizard to see any duplicate records.

To Find Unmatched Records

Occasionally, you may want to find records in one table that have no matching records in another table. For example, you may want to determine which recruiters currently have no clients. The **Find Unmatched Query Wizard** allows you to find unmatched records. The following steps illustrate how to find unmatched records using the Find Unmatched Query Wizard.

1. Click Create on the Ribbon, and then click the Query Wizard button on the Create tab.
2. When Access displays the New Query dialog box, click the Find Unmatched Query Wizard and then click the OK button.
3. Identify the table that may contain unmatched records and then identify the related table.
4. Indicate the fields you want displayed.
5. Finish the wizard to see any duplicate records.

Ordering Records

Normally, Access sequences the records in the Client table by client number whenever listing them because the Client Number field is the primary key. You can change this order, if desired.

To Use the Ascending Button to Order Records

To change the order in which records appear, use the Ascending or Descending buttons. Either button reorders the records based on the field in which the insertion point is located.

The following steps order the records by city using the Ascending button.

1

- Open the Client table in Datasheet view and hide the Navigation Pane.

- Click the City field on the first record to select the field (Figure 3–76).

 Did I have to click the field on the first record?

No. Any other record would have worked as well.

Figure 3–76

2

- Click the Ascending button on the Home tab to sort the records by City (Figure 3–77).

 What if I wanted the cities to appear in reverse alphabetical order?

Click the Descending button.

Figure 3–77

Experiment

Sort the records by city in reverse order. When done, sort the records by city in the original order.

3

- Close the table. When asked if you want to save your changes, click the No button.

Other Ways

1. Right-click field name, click Sort A to Z (for ascending) or Sort Z to A (for descending)

Special Database Operations

The special operations involved in maintaining a database are backup, recovery, compacting a database, and repairing a database.

Backup and Recovery

It is possible to damage or destroy a database. Users can enter data that is incorrect; programs that are updating the database can end abnormally during an update; a hardware problem can occur; and so on. After any such event has occurred, the database may contain invalid data. It even may be totally destroyed.

Obviously, you cannot allow a situation in which data has been damaged or destroyed to go uncorrected. You must somehow return the database to a correct state. This process is called recovery; that is, you **recover** the database.

The simplest approach to recovery involves periodically making a copy of the database (called a **backup copy** or a **save copy**). This is referred to as **backing up** the database. If a problem occurs, you correct the problem by copying this backup copy over the actual database, often referred to as the **live database**.

To backup the database that is currently open, you use the Back Up Database command on the Manage submenu on the Office Button menu. In the process, Access suggests a name that is a combination of the database name and the current date. For example, if you back up the JSP Recruiters database on April 20, 2008, Access will suggest the name JSP Recruiters_2008-04-20. You can change this name if you desire, although it is a good idea to use this name. By doing so, it will be easy to distinguish between all the backup copies you have made to determine which is the most recent. In addition, if you discover that a critical problem occurred on April 18, 2008, you may want to go back to the most recent backup before April 18. If, for example, the database was not backed up on April 17 but was backed up on April 16, you would use JSP Recruiters_2008-04-16.

The following steps back up a database to a file on a hard disk or high-capacity removable disk. You should check with your instructor before completing these steps.

To Back Up a Database

1. Open the database to be backed up.
2. Click the Office Button, and then point to Manage on the Office Button menu.
3. Click Back Up Database on the Manage submenu.
4. Select the desired location in the Save in box. If you do not want the name Access has suggested, enter the desired name in the File name text box.
5. Click the Save button.

Access creates a backup copy with the desired name in the desired location. Should you ever need to recover the database using this backup copy, you can simply copy it over the live version.

Compacting and Repairing a Database

As you add more data to a database, it naturally grows larger. When you delete an object (records, tables, forms, or queries), the space previously occupied by the object does not become available for additional objects. Instead, the additional objects are given new space, that is, space that was not already allocated. To remove this wasted space from the database, you must **compact** the database. The same option that compacts the database also repairs problems that may have occurred in the database.

To Compact and Repair a Database

1. Open the database to be compacted.
2. Click the Office Button, and then point to Manage on the Office Button menu.
3. Click Compact and Repair Database on the Manage submenu.

The database now is the compacted form of the original.

Additional Operations

Additional special operations include opening another database, closing a database without exiting Access, and saving a database with another name. They also include deleting a table (or other object) as well as renaming an object. Finally, you can change properties of a table or other object, such as the object's description.

When you open another database, Access automatically will close the database that had been open. Before deleting or renaming an object, you should ensure that the object has no dependent objects, that is, other objects that depend on the object you wish to delete.

The following steps describe how you could perform these operations.

To Open Another Database

1. Click the Office Button.
2. Click Open on the Office Button menu.
3. Select the database to be opened.
4. Click the Open button.

To Close a Database without Exiting Access

1. Click the Office Button.
2. Click Close Database on the Office Button menu.

To Save a Database with Another Name

1. Click the Office Button.
2. Point to Save As on the Office Button menu.
3. Select the desired format.
4. Enter a name and select a location for the new version.
5. Click the Save button.

To Check for Dependent Objects

1. Ensure that the object you wish to check is selected.
2. Click Database Tools on the Ribbon to display the Database Tools tab.
3. Click the Object Dependencies button on the Database Tools tab.
4. Click the 'Objects that depend on me' option button to display any objects that depend on the selected object.

To Delete a Table or Other Object

1. Right-click the object.
2. Click Delete on the shortcut menu.
3. Click the Yes button in the Microsoft Office Access dialog box.

To Rename an Object

1. Right-click the object.
2. Click Rename on the shortcut menu.
3. Type the new name and press the ENTER key.

To Change Object Properties

1. Right-click the object.

2. Click Table Properties (if the object is a table) or Object Properties on the shortcut menu.

3. Change the desired property and click the OK button.

To Quit Access

You saved all your changes and are ready to quit Access. The following step quits Access.

1 Click the Close button on the right side of the Access title bar to quit Access.

Chapter Summary

In this chapter you have learned how to use a form to add records to a table; search for records; delete records; filter records; create and use Lookup fields; create and use multivalued fields; make mass changes; create validation rules; change the appearance of a datasheet; specify referential integrity; and use subdatasheets. The following list includes all the new Access skills you have learned in this chapter.

1. Create a Simple Form (AC 142)
2. Use a Form to Add Records (AC 144)
3. Search for a Record (AC 145)
4. Update the Contents of a Record (AC 147)
5. Delete a Record (AC 148)
6. Use Filter By Selection (AC 149)
7. Toggle a Filter (AC 151)
8. Clear a Filter (AC 151)
9. Use a Common Filter (AC 152)
10. Use Filter By Form (AC 153)
11. Use Advanced Filter/Sort (AC 155)
12. Delete a Field (AC 157)
13. Add a New Field (AC 157)
14. Create a Lookup Field (AC 158)
15. Add a Multivalued Field (AC 160)
16. Save the Changes and Close the Table (AC 161)
17. Modify Single or Multivalued Lookup Fields (AC 161)
18. Use an Update Query (AC 162)
19. Use a Delete Query (AC 163)
20. Use an Append Query (AC 165)
21. Use a Make-Table Query (AC 165)
22. Specify a Required Field (AC 166)
23. Specify a Range (AC 166)
24. Specify a Default Value (AC 167)
25. Specify a Collection of Allowable Values (AC 167)
26. Specify a Format (AC 168)
27. Save the Validation Rules, Default Values, and Formats (AC 169)
28. Use a Lookup Field (AC 172)
29. Use a Multivalued Lookup Field (AC 173)
30. Resize a Column in a Datasheet (AC 175)
31. Include Totals in a Datasheet (AC 176)
32. Remove Totals from a Datasheet (AC 178)
33. Change Gridlines in a Datasheet (AC 179)
34. Change the Colors and Font in a Datasheet (AC 180)
35. Close the Datasheet Without Saving the Format Changes (AC 181)
36. Query a Multivalued Field Showing Multiple Values on a Single Row (AC 182)
37. Query a Multivalued Field Showing Multiple Values on Multiple Rows (AC 183)
38. Specify Referential Integrity (AC 186)
39. Use a Subdatasheet (AC 190)
40. Find Duplicate Records (AC 191)
41. Find Unmatched Records (AC 191)
42. Use the Ascending Button to Order Records (AC 192)
43. Back up a Database (AC 193)
44. Compact and Repair a Database (AC 193)
45. Open Another Database (AC 194)
46. Close a Database Without Exiting Access (AC 194)
47. Save a Database with Another Name (AC 194)
48. Check for Dependent Objects (AC 194)
49. Delete a Table or Other Object (AC 194)
50. Rename an Object (AC 194)
51. Change Object Properties (AC 194)

 If you have a SAM user profile, you may have access to hands-on instruction, practice, and assessment. Log in to your SAM account (http://sam2007.course.com) to launch any assigned training activities or exams that relate to the skills covered in this chapter.

Learn It Online

Test your knowledge of chapter content and key terms.

Instructions: To complete the Learn It Online exercises, start your browser, click the Address bar, and then enter the Web address scsite.com/ac2007/learn. When the Access 2007 Learn It Online page is displayed, click the link for the exercise you want to complete and then read the instructions.

Chapter Reinforcement TF, MC, and SA
A series of true/false, multiple choice, and short answer questions that test your knowledge of the chapter content.

Flash Cards
An interactive learning environment where you identify chapter key terms associated with displayed definitions.

Practice Test
A series of multiple choice questions that test your knowledge of chapter content and key terms.

Who Wants To Be a Computer Genius?
An interactive game that challenges your knowledge of chapter content in the style of a television quiz show.

Wheel of Terms
An interactive game that challenges your knowledge of chapter key terms in the style of the television show *Wheel of Fortune*.

Crossword Puzzle Challenge
A crossword puzzle that challenges your knowledge of key terms presented in the chapter.

Apply Your Knowledge

Reinforce the skills and apply the concepts you learned in this chapter.

Specifying Validation Rules, Updating Records, Formatting a Datasheet, and Creating Relationships
Instructions: Start Access. Open The Bike Delivers database that you modified in Apply Your Knowledge in Chapter 2 on page AC 128. (If you did not complete this exercise, see your instructor for a copy of the modified database.)

Perform the following tasks:
1. Open the Customer table in Design view as shown in Figure 3–78.

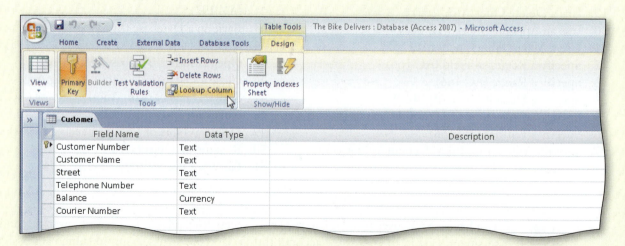

Figure 3–78

2. Format the Customer Number field so any lowercase letters appear in uppercase and make the Customer Name field a required field.

3. Specify that balance amounts must be between $0.0 and $1,000. Include validation text.

4. Save the changes to the Customer table.

5. Create a simple form for the Customer table and find the record for ME71 and change the customer name to Mentor Group Limited. Save the form as Customer Simple Form and close the form.

6. Open the Customer table in Datasheet view and use Filter By Selection to find the record for CI76. Delete the record. Remove the filter.

7. Resize all columns to best fit and remove the gridlines from the datasheet. Save the changes to the layout of the table. Close the Customer table.

8. Establish referential integrity between the Courier table (the one table) and the Customer table (the many table). Cascade the update but do not cascade the delete.

9. Submit the revised database in the format specified by your instructor.

Extend Your Knowledge

Extend the skills you learned in this chapter and experiment with new skills. You may need to use Help to complete the assignment.

Creating Action Queries, Changing Table Properties

Instructions: See the inside back cover of this book for instructions for downloading the Data Files for Students, or see your instructor for information on accessing the files required in this book.

Backyard is a retail business that specializes in products for the outdoors. The owner has created an Access database in which to store information about the products he sells. He recently acquired the inventory of a store that is going out of business. The inventory currently is stored in the Inventory database.

Perform the following tasks:

1. The owner needs to add the items stored in the Product table of the Inventory database to the Item table of the Backyard database. Create and run an append query to create the Item table for the Backyard database shown in Figure 3–79.

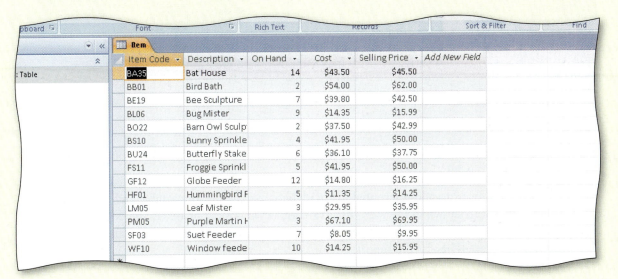

Item Code	Description	On Hand	Cost	Selling Price	Add New Field
BA35	Bat House	14	$43.50	$45.50	
BB01	Bird Bath	2	$54.00	$62.00	
BE19	Bee Sculpture	7	$39.80	$42.50	
BL06	Bug Mister	9	$14.35	$15.99	
BO22	Barn Owl Sculp	2	$37.50	$42.99	
BS10	Bunny Sprinkle	4	$41.95	$50.00	
BU24	Butterfly Stake	6	$36.10	$37.75	
FS11	Froggie Sprinkl	5	$41.95	$50.00	
GF12	Globe Feeder	12	$14.80	$16.25	
HF01	Hummingbird F	5	$11.35	$14.25	
LM05	Leaf Mister	3	$29.95	$35.95	
PM05	Purple Martin H	3	$67.10	$69.95	
SF03	Suet Feeder	7	$8.05	$9.95	
WF10	Window feede	10	$14.25	$15.95	

Figure 3–79

Continued >

Extend Your Knowledge *continued*

2. Open the Item table in the Backyard database and change the description for WF10 to Window Bird Feeder. Resize all columns to best fit the data.

3. Sort the datasheet in ascending order by Description.

4. Add a totals row to the datasheet and display the sum of the on hand items, and the average cost and average selling price.

5. Save the changes to the layout of the table. Close the table and rename it Product.

6. Update the table properties for the Product table to include the description, Updated to include items from Inventory database.

7. Using a query, delete all records in the Product table where the description starts with the letter S. Save the query as Delete Query.

8. Change the database properties, as specified by your instructor. Submit the revised database in the format specified by your instructor.

Make It Right

Analyze a database and correct all errors and/or improve the design.

Correcting Table Design Errors

Instructions: Start Access. Open the Care4Pets database. See the inside back cover of this book for instructions for downloading the Data Files for Students, or see your instructor for information on accessing the files required in this book.

Care4Pets provides a variety of services to pet owners. The owner of Care4Pets has decided that she could better manage her business if she added a multivalued field that lists the various types of pets her customers have. She created the field shown in Figure 3–80 but forgot to add Rabbit as one of the pet types. Modify the multivalued Lookup field to include Rabbit as a pet type.

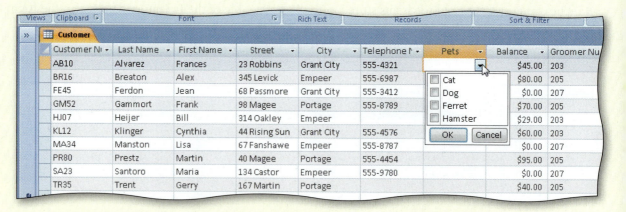

Figure 3–80

Finally, she wanted to add referential integrity between the Groomer table and the Customer table. The relationship shown in Figure 3–81 is not correct and must be fixed. She does not want to cascade the update or the delete. She also wants to create a report for the relationship. Use the name Relationships for Care4Pets for the report.

Figure 3–81

Submit the revised database in the format specified by your instructor.

In the Lab

Design, create, modify, and/or use a database following the guidelines, concepts, and skills presented in this chapter. Labs are listed in order of increasing difficulty.

Lab 1: Maintaining the JMS TechWizards Database

Problem: JMS TechWizards is expanding rapidly and needs to make some database changes to handle the expansion. The company needs to know more about its clients, such as the type of business, and it needs to ensure that data that is entered is valid. It also needs to update the records in the database.

Instructions: Use the database created in the In the Lab 1 of Chapter 1 on page AC 67 for this assignment or see your instructor for information on accessing the files required for this book.

Perform the following tasks:

1. Open the JMS TechWizards database and then open the Client table in Design view.

2. Add a Lookup field, Client Type, to the Client table. The field should appear after the Telephone Number field. The field will contain data on the type of client. The client types are MAN (Manufacturing), RET (Retail), and SER (Service). Save these changes to the structure.

3. Using a query, change all the entries in the Client Type column to RET. Save the query as Client Type Update Query.

4. Open the Client table and make the following changes. You can use the Find button, the Replace button, or Filter By Selection to locate the records to change:

   a. Change the client type for clients AM53 and SA56 to MAN.

   b. Change the client type for clients GR56, JE77, and ME17 to SER.

   c. Change the name of client SA56 to Sawyer Industries.

   d. Change the name of client ST21 to Steed's Department Store.

5. Resize all columns to best fit the data and remove the vertical gridlines. Save the changes to the layout of the table.

Continued >

6. Create the following validation rules for the Client table and save the changes.

   a. Specify the legal values MAN, RET, and SER for the Client Type field. Include validation text.

   b. Assign a default value of RET to the Client Type field.

   c. Ensure that any letters entered in the Client Number field appear as uppercase.

   d. Specify that the billed amount must be less than or equal to $1,500.00. Include validation text.

7. Open the Client table and use Filter By Form to find all records where the client is located in Anderson and has a client type of SER. Delete these records.

8. JMS has signed up a new retail store, Cray Meat Market (Client Number CR21) and needs to add the record to the Client table. The Meat Market is at 72 Main in Anderson, TX 78077. The phone number is 512-555-7766. Lee Torres is the technician assigned to the account. To date, they have not been billed for any services. Create a split form for the Client table and use this split form to add the record.

9. Specify referential integrity between the Technician table (the one table) and the Client table (the many table). Cascade the update but not the delete.

10. Compact the database and then back up the database.

11. Submit the revised database in the format specified by your instructor.

In the Lab

Lab 2: Maintaining the Hockey Fan Zone Database

Problem: The management of the Hockey Fan Zone store needs to change the database structure, add validation rules, and update records.

Instructions: Use the database created in the In the Lab 2 of Chapter 1 on page AC 68 for this assignment, or see your instructor for information on accessing the files required for this book.

Perform the following tasks:

1. Open the Hockey Fan Zone database and then open the Item table in Design view.

2. Add a Lookup field, Item Type to the Item table. The field should appear after the Description field. The field will contain data on the type of item for sale. The item types are CAP (caps and hats), CLO (clothing), and NOV (Novelties).

3. Make the following changes to the Item table:

   a. Change the field size for the On Hand field to Integer. The Format should be fixed and the decimal places should be 0.

   b. Make Description a required field.

   c. Specify the legal values CAP, CLO, and NOV for the Item Type field. Include validation text.

   d. Specify that number on hand must be between 0 and 75. Include validation text.

4. Save the changes to the table design. If a dialog box appears indicating that some data may be lost, click the Yes button.

5. Using a query, assign the value NOV to the Item Type field for all records. Save the query as Update Query.

6. Delete the split form for the Item table that you created in Chapter 1. The form does not include the Item Type field. Recreate the split form for the Item table.

7. Use the split form to change the item type for item numbers 3663 and 7930 to CAP. Change the item type for item numbers 5923 and 7810 to CLO.

8. Add the following items to the Item table.

3673	Blanket	NOV	5	$29.90	$34.00	AC
6078	Key Chain	NOV	20	$3.00	$5.00	MN
7550	Sweatshirt	CLO	8	$19.90	$22.95	LG

9. Create an advanced filter for the Item table. The filter should display the item number, item type, description, and number on hand for all items with less than 10 items on hand. Sort the filter by item type and description. Save the filter settings as a query and name the filter Reorder Filter.

10. Resize all columns in the Item table and the Supplier table to best fit.

11. Using a query, delete all records in the Item table where the description starts with the letter F. Save the query as Delete Query.

12. Specify referential integrity between the Supplier table (the one table) and the Item table (the many table). Cascade the update but not the delete.

13. Compact the database.

14. Submit the revised database in the format specified by your instructor.

In the Lab

Lab 3: Maintaining the Ada Beauty Supply Database

Problem: The management of Ada Beauty Supply has determined that some changes must be made to the database structure. A multivalued field must be added. Validation rules need to be added. Finally, some additions and deletions are required to the database.

Instructions: Use the Ada Beauty Supply database created in the In the Lab 3 of Chapter 1 on page AC 69 for this assignment, or see your instructor for information on accessing the files required for this book. Submit the revised database in the format specified by your instructor.

Instructions Part 1: Several changes must be made to the database structure. For example, management would like a multivalued field that lists the type of services each beauty salon offers. This knowledge can help the sales representatives better meet the needs of their customers. Table 3-2 lists the service abbreviations and descriptions that management would like in a Services Offered multivalued field.

Table 3–2 Service Abbreviations and Descriptions	
Service Abbreviation	**Description**
FAC	Facial
HRS	Hair Styling
MNC	Manicure
PED	Pedicure
MST	Massage Therapy
TAN	Tanning

Management wants to ensure that an entry always appears in the Customer Name field and that any letters entered in the Customer Number field appear in uppercase. It also requires that the amount in the Balance field is never less than 0 or greater than $1,000. Make the changes to the database structure. Place the Services Offered field after the Telephone field.

Continued >

In the Lab *continued*

Instructions Part 2: The data for the Services Offered field shown in Figure 3–82 must be added to the database. The address for Elegante is incorrect. It should be 180 Broadway. Le Beauty has changed its name to Le Beauty Day Spa. Nancy's Place has gone out of business. A new salon, PamperMe Day Spa, just opened. The address for the spa is 2125 Lawrence and the phone number is 555-2401. The spa provides all services except hair styling and tanning.

Management wants to use PA10 as the customer number and Terry Sinson is the sales rep. The new spa has purchased $750 worth of supplies but has not paid for them. Format the datasheet to best fit the data.

Customer Nu ▾	Customer Na ▾	Street ▾	Telephone ▾	Services Offered ▾	Balance ▾	Amount Paid ▾	Sales Rep Ni ▾
AM23	Amy's Salon	223 Johnson	555-2150	HRS, MNC	$195.00	$1,695.00	44
BB34	Bob the Barber	1939 Jackson	555-1939	HRS	$150.00	$0.00	51
BL15	Blondie's	3294 Devon	555-7510	HRS, MNC, PED, TAN	$555.00	$1,350.00	49
CM09	Cut Mane	3140 Halsted	555-0604	HRS, MNC	$295.00	$1,080.00	51
CS12	Curl n Style	1632 Clark	555-0804	HRS, MNC, PED	$145.00	$710.00	49
EG07	Elegante	1805 Boardway	555-1404	FAC, MNC, PED	$0.00	$1,700.00	44
JS34	Just Cuts	2200 Lawrence	555-0313	HRS	$360.00	$700.00	49
LB20	Le Beauty	13 Devon	555-5161	FAC, MNC, MST, PED	$200.00	$1,250.00	49
NC25	Nancy's Place	1027 Wells	555-4210	HRS	$240.00	$550.00	44
RD03	Rose's Day Spa	787 Monroe	555-7657	FAC, MNC, MST, PED	$0.00	$975.00	51
TT21	Tan and Tone	1939 Congress	555-6554	HRS, MNC, TAN	$160.00	$725.00	44

Figure 3–82

Instructions Part 3: Because the sales reps work on commission, management wants to make sure that customers are not assigned to a sales rep who is not in the database. It also wants the ability to change a sales rep number in the Sales Rep table and have the change applied to the Customer table. Create the appropriate relationship that would satisfy management's needs.

Cases and Places

Apply your creative thinking and problem solving skills to design and implement a solution.

• EASIER   •• MORE DIFFICULT

• 1: Maintaining the Second Hand Goods Database

Use the Second-Hand Goods database you created in Cases and Places 1 in Chapter 1 on page AC 71 for this assignment, or see your instructor for information on accessing the files required for this book. Perform each of the following tasks:

a. The Condition field should be a Lookup field. Only the current values in the database should be legal values.

b. A better description for the bookcases is 3-Shelf Bookcase.

c. The duvet has been sold.

d. The minimum price of any item is $2.00.

e. It would be easier to find items for sale if the default sort order for the item table were by description rather than by item number. Also, some of the descriptions are not displayed completely in Datasheet view.

f. Specify referential integrity. Cascade the update and the delete.

Submit the revised database in the format specified by your instructor.

• 2: Maintaining the BeachCondo Rentals database

Use the BeachCondo Rentals database you created in Cases and Places 2 in Chapter 1 on page AC 71 for this assignment, or see your instructor for information on accessing the files required for this book. Perform each of the following tasks:

a. Add the field, For Sale to the Condo Unit table, to indicate whether a condo unit is for sale. The field is a Yes/No field and should appear after the weekly rate.

b. All units owned by Alonso Bonita are for sale.

c. The Bedrooms, Bathrooms, and Sleeps fields always should contain data.

d. Most common condo units have one bedroom, one bathroom, and sleep two people. All condo units should have a minimum of one bedroom, one bathroom, and sleep two people.

e. No unit rents for less than $700 or more than $1,500.

f. Management has just received a new listing from Mark Graty. It is unit 300. The unit sleeps 10, has three bedrooms, has 2.5 bathrooms, and includes linens. The weekly rate is $1,400 and the owner is interested in selling the unit.

g. Specify referential integrity. Do not cascade the update or the delete.

Submit the revised database in the format specified by your instructor.

•• 3: Maintaining the Restaurant Database

Use the restaurant database you created in Cases and Places 3 in Chapter 1 on page AC 71 for this assignment, or see your instructor for information on accessing the files required for this book. Using the Plan Ahead guidelines presented in this chapter, determine what changes need to be made to your database. For example, a multivalued field could be useful to record opening days and times of a restaurant. Another multivalued field could record restaurant specialties. Create any necessary relationships. Examine the relationships to determine if the default join type is appropriate and whether you need to cascade the update and/or delete. Use a word processing program, such as

Continued >

Cases and Places *continued*

Microsoft Word, to explain the changes you need to make to the database. Then, make the changes to the database. Submit the Word document and the revised database in the format specified by your instructor.

•• 4: Updating Your Contacts Database

Make It Personal

Use the contacts database you created in Cases and Places 4 in Chapter 1 on page AC 71 for this assignment, or see your instructor for information on accessing the files required for this book. Consider your own personal job situation. Has the focus of your job search changed? Are there specific jobs within the companies of interest that appeal to you? Have you contacted an individual within a company to express your interest? If so, consider creating another table with a one-to-one relationship between the individual contact and the company. Create a multivalued field to store those specific positions that would interest you. Review the fields in the contacts database. Are there any fields you need to add? Are there any fields you need to delete? Are there any tables that need to be deleted? Are there companies that need to be added to your database? Make any necessary changes to your database structure and update the database. Using a word processing program, such as Microsoft Word, explain what changes you made to your database and why you made the changes. Submit the Word document and the revised database in the format specified by your instructor.

•• 5: Understanding Action Queries, Query Wizards, and Table Design Changes

Working Together

With a make-table query, a user can create a new table from one or more tables in the database. The table can be stored in the same database or a new database. As a team, use the Access Help system to learn more about make-table queries. Then, choose either the Cases and Places 1 database or the Cases and Places 2 database and create a make-table query. For example, for the Hockey Fan Zone, the management could create a table named Supplier Call List that would include the item code, description, and cost of each item as well as the supplier name and telephone number. Write a one-page paper that (1) explains the purpose for which the new table is intended and (2) suggests at least two additional uses for make-table queries. Submit the paper and the database in the format specified by your instructor.

Open the Students database that you created in Chapter 1. As a team, review the data types for each of the fields that are in the database. Do any of these data types need to be changed? For example, is there a field that should store multiple values? Are there any fields that should contain validation rules? Change the data types and add validation rules as necessary. Examine the tables in your database. Delete any tables that you do not need. Determine the relationships among the remaining tables. Are there any one-to-one relationships or one-to-many relationships? Write a one-page paper that explains your reasons for changing (or not changing) the structure of the database. Submit the paper and the database in the format specified by your instructor.

Save the Ada Beauty Supply database as AdaTeam Beauty Supply. Research the purpose of the Find Unmatched Query Wizard and the Find Duplicates Query Wizard. Use the AdaTeam database and create queries using each of these wizards. Did the queries perform as expected? Open each query in Design view and modify it, for example, add another field to the query. What happened to the query results? Write a one-page paper that explains the purpose of each query wizard and describes the team's experiences with creating and modifying the queries. Submit the paper and database in the format specified by your instructor.

Integration Feature

Sharing Data Among Applications

Objectives

You will have mastered the material in this Integration Feature when you can:

- Import from or link to an Excel worksheet
- Import from or link to an Access database
- Import from or link to a text file
- Export data to Excel, Word, and text files
- Publish a report
- Export and import XML data

Integration Feature Introduction

It is not uncommon for people to use an application for some specific purpose, only to find later that another application may be better suited. For example, an organization initially might use Excel to maintain data on inventory only to discover later that the data would be better maintained in an Access database. This feature shows how to use data from other applications in Access. It also shows how to make Access data available to other applications.

Project — Sharing Data Among Applications

Camashaly specializes in sales of used computers and computer equipment. Employees have been using Microsoft Excel to automate a variety of tasks for several years. When determining to keep track of prices, item descriptions, serial numbers, and other data on the items for sale, the administrators originally decided to maintain the data as an Excel worksheet. Employees recently completed Microsoft Office training and now have decided they need to maintain the data in an Access database. They have two choices. They can **import** the data, which means to make a copy of the data as a table in the Access database. In this case, any changes made to the data in Access would not be reflected in the Excel worksheet. The other option is to **link** to the data in the worksheet. When data is linked, the data appears as a table in the Access database, but is, in fact, maintained in its original form in Excel. Any changes to the Excel data are thus automatically reflected when the linked table is viewed in Access. In this arrangement, Access would typically be used as a vehicle for viewing and querying the data, with actual updates being made in Excel.

Figure 1 illustrates the conversion process. The type of worksheet that can be converted is one in which the data is stored as a **list**, that is, a collection of rows and columns in which all the entries in a column represent the same type of data. In this type of list, the first row contains column headings rather than data. In the worksheet in Figure 1a, the first row contains the labels, which are entries indicating the type of data found in the column. The entry in the first column, for example, is Item Id, indicating that all the other values in the column are Item Ids. The entry in the second column is Description, indicating that all the other values in the column are descriptions. Other than the first row, which contains the labels, all the rows contain precisely the same type of data shown in the Access database in Figure 1b: an item Id in the first column, a description in the second column, the number of units on hand in the third column, and so on.

(a) Microsoft Excel Worksheet

(b) Microsoft Access Table

Figure 1

As the figures illustrate, the worksheet, shown in Figure 1a, is copied to an Access table, shown in Figure 1b. The columns in the worksheet become the fields. The column headings in the first row of the worksheet become the field names. The rows of the worksheet, other than the first row, which contains the labels, become the records in the table. In the process, each field will be assigned the data type that seems the most reasonable, given the data currently in the worksheet.

Organizations that currently use Access for their data needs often find that they need to export the data to other applications. JSP Recruiters has determined that it needs to make some of the data in its database available to other applications. Some users need the data in Excel; others want it placed in a Microsoft Word document. Still others want the ability to receive a report by e-mail.

You can **export** (copy) data from an Access database so that another application (for example, Excel) can use the data. Figure 2a on the next page shows the Recruiter-Client query exported to Excel and Figure 2b on the next page shows the same query exported to Word.

At times you may want to send a report to a user by e-mail. It would be prohibitive to send the whole database to the other user, just so the user could print or view the report. In addition, doing so would require the other user to have Microsoft Access installed. A better way is to publish the report as either a PDF or XPS (XML Paper Specification) file. A user with the appropriate software then can view and print the file. In Figure 2c, the report appears in the XML Paper Specification viewer. It looks just as it does in Access.

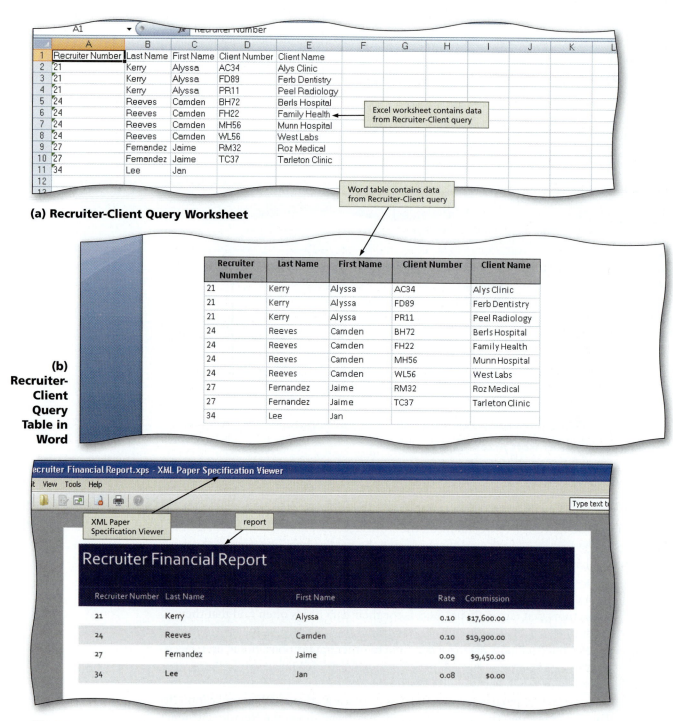

(a) Recruiter-Client Query Worksheet

(b) Recruiter-Client Query Table in Word

(c) XPS Version of Recruiter Financial Report

Figure 2

JSP Recruiters also would like to export the Client and Recruiter tables in such a way that they can be imported easily to a database used by a related organization, JSP Consulting, that handles various accounting functions for JSP Recruiters. The users have learned that the easiest way to do this is to use XML (Extensible Markup Language), which is a language that defines data records on a page, allowing for exchange of data between dissimilar applications. The XML format allows you to export and import both data and structure of multiple related tables in a single operation.

Overview

As you read through this feature, you will learn how to share data among applications by performing these general tasks:

- Import an Excel worksheet into an Access table
- Export a query to Excel
- Export a query to Word
- Publish a report as an XPS file
- Export multiple tables to an XML file
- Import multiple tables from an XML file

BTW

PDF and XPS Formats
Before you export to PDF and XPS formats, check to make sure you have the PDF or XPS button in the Export group on the External Data tab. If not, you must first install a free add-in program. To learn more about installing the add-in, type PDF in the Access Help window and follow the instructions. If you are using a computer in a school or work setting, check with your instructor or IT staff before installing any add-in program.

Plan Ahead

Guidelines for Sharing Data Among Applications

1. **Identify sources of external data for the database.** Does data already exist that you should incorporate into your database? Determine whether the data is in an Excel worksheet, another database, a text file, or some other application.

2. **Determine whether the data you have identified is in an appropriate format.** Is it a collection of rows and columns in which all the entries in a column represent the same type of data? Does the first row contain column headings rather than data? Is the data separated by tabs or by commas?

3. **Determine whether changes made to the data in the original data source should be reflected in the Access table.** If so, linking to the data source is the appropriate action. If not, importing the data would be appropriate.

4. **If the source of data is an Access database, determine whether, in addition to the tables, there are other objects to be imported.** If you import tables, you also can import queries, forms, and reports based on those tables. If, for example, the other database contained a report based on a table you are importing, you can import the report as well, thus saving you the effort of having to recreate the report.

5. **For data in your database that you want to make available to others, determine whether exporting the data is appropriate.** If you export the data, any changes that others make to the data will not be reflected in your database. If it is acceptable that these changes are not reflected, then exporting is appropriate. If not, the data will need to be linked. Linking must take place within the other application.

6. **If data is to be exported, determine the destination application.** The application that will receive the data determines the export process to be used. Common choices are Excel and Word. You also can export to text files in a variety of formats. For applications to which you cannot directly export data, you often can export an appropriately formatted text file that the other application can import. To make reports available to others, rather than exporting the report, you can publish the report, which is the process of making the report available to others on the Web. You can publish the report in either PDF or XPS format, so you would need to determine which is appropriate for the person who wants to be able to view the report.

When necessary, more specific details concerning the above decisions and/or actions are presented at appropriate positions within the feature. The feature also will identify the use of these guidelines in sharing data as shown in Figures 1 and 2.

Starting Access

If you are using a computer to step through the project in this chapter and you want your screen to match the figures in this book, you should change your screen's resolution to 1024 × 768. For information about how to change a computer's resolution, read Appendix E.

To Start Access

The following steps, which assume Windows is running, start Access.

Note: If you are using Windows XP, see Appendix F for alternate steps.

1 Click the Start button on the Windows taskbar to display the Start menu.

2 Click All Programs at the bottom of the left pane on the Start menu to display the All Programs list and then click Microsoft Office in the All Programs list to display the Microsoft Office list.

3 Click Microsoft Office Access 2007 on the Microsoft Office submenu to start Access and display the Getting Started with Microsoft Office Access window.

4 If the Access window is not maximized, click the Maximize button on its title bar to maximize the window.

To Create a New Database

Before importing data from another application to an Access database, you must ensure that a database exists. If there is no database, then you need to create one. The following steps create a database on a USB flash drive that will store the items for Camashaly.

Note: If you are using Windows XP, see Appendix F for alternate steps.

1 With a USB flash drive connected to one of the computer's USB ports, click Blank Database in the Getting Started with Microsoft Office Access screen to create a new blank database.

2 Type Camashaly in the File Name text box and then click the 'Browse for a location to put your database' button to display the File New Database dialog box.

3 Click Computer in the Favorite Links section to display a list of available drives and folders and then double-click UDISK 2.0 (E:) (your letter may be different) in the Computer list to select the USB flash drive as the new save location.

4 Click the OK button to select the USB flash drive as the location for the database and to return to the Getting Started with Microsoft Office Access screen.

5 Click the Create button to create the database on the USB flash drive with the file name, Camashaly.

Importing or Linking Data from Other Applications to Access

The process of importing or linking an Access database uses a wizard. Specifically, if the data is imported from an Excel worksheet, the process will use the **Import Spreadsheet Wizard**; if the data is linked to an Excel worksheet, the process will use the **Link Spreadsheet Wizard**. The wizard takes you through some basic steps, asking a few simple questions. After you have answered the questions, the wizard will import or link the data.

Identify sources of external data for the database: Excel worksheet.
You need to decide whether it is appropriate for data you currently keep in an Excel worksheet to be kept in a database instead. The following are some common reasons for using a database instead of a worksheet:

1. The worksheet contains a great deal of redundant data. As discussed in Chapter 1 on pages AC 10 and AC 12, databases can be designed to eliminate redundant data.

2. The data to be maintained consists of multiple interrelated items. For example, the JSP Recruiters database maintains data on two items, clients and recruiters, and these items are interrelated. A client has a single recruiter and each recruiter is responsible for several clients. The JSP Recruiters database is a very simple one. Databases easily can contain many separate, but interrelated, items.

3. You want to use the powerful query and report capabilities of Microsoft Access.

Plan Ahead

Determine whether the data you have identified is in an appropriate format: Excel worksheet.
Before importing or linking the Excel worksheet you have identified, you need to make sure it is in an appropriate format. The following are some of the actions you should take to ensure correct format:

1. Make sure the data is in the form of a list, a collection of rows and columns in which all the entries in a column represent the same type of data.

2. Make sure that there are no blank rows within the list. If there are, remove them prior to importing or linking.

3. Make sure there are no blank columns within the list. If there are, remove them prior to importing or linking.

4. Determine whether the first row contains column headings that will make appropriate field names in the resulting table. If not, you might consider adding such a row. In general, the process is simpler if the first row in the worksheet contains appropriate column headings.

Plan Ahead

To Import an Excel Worksheet

After Camashaly managers identified that a worksheet named Computer Items contains data that should be in a table in the database, they would import the data. You import a worksheet by using the Import Spreadsheet Wizard. In the process, you will indicate that the first row in the Computer Items worksheet contains the column headings. These column headings then will become the field names in the Access table. In addition, you will indicate the primary key for the table. As part of the process, you could, if appropriate, choose not to include all the fields from the worksheet in the resulting table.

The following steps import the Computer Items Excel worksheet.

Note: If you are using Windows XP, see Appendix F for alternate steps.

• Click External Data on the Ribbon to display the External Data tab (Figure 3).

Figure 3

2

• Click the Excel button in the Import group on the External Data tab to display the Get External Data – Excel Spreadsheet dialog box.

• Click the Browse button in the Get External Data – Excel Spreadsheet dialog box.

• If necessary, click the Look in box arrow and then click UDISK 2.0 (E:) to select the USB flash drive in the Look in list as the new open location. (Your drive letter might be different.)

• Click the Computer Items workbook, and then click the Open button to select the workbook (Figure 4).

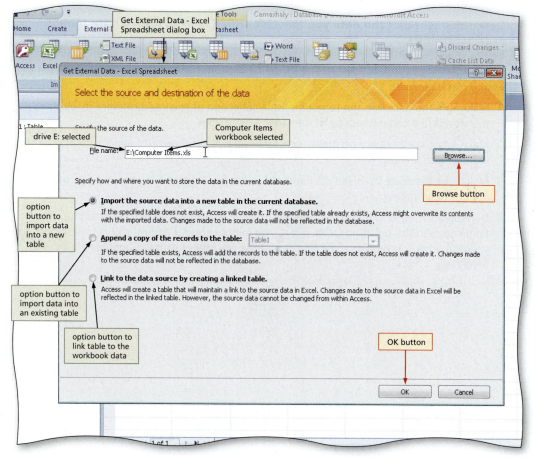

Figure 4

3

- With the option button to import the data to a new table selected, click the OK button to display the Import Spreadsheet Wizard dialog box (Figure 5).

Q&A What happens if I select the option button to append records to an existing table?

Instead of the records being placed in a new table, they will be added to the existing table, provided the value in the primary key field does not duplicate that on an existing record.

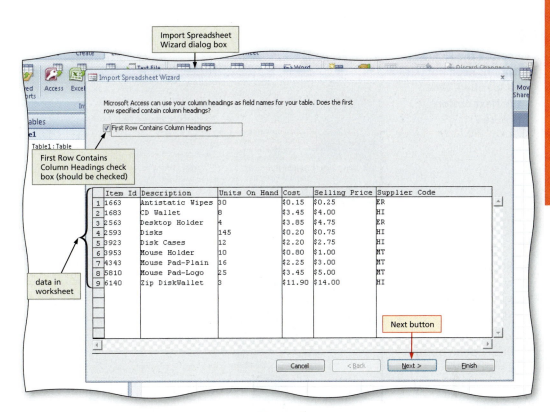

Figure 5

4

- If necessary, click First Row Contains Column Headings to select it.

- Click the Next button (Figure 6).

Q&A When would I use the options on this screen?

You would use these options if you wanted to change properties for one or more fields. You can change the name, the data type, and whether the field is indexed. You also can indicate that some fields are not to be imported.

Figure 6

5

- Because the Field Options need not be specified, click the Next button (Figure 7).

Figure 7

6

- Click the 'Choose my own primary key.' option button (Figure 8).

Q&A

How do I decide which option button to select?

If one of the fields is an appropriate primary key, choose your own primary key from the list of fields. If you are sure you do not want a primary key, choose No primary key. Otherwise, let Access add the primary key.

Figure 8

7

- Because the Item Id field, which is the correct field, is already selected as the primary key, click the Next button.

- Be sure Item appears in the Import to Table text box.

- Click the Finish button to import the data (Figure 9).

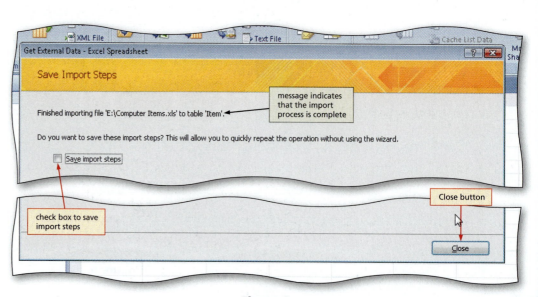

Figure 9

8

- Click the Save import steps check box to display the Save import steps options.

- If necessary, type `Import-Computer Items` in the Save as text box.

- Type `Import data from Computer Items workbook into Item table` in the Description text box (Figure 10).

Q&A

When would I create an Outlook task?

If the import operation is one you will repeat on a regular basis, you can create and schedule the import process just as you can schedule any other Outlook task.

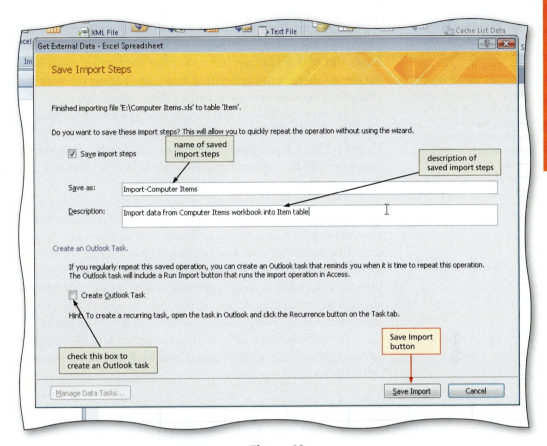

Figure 10

9

- Click the Save Import button to save the import steps (Figure 11).

Figure 11

Other Ways

1. Right-click Table1 : Table in Navigation Pane, point to Import, click appropriate file format

Using the Access Table

After the Access version of the table has been created, you can use it as you would any other table. You can open the table in Datasheet view (Figure 1b on page AC 207). You can make changes to the data. You can create queries or reports that use the data in the table.

By clicking Design View on the table's shortcut menu, you can view the table's structure and make any necessary changes to the structure. The changes may include changing field sizes and types (for those that may not be correct), creating indexes, specifying the primary key, or adding additional fields. If you have imported multiple tables that are to be related, you will need to relate the tables. To accomplish any of these tasks, use the same steps you used in Chapter 3.

BTW

Saving Import Steps
When you save the steps that import data from a Microsoft Office Excel 2007 workbook, Access stores the name of the Excel workbook, the name of the destination database, and other details, including whether the data was appended to a table or added to a new table, primary key information, field names, and so on.

Linking versus Importing

When an external table or worksheet is imported, or converted, into an Access database, a copy of the data is placed as a table in the database. The original data still exists, just as it did before, but no further connection exists between it and the data in the database. Changes to the original data do not affect the data in the database. Likewise, changes in the database do not affect the original data.

It also is possible to link data stored in a variety of formats to Access databases by selecting the 'Link to the data source by creating a linked table' option button on the Get External Data - Excel Spreadsheet dialog box rather than the 'Import the source data into a new table in the current database' option button (Figure 4 on page AC 212). With linking, the connection is maintained.

When an Excel worksheet is linked, for example, the worksheet is not stored in the database. Instead Access simply establishes a connection to the worksheet so you can view the data in either Access or Excel. Any change made in the worksheet will be visible immediately in the table. For example, if you change an address in Excel and then view the table in Access, you would see the new address. If you add a new row in Excel and then view the table in Access, the row would appear as a new record. You cannot make changes to the table in Access. If you want to add, change, or delete data, you must make the changes in the worksheet because the data is stored in an Excel workbook.

To identify that a table is linked to other data, Access places an arrow in front of the table (Figure 12). In addition, the Excel icon in front of the name indicates that the data is linked to an Excel worksheet.

Figure 12

The Linked Table Manager

After you link tables between a worksheet and a database or between two databases, you can modify many of the linked table's features. For example, you can rename the linked table, set view properties, and set links between tables in queries. If you move, rename, or modify linked tables, you can use the **Linked Table Manager** to update the links. To do so, click Database Tools on the Ribbon to display the Database Tools tab. Then click the Linked Table Manager button on the Database Tools tab. The Linked Table Manager dialog box that appears includes instructions on how to update the links.

To Close a Database

The following steps show how to close the database.

1 Click the Office Button to display the Office Button menu.

2 Click Close Database on the Office Button menu.

Importing from or Linking to Data in Another Access Database

Just as you can import data from an Excel worksheet, you can import data from another Access database. Similarly, just as you can link to data in an Excel worksheet, you can link to data in another Access database.

Identify sources of external data for the database: Access database.
You need to decide whether it is appropriate for you to import or link data in another Access database. The following are some common reasons for importing from or linking to another database:

1. You want to combine two databases into one. By importing, you can copy all objects (tables, queries, forms, reports, and so on) from one database to the other.

2. You want to create tables that are similar to tables in another database. When importing, you can choose to copy the table structure without the data. The table created in the process will have all the fields and field properties of the original, but will be empty.

3. You want to copy a collection of related objects from another database. In one operation you could, for example, copy a table along with all queries, forms, and reports that are based on that table.

4. You have several databases, but data in some tables is the same, for example, the Client table must be shared between some of the databases. By linking, any updates to the table in the source database are immediately available to anyone using any of the other databases.

Plan Ahead

To Import Data from Another Access Database

The following steps would import data from another Access database into the database that is currently open.

1. Click the Access button in the Import group on the External Data tab.

2. Select the database containing the data to be imported.

3. Be sure the 'Import tables, queries, forms, reports, macros, and modules into the current database' option button is selected and click the OK button.

4. In the Import Objects dialog box, select the tables, queries, forms, reports, macros, and/or modules you wish to import and then click the OK button.

5. Decide if you wish to save the import steps.

To Link to Data in Another Access Database

The following steps would link tables in another Access database into the database that is currently open.

1. Click the Access button in the Import group on the External Data tab.

2. Select the database containing the tables to be linked.

3. Click the 'Link to the data source by creating a linked table' option button to link and then click the OK button.

4. In the Link tables dialog box, select the tables you wish to link and then click the OK button.

Text Files

Text files contain unformatted characters including both readable characters, such as numbers and letters, and some special characters, such as tabs, carriage returns, and line feeds. Typical extensions for text files that can be imported or linked into Access databases are txt, csv, asc, and tab.

To be able to use a text file for importing or linking, it must be organized into records (rows) and fields (columns). Records and fields can be organized in two ways: delimited files and fixed-width files.

In **delimited files**, each record is on a separate line and the fields are separated by a special character, called the **delimiter**. Common delimiters are tabs, semicolons, commas, and spaces. You also can choose any other value that does not appear within the field contents. The csv (comma separated values) file often used in Excel is an example of a delimited file.

In **fixed-width files**, the width of any field is the same on every record. For example, if the width of the first field on the first record is 12 characters, the width of the first field on every other record also must be 12 characters.

Plan Ahead

Identify sources of external data for the database: text file.
You need to decide whether it is appropriate for you to use external data stored in a text file. The following are some common reasons for using a text file for this purpose:

1. Data that you want to import is not available in a format that Access recognizes. You first would export the data from the original application to a text file and then import that text file into Access.

2. You manage data in Access but regularly receive data in text files from other users that needs to be incorporated into your database.

Plan Ahead

Determine whether the data you have identified is in an appropriate format: text file.
Before importing or linking the text file you have identified, you need to make sure it is in an appropriate format. The following are some of the actions you should take to ensure correct format:

1. Make sure the data in the text file consistently follows one of the available formats (delimited or fixed width). If the file is delimited, identify the delimiter and make sure the same one is used throughout. If the file is fixed-width, make sure each field on each record is the same width.

2. Make sure that there are no blank records within the file. If there are, remove them prior to importing or linking.

3. Make sure there are no blank fields within the list. If there are, remove them prior to importing or linking.

4. For each field, make sure the entries in each record represent the same type of data.

5. If it is a delimited file, determine whether the first row contains column headings that will make appropriate field names in the resulting table. If not, you should add such a row. In general, the process is simpler if the first row in a delimited file contains appropriate column headings.

6. Make sure there are no extra paragraph (carriage) returns at the end of the file. If there are, remove them prior to importing or linking.

To Import Data from or Link Data to a Text File

To import data from or link data to a text file, you would use the following steps.

1. Click the Text File button in the Import group on the External Data tab.

2. Select the text file containing the data to be imported.

3. Be sure the 'Import the source into a new table in the current database' option button is selected if you wish to create a new table. Click the 'Append a copy of the records to the table' option button if you wish to add to an existing table, and then select the table. Click the 'Link to the data source by creating a linked table' option button if you wish to link the data. Once you have selected the correct option button, click the OK button.

4. Select the Delimited option button for a delimited file or the Fixed Width option button for a fixed-width file, and then click the Next button.

5a. For a delimited file, select the character that delimits the field values. If you know the file uses a text qualifier, which is a symbol used to enclose character values, select either the double quotation mark (") or the single quotation mark ('). If the first row contains field names, click the First Row contains Field Names check box. Once you have made your selections, click the Next button.

5b. For a fixed-width file, review the structure that Access recommends. If the recommended structure is not appropriate, follow the directions on the screen to add, remove, or adjust the lines. Once you have finished, click the Next button.

6. You can use the next screen if you need to change properties of one or more fields. When finished, click the Next button.

7. If you are importing, select the appropriate primary key, and then click the Next button. If you are linking, you will not have an opportunity to select a primary key.

8. Be sure the table name is correct, and then click the Finish button to import or link the data. Decide if you wish to save the import steps.

Using Saved Import Steps

You can use a set of saved import steps from within Access by clicking the Saved Imports button on the External Data tab. You then will see the Manage Data Tasks dialog box, as shown in Figure 13 on the next page. Select the set of saved import steps you want to repeat. (In this case only the import named Import-Computer Items exists.) Click the Run button to repeat the import steps you saved earlier. If you have created an Outlook task, you can schedule the import operation just as you schedule any other Outlook task.

Figure 13

Exporting Data from Access to Other Applications

Exporting is the process of copying database objects to another database, to a worksheet, or to some other format so another application (for example, Excel) can use the data. Businesses need the flexibility of using the same data in different applications. For example, numerical data in a table exported to Excel could be analyzed using Excel's powerful statistical functions. Data also could be exported as an RTF file for use in marketing brochures.

To Open a Database

Before exporting the JSP Recruiters data, you first must open the database. The following steps open the database.

Note: If you are using Windows XP, see Appendix F for alternate steps.

1 With your USB flash drive connected to one of the computer's USB ports, click the More button to display the Open dialog box.

2 If the Folders list is displayed below the Folders button, click the Folders button to remove the Folders list.

3 If necessary, click Computer in the Favorite Links section and then double-click UDISK 2.0 (E:) to select the USB flash drive as the new open location. (Your drive letter might be different.)

4 Click JSP Recruiters to select the file name.

5 Click the Open button to open the database.

6 If a Security Warning appears, click the Options button to display the Microsoft Office Security Options dialog box.

7 Click the 'Enable this content' option button and then click the OK button to enable the content.

To Export Data to Excel

Once JSP Recruiters has decided to make the Recruiter-Client Query available to Excel users, it needs to export the data. To export data to Excel, select the table or query to be exported, and then click the Excel button in the Export group on the External Data tab. The following steps export the Client-Recruiter Query to Excel and save the export steps.

1

• Click the Recruiter-Client Query in the Navigation Pane to select it.

• Click External Data on the Ribbon to display the External Data tab (Figure 14).

Figure 14

2

- Click the Excel button in the Export group on the External Data tab to display the Export – Excel Spreadsheet dialog box.

- Click the Browse button and select your USB flash drive as the file location.

- Be sure the file name is Recruiter-Client Query and then click the Save button (Figure 15).

Q&A Did I need to browse?

No. You could type the appropriate file location.

Q&A Could I change the name of the file?

You could change it. Simply replace the current file name with the one you want.

Q&A What if the file I want to export already exists?

Access will indicate that the file already exists and ask if you want to replace it. If you click the Yes button, the file you export will replace the old file. If you click the No button, you must either change the name of the export file or cancel the process.

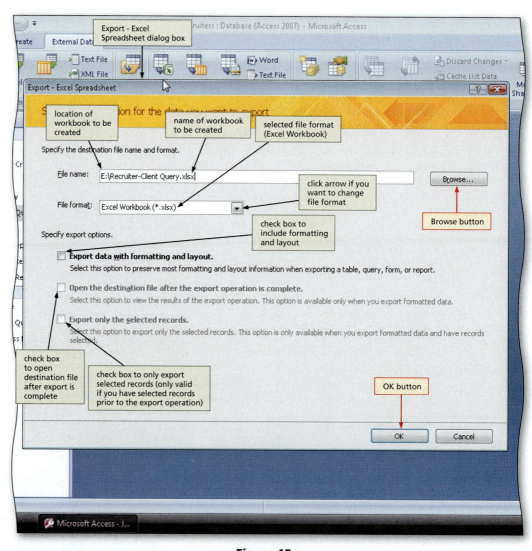

Figure 15

3

- Click the OK button to export the data (Figure 16).

4

- Click the Save export steps check box to display the Save export steps options.

- If necessary, type Export-Recruiter-Client Query in the Save as text box.

- Type Export the Recruiter-Client Query without formatting in the Description text box.

- Click the Save Export button to save the export steps.

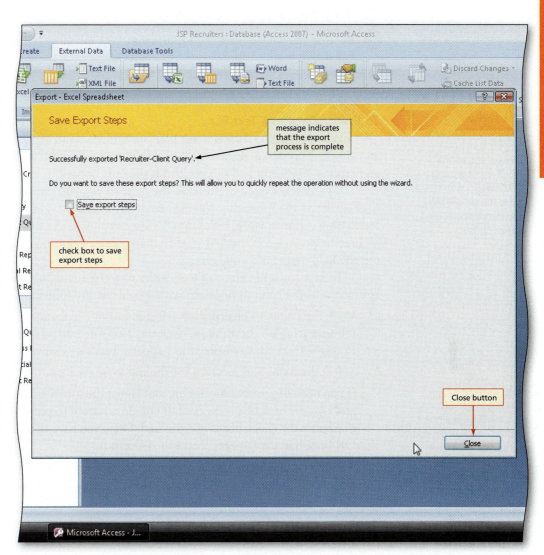

Figure 16

Other Ways

1. Right-click database object in Navigation Pane, point to Export, click appropriate file format

To Export Data to Word

Once JSP Recruiters has decided to also make the Recruiter-Client Query available to Word, it needs to export the data. There is a problem, however. It is not possible to export data to the standard Word format. It is possible, however to export the data as an RTF (rich text file), which Word can access. The following steps export the data to an RTF file. They do not save the export steps.

1 With the Recruiter-Client Query selected in the Navigation Pane and the External Data tab appearing on the screen, click the Word button in the Export group on the External Data tab to display the Export - RTF File dialog box.

2 Select your USB drive as the file location and make sure that Recruiter-Client Query is the file name.

3 If necessary, click the Save button and then click the OK button to export the data.

4 Because you will not save the export steps, click the Close button to close the Export - RTF File dialog box.

BTW

XPS Format
To view a file in XPS format, you need a viewer. You or the recipient of your file can download a free viewer from the Downloads section of Microsoft Office Online.

TO EXPORT DATA TO A TEXT FILE

When exporting data to a text file, you can choose to export the data with formatting and layout. This option preserves much of the formatting and layout in tables, queries, forms, and reports. For forms and reports, this is the only option.

If you do not need to preserve the formatting, you can choose either delimited or fixed-width as the format for the exported file. The most common option, especially if formatting is not an issue, is delimited. You can choose the delimiter and also whether to include field names on the first row. In many cases, delimiting with a comma and including the field names is a good choice.

To export data from a table or query to a comma-delimited file in which the first row contains the column headings, you would use the following steps.

1. With the object to be exported selected in the Navigation Pane and the External Data tab appearing on the Ribbon, click the Text File button in the Export group on the External Data tab to display the Export - Text File dialog box.

2. Select the name and location for the file to be created.

BTW

PDF Format
To view a PDF file, you must have a PDF reader installed on your computer. One such reader is the Acrobat Reader, available for free from Adobe Systems.

3. If you need to preserve formatting and layout, be sure the 'Export data with formatting and layout' check box is checked. If you do not need to preserve formatting and layout, make sure the check box is not checked. Once you have made your selection, click the OK button in the Export - Text File dialog box.

4. To create a delimited file, be sure the Delimited option button is selected. To create a fixed-width file, be sure the Fixed Width option button is selected. Once you have made your selection, click the Next button.

5a. If you are exporting to a delimited file, choose the delimiter that you want to separate your fields, such as a comma. Decide whether to include field names on the first row and, if so, click the Include Field Names on First Row check box. If you want to select a text qualifier, select it in the Text Qualifier list. When you have made your selections, click the Next button.

5b. If you are exporting to a fixed-width file, review the position of the vertical lines that separate your fields. If any lines are not positioned correctly, follow the directions on the screen to reposition them. When you have finished, click the Next button.

6. Click the Finish button to export the data.

7. Save the export steps if you wish, or simply click the Close button in the Export - Text File dialog box to close the dialog box without saving the export steps.

To Publish a Report

At JSP Recruiters, the staff would like to make the Recruiter Financial Report available through e-mail, which they can do by publishing the report as either a PDF or XPS file. The following steps publish the Recruiter Financial Report as an XPS file.

Note: If you are using Windows XP, see Appendix F for alternate steps.

- Click the Recruiter Financial Report in the Navigation Pane to select it.

- Click the 'PDF or XPS' button in the Export group on the External Data tab (see Figure 14 on page AC 221) to display the Publish as PDF or XPS dialog box.

- Select your USB drive as the file location. Make sure that Recruiter Financial Report is the file name and that XPS Document is the file type. If necessary, remove the check mark in the 'Open file after publishing' check box.

- Click the 'Standard (publishing online and printing)' option button to create a file that is appropriate for both publishing online and printing (Figure 17).

Q&A

How do I publish as PDF?

Change XPS Document to PDF in the Save as type box.

Figure 17

- Click the Publish button to publish the report as an XPS file.

- Because you will not save the export steps, click the Close button to close the Export - XPS dialog box.

Using Saved Export Steps

You can use a set of saved Export steps from within Access by clicking the Saved Exports button on the External Data tab. You then select the set of saved export steps you want to repeat and click the Run button in the Manage Data Tasks dialog box. If you have created an Outlook task, you can schedule the export operation just as you can schedule any other Outlook task.

BTW

Viewing or Printing the Report

To view or print the report stored in the XPS file, use the XML Paper Specification Viewer. If the XML Paper Specification Viewer is not installed on your system, you can obtain it from Microsoft. If you are unable to view or print XPS files, you alternatively can publish the report as a PDF. To do so, change the Save as type from XPS Document to PDF before clicking the Publish button.

Saving Export Steps
When you save the steps that export formatted data to Microsoft Office Excel or Word 2007, the current filter and column settings of the source object in Access are saved. If the source object (table, query, form, or report) is open when you run the export steps, Access exports only the data that is currently displayed in the view.

XML

Just as Hypertext Markup Language (HTML) is the standard language for creating and displaying Web pages, **Extensible Markup Language (XML)** is the standard language for describing and delivering data on the Web. Another way of viewing the difference is that HTML handles the *appearance* of data within a Web page, whereas XML handles the *meaning* of data. XML is a data interchange standard that allows you to exchange data between dissimilar systems or applications. With XML, you can describe both the data and the structure **(schema)** of the data. You can export tables, queries, forms, or reports.

When exporting XML data, you can choose to export multiple related tables in a single operation to a single XML file. If you later import this XML data to another database, you will import all the tables in a single operation. Thus, the new database would contain each of the tables. All the fields would have the correct data types and sizes and the primary keys would be correct.

To Export XML Data

In exporting XML data, you indicate whether to just save the data or to save both the data and the schema (that is, the structure). If you have made changes to the appearance of the data, such as changing the font, and want these changes saved as well, you save what is known as the **presentation**. The data is saved in a file with the XML extension, the schema is saved in a file with the XSD extension, and the presentation is saved in a file with the XSL extension. The default choice, which usually is appropriate, is to save both the data and schema, but not the presentation. If multiple tables are related, such as the Client and Recruiter tables in the JSP Recruiters data, you can export both tables to a single file.

The following steps export both the Client and Recruiter tables to a single XML file called Client. The steps save the data and the schema, but do not save the presentation.

1
- Click the Client table in the Navigation Pane to select it.
- Click the More button in the Export group on the External Data tab to display the More button menu with additional export options (Figure 18).

Figure 18

2
- Click XML File on the More button menu to display the Export - XML File dialog box.
- Select your USB drive as the file location and make sure that Client is the file name (Figure 19).

Figure 19

3

- Click the OK button to display the Export XML dialog box (Figure 20).

Figure 20

4

- Click the More Options button to specify additional options (Figure 21).

Q&A

What is the purpose of the other tabs in this dialog box?

You can use the Schema tab to indicate whether you want primary key, index information, table properties, and field properties included (normally they are) and whether the schema information is to be stored in a separate file (normally it is). If you want to export the presentation, you can use the Presentation tab to indicate this fact and also specify options concerning how the Presentation will be exported.

Figure 21

5

- Click the expand indicator (the plus sign) to the left of [Lookup Data], and then click the Recruiter check box to select the Recruiter table (Figure 22).

6

- Click the OK button to export the data.

- Because you will not save the export steps, click the Close button to close the Export - XML File dialog box.

- Click the Close Database command on the Office Button menu.

Figure 22

To Create a New Database

Before importing the data from the JSP Recruiters database, you need to create the new JSP Consulting database that will contain the data. The following steps create the JSP Consulting database on a USB flash drive.

1 With a USB flash drive connected to one of the computer's USB ports, click Blank Database in the Getting Started with Microsoft Office Access screen to create a new blank database.

2 Type `JSP Consulting` in the File Name text box and then click the 'Browse for a location to put your database' button to display the File New Database dialog box.

BTW

Quick Reference
For a table that lists how to complete the tasks covered in this book using the mouse, Ribbon, shortcut menu, and keyboard, see the Quick Reference Summary at the back of this book, or visit the Access 2007 Quick Reference Web page (scsite.com/ac2007/qr).

3 Click Computer in the Favorite Links section to display a list of available drives and folders and then click UDISK 2.0 (E:) (your letter may be different) in the Computer list to select the USB flash drive as the new save location.

4 Click the OK button to select the USB flash drive as the location for the database and to return to the Getting Started with Microsoft Office Access screen.

5 Click the Create button to create the database on the USB flash drive with the file name, JSP Consulting.

To Import XML Data

The following steps import both the Client and Recruiter tables stored in the XML file called Client. In addition to having the same data, the fields in both tables will have precisely the same data types and sizes as in the original database. Also, the same fields will have been designated primary keys.

1

• With the JSP Consulting database open, click External Data on the Ribbon to display the External Data tab.

• Click the XML File button in the Import group on the External Data tab to display the Get External Data - XML File dialog box.

• Click the Browse button in the Get External Data - XML File dialog box to display the File Open dialog box.

• Click Computer and then double-click UDISK 2.0 (E:).

• Click the Client file to select it (Figure 23).

Q&A

Should I click the xsd version?

No. If you do, you will import both tables, but none of the data. That is, the tables will be empty.

Figure 23

- Click the Open button to return to the Get External Data - XML File dialog box (Figure 24).

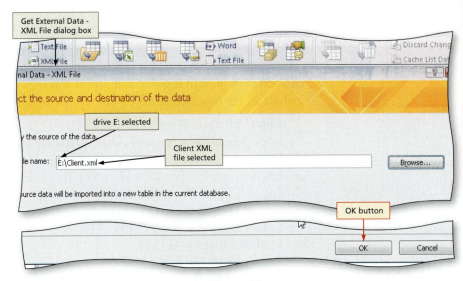

Figure 24

3
- Click the OK button to display the Import XML dialog box (Figure 25).

4
- Be sure the Structure and Data option button is selected and then click the OK button to import the data.

- Because you will not save the import steps, click the Close button to close the Get External Data - XML File dialog box.

Figure 25

To Quit Access

You are ready to quit Access. The following step quits Access.

1 Click the Close button on the right side of the Access title bar to quit Access.

BTW

Certification
The Microsoft Certified Application Specialist (MCAS) program provides an opportunity for you to obtain a valuable industry credential — proof that you have the Access 2007 skills required by employers. For more information, see Appendix G or visit the Access 2007 Certification Web page (scsite.com/ac2007/cert).

Feature Summary

In this feature you have learned to import from and link to data in Excel worksheets, other Access databases, and text files; export data to Excel worksheets, Word documents, and text files; publish reports; and export and import XML data. The items listed below include all the new Access skills you have learned in this chapter.

1. Import an Excel Worksheet (AC 212)
2. Import Data from Another Access Database (AC 217)
3. Link to Data in Another Access Database (AC 217)
4. Import Data from or Link Data to a Text File (AC 219)
5. Export Data to Excel (AC 221)
6. Export Data to Word (AC 223)
7. Export Data to a Text File (AC 224)
8. Publish a Report (AC 225)
9. Export XML Data (AC 226)
10. Import XML Data (AC 228)

If you have a SAM user profile, you may have access to hands-on instruction, practice, and assessment. Log in to your SAM account (http://sam2007.course.com) to launch any assigned training activities or exams that relate to the skills covered in this feature.

In the Lab

Design, create, modify, and/or use a database following the guidelines, concepts, and skills presented in this feature.

Lab 1: Importing Data to an Access Database

Problem: TAL Woodworks sells custom wood accessories for the home. TAL uses worksheets to keep track of inventory and customers. TAL realizes that customer data would be better handled if maintained in an Access database. The company wants to maintain the products inventory in Excel but also would like to be able to use the query and report features of Access.

Instructions: For this assignment, you will need two files: Customer.csv and Product.xlsx. See the inside back cover of this book for instructions for downloading the Data Files for Students, or see your instructor for information on accessing the files required in this book. Perform the following tasks:

1. Start Access and create a new database in which to store all the objects for TAL Woodworks. Call the database TAL Woodworks.

2. Import the Customer worksheet shown in Figure 26 into Access. The worksheet is saved as a .csv file.

	A	B	C	D	E	F	G	H	I	J	K
1	Customer Number	Name	Address	City	State	Balance					
2	AD23	Adson Gifts	407 Mallory	Tourin	CO	$ 205.00					
3	AR75	Arthur's Interiors	200 Mimberly	Denton	CO	$ 180.00					
4	BE28	Becker Design	224 Harbor Oak	Charleston	CO	$ 170.00					
5	CR66	Casa Grande	506 Mallory	Tourin	CO	$0.00					
6	DL60	Dee's Things	123 Village	Denton	CO	$ 235.00					
7	GR36	Grande Casa	1345 Fern	Charleston	CO	$ 204.00					
8	HA09	Hal's Gifts	568 Denmer	Berridge	CO	$ 245.00					
9	ME17	My House	879 Vinca	Berls	CO	$ 268.00					
10	RO44	Royal Interiors	677 Liatris	Berridge	CO	$0.00					
11	ST22	Steedman's	889 Lantana	Berls	CO	$ 123.00					
12											
13											
14											

Figure 26

3. Use Customer as the name of the table and Customer Number as the primary key.

4. Save the import steps. Be sure to enter a description for the saved steps.

5. Link the Product worksheet shown in Figure 27 to the database.

	A	B	C	D	E	F	G	H	I	J	K	L
1	Product Code	Description	On Hand	Cost	Selling Price							
2	101	Candy Dish	10	$4.00	$6.00							
3	103	Letter Opener	15	$2.00	$3.00							
4	104	Tray	5	$10.00	$15.00							
5	106	Salad Tongs	20	$3.00	$5.00							
6	110	Lazy Susan	8	$16.00	$20.00							
7	112	Spoon Set	21	$12.00	$14.00							
8	113	Salad Bowl	9	$18.00	$25.00							
9	115	Desk Organizer	8	$22.00	$30.00							
10	120	Book Ends	4	$27.00	$34.00							
11	121	Mobile	7	$34.00	$40.00							
12												
13												
14												

Figure 27

6. Rename the linked Product table as Inventory. Then, use the Linked Table Manager to update the link between the Excel worksheet and the Access table.

7. Import the Sales Rep table from the Ada Beauty Supply database that you modified in In the Lab 3 in Chapter 3 on page AC 201. (If you did not complete this exercise, see your instructor for a copy of the modified database.) Sales reps of Ada often sell gift items to salons.

8. Change the database properties, as specified by your instructor. Submit the database in the format specified by your instructor.

In the Lab

Lab 2: Exporting Data to Other Applications

Problem: JMS TechWizards wants to be able to export some of the data in its Access database to other applications. JMS wants to export the City-Technician Crosstab query for further processing in Excel. It also wants to use the Technician table in a Word document as well as e-mail the Salary Report to the company's accounting firm. The company has decided to branch out and offer consulting services. It wants to export the Client and Technician tables as a single XML file and then import it to a new database.

Instructions: Start Access. Open the JMS TechWizards database that you modified in In the Lab 1 in Chapter 3 on page AC 195. (If you did not complete this exercise, see your instructor for a copy of the modified database.) Perform the following tasks:

1. Export the City-Technician Crosstab query to Excel as shown in Figure 28. Save the export steps. Be sure to include a description.

Figure 28

2. Export the Technician table to a Word document. Do not save the export steps.

3. Publish the Salary Report as an XPS file.

4. Export both the Client and Technician tables in XML format. Be sure that both tables are exported to the same file. Do not save the export steps.

5. Create a new database called JMS TechConsultants.

6. Import the Client XML file containing both the Client and Technician tables to the JMS TechConsultants database.

7. Submit the Excel workbook, Word document, XPS file, and JMS TechConsultants database in the format specified by your instructor.

Appendix A
Project Planning Guidelines

Using Project Planning Guidelines

The process of communicating specific information to others is a learned, rational skill. Computers and software, especially Microsoft Office 2007, can help you develop ideas and present detailed information to a particular audience.

Using Microsoft Office 2007, you can create projects such as Word documents, Excel spreadsheets, Access databases, and PowerPoint presentations. Computer hardware and productivity software such as Microsoft Office 2007 minimizes much of the laborious work of drafting and revising projects. Some communicators handwrite ideas in note-books, others compose directly on the computer, and others have developed unique strategies that work for their own particular thinking and writing styles.

No matter what method you use to plan a project, follow specific guidelines to arrive at a final product that presents information correctly and effectively (Figure A–1). Use some aspects of these guidelines every time you undertake a project, and others as needed in specific instances. For example, in determining content for a project, you may decide that a bar chart communicates trends more effectively than a paragraph of text. If so, you would create this graphical element and insert it in an Excel spreadsheet, a Word document, or a PowerPoint slide.

Determine the Project's Purpose

Begin by clearly defining why you are undertaking this assignment. For example, you may want to track monetary donations collected for your club's fundraising drive. Alternatively, you may be urging students to vote for a particular candidate in the next election. Once you clearly understand the purpose of your task, begin to draft ideas of how best to communicate this information.

Analyze your Audience

Learn about the people who will read, analyze, or view your work. Where are they employed? What are their educational backgrounds? What are their expectations? What questions do they have?

PROJECT PLANNING GUIDELINES

1. DETERMINE THE PROJECT'S PURPOSE
Why are you undertaking the project?

2. ANALYZE YOUR AUDIENCE
Who are the people who will use your work?

3. GATHER POSSIBLE CONTENT
What information exists, and in what forms?

4. DETERMINE WHAT CONTENT TO PRESENT TO YOUR AUDIENCE
What information will best communicate the project's purpose to your audience?

Figure A–1

Design experts suggest drawing a mental picture of these people or finding photographs of people who fit this profile so that you can develop a project with the audience in mind.

By knowing your audience members, you can tailor a project to meet their interests and needs. You will not present them with information they already possess, and you will not omit the information they need to know.

Example: Your assignment is to raise the profile of your college's nursing program in the community. How much do they know about your college and the nursing curriculum? What are the admission requirements? How many of the applicants admitted complete the program? What percent pass the state Boards?

Gather Possible Content

Rarely are you in a position to develop all the material for a project. Typically, you would begin by gathering existing information that may reside in spreadsheets or databases. Web sites, pamphlets, magazine and newspaper articles, and books could provide insights of how others have approached your topic. Personal interviews often provide perspectives not available by any other means. Consider video and audio clips as potential sources for material that might complement or support the factual data you uncover.

Determine What Content to Present to your Audience

Experienced designers recommend writing three or four major ideas you want an audience member to remember after reading or viewing your project. It also is helpful to envision your project's endpoint, the key fact you wish to emphasize. All project elements should lead to this ending point.

As you make content decisions, you also need to think about other factors. Presentation of the project content is an important consideration. For example, will your brochure be printed on thick, colored paper or transparencies? Will your PowerPoint presentation be viewed in a classroom with excellent lighting and a bright projector, or will it be viewed on a notebook computer monitor? Determine relevant time factors, such as the length of time to develop the project, how long readers will spend reviewing your project, or the amount of time allocated for your speaking engagement. Your project will need to accommodate all of these constraints.

Decide whether a graph, photograph, or artistic element can express or emphasize a particular concept. The right hemisphere of the brain processes images by attaching an emotion to them, so audience members are more apt to recall these graphics long term rather than just reading text.

As you select content, be mindful of the order in which you plan to present information. Readers and audience members generally remember the first and last pieces of information they see and hear, so you should put the most important information at the top or bottom of the page.

Summary

When creating a project, it is beneficial to follow some basic guidelines from the outset. By taking some time at the beginning of the process to determine the project's purpose, analyze the audience, gather possible content, and determine what content to present to the audience, you can produce a project that is informative, relevant, and effective.

Appendix B

Introduction to Microsoft Office 2007

What Is Microsoft Office 2007?

Microsoft Office 2007 is a collection of the more popular Microsoft application software. It is available in Basic, Home and Student, Standard, Small Business, Professional, Ultimate, Professional Plus, and Enterprise editions. Each edition consists of a group of programs, collectively called a suite. Table B–1 lists the suites and their components. **Microsoft Office Professional Edition 2007** includes these six programs: Microsoft Office Word 2007, Microsoft Office Excel 2007, Microsoft Office Access 2007, Microsoft Office PowerPoint 2007, Microsoft Office Publisher 2007, and Microsoft Office Outlook 2007. The programs in the Office suite allow you to work efficiently, communicate effectively, and improve the appearance of the projects you create.

Table B–1

	Microsoft Office Basic 2007	Microsoft Office Home & Student 2007	Microsoft Office Standard 2007	Microsoft Office Small Business 2007	Microsoft Office Professional 2007	Microsoft Office Ultimate 2007	Microsoft Office Professional Plus 2007	Microsoft Office Enterprise 2007
Microsoft Office Word 2007	✓	✓	✓	✓	✓	✓	✓	✓
Microsoft Office Excel 2007	✓	✓	✓	✓	✓	✓	✓	✓
Microsoft Office Access 2007					✓	✓	✓	✓
Microsoft Office PowerPoint 2007		✓	✓	✓	✓	✓	✓	✓
Microsoft Office Publisher 2007				✓	✓	✓	✓	✓
Microsoft Office Outlook 2007	✓		✓				✓	✓
Microsoft Office OneNote 2007		✓				✓		
Microsoft Office Outlook 2007 with Business Contact Manager				✓	✓	✓		
Microsoft Office InfoPath 2007						✓	✓	✓
Integrated Enterprise Content Management						✓	✓	✓
Electronic Forms						✓	✓	✓
Advanced Information Rights Management and Policy Capabilities						✓	✓	✓
Microsoft Office Communicator 2007							✓	✓
Microsoft Office Groove 2007						✓		✓

Microsoft has bundled additional programs in some versions of Office 2007, in addition to the main group of Office programs. Table B–1 on the previous page lists the components of the various Office suites.

In addition to the Office 2007 programs noted previously, Office 2007 suites can contain other programs. Microsoft Office OneNote 2007 is a digital notebook program that allows you to gather and share various types of media, such as text, graphics, video, audio, and digital handwriting. Microsoft Office InfoPath 2007 is a program that allows you to create and use electronic forms to gather information. Microsoft Office Groove 2007 provides collaborative workspaces in real time. Additional services that are oriented toward the enterprise solution also are available.

Office 2007 and the Internet, World Wide Web, and Intranets

Office 2007 allows you to take advantage of the Internet, the World Wide Web, and intranets. The Microsoft Windows operating system includes a **browser**, which is a program that allows you to locate and view a Web page. The Windows browser is called Internet Explorer.

One method of viewing a Web page is to use the browser to enter the Web address for the Web page. Another method of viewing a Web page is clicking a hyperlink. A **hyperlink** is colored or underlined text or a graphic that, when clicked, connects to another Web page. Hyperlinks placed in Office 2007 documents allow for direct access to a Web site of interest.

An **intranet** is a private network, such as a network used within a company or organization for internal communication. Like the Internet, hyperlinks are used within an intranet to access documents, pages, and other destinations on the intranet. Unlike the Internet, the materials on the network are available only for those who are part of the private network.

Online Collaboration Using Office

Organizations that, in the past, were able to make important information available only to a select few, now can make their information accessible to a wider range of individuals who use programs such as Office 2007 and Internet Explorer. Office 2007 allows colleagues to use the Internet or an intranet as a central location to view documents, manage files, and work together.

Each of the Office 2007 programs makes publishing documents on a Web server as simple as saving a file on a hard disk. Once placed on the Web server, users can view and edit the documents and conduct Web discussions and live online meetings.

Using Microsoft Office 2007

The various Microsoft Office 2007 programs each specialize in a particular task. This section describes the general functions of the more widely used Office 2007 programs, along with how they are used to access the Internet or an intranet.

Microsoft Office Word 2007

Microsoft Office Word 2007 is a full-featured word processing program that allows you to create many types of personal and business documents, including flyers, letters, resumes, business documents, and academic reports.

Word's AutoCorrect, spelling, and grammar features help you proofread documents for errors in spelling and grammar by identifying the errors and offering suggestions for corrections as you type. The live word count feature provides you with a constantly updating word count as you enter and edit text. To assist with creating specific documents, such as a business letter or resume, Word provides templates, which provide a formatted document before you type the text of the document. Quick Styles provide a live preview of styles from the Style gallery, allowing you to preview styles in the document before actually applying them.

Word automates many often-used tasks and provides you with powerful desktop publishing tools to use as you create professional looking brochures, advertisements, and newsletters. SmartArt allows you to insert interpretive graphics based on document content.

Word makes it easier for you to share documents for collaboration. The Send feature opens an e-mail window with the active document attached. The Compare Documents feature allows you easily to identify changes when comparing different document versions.

Word 2007 and the Internet   Word makes it possible to design and publish Web pages on the Internet or an intranet, insert a hyperlink to a Web page in a word processing document, as well as access and search the content of other Web pages.

Microsoft Office Excel 2007

Microsoft Office Excel 2007 is a spreadsheet program that allows you to organize data, complete calculations, graph data, develop professional looking reports, publish organized data to the Web, and access real-time data from Web sites.

In addition to its mathematical functionality, Excel 2007 provides tools for visually comparing data. For instance, when comparing a group of values in cells, you can set cell backgrounds with bars proportional to the value of the data in the cell. You can also set cell backgrounds with full-color backgrounds, or use a color scale to facilitate interpretation of data values.

Excel 2007 provides strong formatting support for tables with the new Style Preview gallery.

Excel 2007 and the Internet   Using Excel 2007, you can create hyperlinks within a worksheet to access other Office documents on the network or on the Internet. Worksheets saved as static, or unchanging Web pages can be viewed using a browser. The person viewing static Web pages cannot change them.

In addition, you can create and run queries that retrieve information from a Web page and insert the information directly into a worksheet.

Microsoft Office Access 2007

Microsoft Office Access 2007 is a comprehensive database management system (DBMS). A **database** is a collection of data organized in a manner that allows access, retrieval, and use of that data. Access 2007 allows you to create a database; add, change, and delete data in the database; sort data in the database; retrieve data from the database; and create forms and reports using the data in the database.

Access 2007 and the Internet   Access 2007 lets you generate reports, which are summaries that show only certain data from the database, based on user requirements.

Microsoft Office PowerPoint 2007

Microsoft Office PowerPoint 2007 is a complete presentation graphics program that allows you to produce professional looking presentations. With PowerPoint 2007, you can create informal presentations using overhead transparencies, electronic presentations using a projection device attached to a personal computer, formal presentations using 35mm slides or a CD, or you can run virtual presentations on the Internet.

PowerPoint 2007 and the Internet   PowerPoint 2007 allows you to publish presentations on the Internet or other networks.

Microsoft Office Publisher 2007

Microsoft Office Publisher 2007 is a desktop publishing program (DTP) that allows you to design and produce professional quality documents (newsletters, flyers, brochures, business cards, Web sites, and so on) that combine text, graphics, and photographs. Desktop publishing software provides a variety of tools, including design templates, graphic manipulation tools, color schemes or libraries, and various page wizards and templates. For large jobs, businesses use desktop publishing software to design publications that are **camera ready**, which means the files are suitable for production by outside commercial printers. Publisher 2007 also allows you to locate commercial printers, service bureaus, and copy shops willing to accept customer files created in Publisher.

Publisher 2007 allows you to design a unique image, or logo, using one of more than 45 master design sets. This, in turn, permits you to use the same design for all your printed documents (letters, business cards, brochures, and advertisements) and Web pages. Publisher includes 70 coordinated color schemes; 30 font schemes; more than 10,000 high-quality clip art images; 1,500 photographs; 1,000 Web-art graphics; 340 animated graphics; and hundreds of unique Design Gallery elements (quotations, sidebars, and so on). If you wish, you also can download additional images from the Microsoft Office Online Web page on the Microsoft Web site.

Publisher 2007 and the Internet   Publisher 2007 allows you easily to create a multipage Web site with custom color schemes, photographic images, animated images, and sounds.

Microsoft Office Outlook 2007

Microsoft Office Outlook 2007 is a powerful communications and scheduling program that helps you communicate with others, keep track of your contacts, and organize your schedule. Outlook 2007 allows you to view a To-Do bar containing tasks and appointments from your Outlook calendar. Outlook 2007 allows you to send and receive electronic mail (e-mail) and permits you to engage in real-time communication with family, friends, or coworkers using instant messaging. Outlook 2007 also provides you with the means to organize your contacts, and you can track e-mail messages, meetings, and notes with a particular contact. Outlook's Calendar, Contacts, Tasks, and Notes components aid in this organization. Contact information is available from the Outlook Calendar, Mail, Contacts, and Task components by accessing the Find a Contact feature. **Personal information management (PIM)** programs such as Outlook provide a way for individuals and workgroups to organize, find, view, and share information easily.

Microsoft Office 2007 Help

At any time while you are using one of the Office programs, you can interact with **Microsoft Office 2007 Help** for that program and display information about any topic associated with the program. Several categories of help are available. In all programs, you can access Help by pressing the F1 key on the keyboard. In Publisher 2007 and Outlook 2007, the Help window can be opened by clicking the Help menu and then selecting Microsoft Office Publisher or Outlook Help command, or by entering search text in the 'Type a question for help' text box in the upper-right corner of the program window. In the other Office programs, clicking the Microsoft Office Help button near the upper-right corner of the program window opens the program Help window.

The Help window in all programs provides several methods for accessing help about a particular topic, and has tools for navigating around Help. Appendix C contains detailed instructions for using Help.

Collaboration and SharePoint

While not part of the Microsoft Office 2007 suites, SharePoint is a Microsoft tool that allows Office 2007 users to share data using collaborative tools that are integrated into the main Office programs. SharePoint consists of Windows SharePoint Services, Office SharePoint Server 2007, and, optionally, Office SharePoint Designer 2007.

Windows SharePoint Services provides the platform for collaboration programs and services. Office SharePoint Server 2007 is built on top of Windows SharePoint Services. The result of these two products is the ability to create SharePoint sites. A SharePoint site is a Web site that provides users with a virtual place for collaborating and communicating with their colleagues while working together on projects, documents, ideas, and information. Each member of a group with access to the SharePoint site has the ability to contribute to the material stored there. The basic building blocks of SharePoint sites are lists and libraries. Lists contain collections of information, such as calendar items, discussion points, contacts, and links. Lists can be edited to add or delete information. Libraries are similar to lists, but include both files and information about files. Types of libraries include document, picture, and forms libraries.

The most basic type of SharePoint site is called a Workspace, which is used primarily for collaboration. Different types of Workspaces can be created using SharePoint to suit different needs. SharePoint provides templates, or outlines of these Workspaces, that can be filled in to create the Workspace. Each of the different types of Workspace templates contain a different collection of lists and libraries, reflecting the purpose of the Workspace. You can create a Document Workspace to facilitate collaboration on documents. A Document Workspace contains a document library for documents and supporting files, a Links list that allows you to maintain relevant resource links for the document, a Tasks list for listing and assigning To-Do items to team members, and other links as needed. Meeting Workspaces allow users to plan and organize a meeting, with components such as Attendees, Agenda, and a Document Library. Social Meeting Workspaces provide a place to plan social events, with lists and libraries such as Attendees, Directions, Image/Logo, Things To Bring, Discussions, and Picture Library. A Decision Meeting Workspace is a Meeting Workspace with a focus on review and decision-making, with lists and libraries such as Objectives, Attendees, Agenda, Document Library, Tasks, and Decisions.

Users also can create a SharePoint site called a WebParts page, which is built from modules called WebParts. WebParts are modular units of information that contain a title bar and content that reflects the type of WebPart. For instance, an image WebPart would contain a title bar and an image. WebParts allow you quickly to create and modify a SharePoint site, and allow for the creation of a unique site that can allow users to access and make changes to information stored on the site.

Large SharePoint sites that include multiple pages can be created using templates as well. Groups needing more refined and targeted sharing options than those available with SharePoint Server 2007 and Windows SharePoint Services can add SharePoint Designer 2007 to create a site that meets their specific needs.

Depending on which components have been selected for inclusion on the site, users can view a team calendar, view links, read announcements, and view and edit group documents and projects. SharePoint sites can be set up so that documents are checked in and out, much like a library, to prevent multiple users from making changes simultaneously. Once a SharePoint site is set up, Office programs are used to perform maintenance of the site. For example, changes in the team calendar are updated using Outlook 2007, and changes that users make in Outlook 2007 are reflected on the SharePoint site. Office 2007 programs include a Publish feature that allows users easily to save file updates to a SharePoint site. Team members can be notified about changes made to material on the site either by e-mail or by a news feed, meaning that users do not have to go to the site to check to see if anything has been updated since they last viewed or worked on it. The search feature in SharePoint allows users quickly to find information on a large site.

Appendix C

Microsoft Office Access 2007 Help

Using Microsoft Office 2007 Access Help

This appendix shows how to use Microsoft Office Access Help. At any time while you are using one of the Microsoft Office 2007 programs, you can use Office Help to display information about all topics associated with the program. This appendix uses Microsoft Office Access 2007 to illustrate the use of Office Help. Help in other Office 2007 programs responds in a similar fashion.

In Office 2007, Help is presented in a window that has Web browser-style navigation buttons. Each Office 2007 program has its own Help home page, which is the starting Help page that is displayed in the Help window. If your computer is connected to the Internet, the contents of the Help page reflect both the local help files installed on the computer and material from Microsoft's Web site. As shown in Figure C–1, two methods for accessing Access's Help are available:

1. Microsoft Office Access Help button near the upper-right corner of the Access window
2. Function key F1 on the keyboard

Figure C–1

To Open the Access Help Window

The following steps open the Access Help window and maximize the window.

- Start Microsoft Access, if necessary. Click the Microsoft Office Access Help button near the upper-right corner of the Access window to open the Access Help window (Figure C–2).

Figure C–2

- Click the Maximize button on the Help title bar to maximize the Help window (Figure C–3).

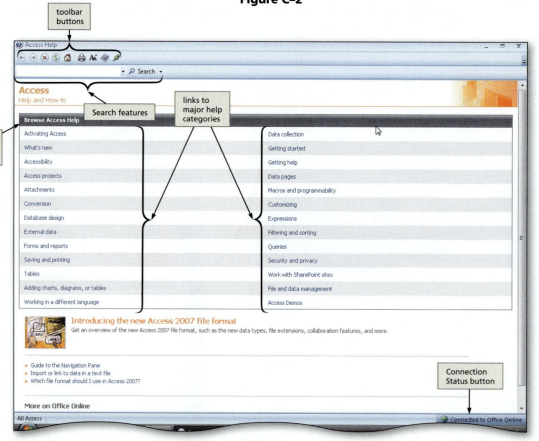

Figure C–3

The Access Help Window

The Access Help window provides several methods for accessing help about a particular topic, and also has tools for navigating around Help. Methods for accessing Help include searching the help content installed with Access, or searching the online Office content maintained by Microsoft.

Figure C–3 shows the main Access Help window. To navigate Help, the Access Help window includes search features that allow you to search on a word or phrase about which you want help; the Connection Status button, which allows you to control where Access Help searches for content; toolbar buttons; and links to major Help categories.

Search Features

You can perform Help searches on words or phrases to find information about any Access feature using the 'Type words to search for' text box and the Search button (Figure C–4a). Click the 'Type words to search for' text box and then click the Search button or press the ENTER key to initiate a search of Access Help.

Figure C–4

Access Help offers the user the option of searching the online Help Web pages maintained by Microsoft or the offline Help files placed on your computer when you install Access. You can specify whether Access Help should search online or offline from two places: the Connection Status button on the status bar of the Access Help window, or the Search button arrow on the toolbar. The Connection Status button indicates whether Help currently is set up to work with online or offline information sources. Clicking the Connection Status button provides a menu with commands for selecting online or offline searches (Figure C–4b). The Connection Status menu allows the user to select whether help searches will return content only from the computer (offline), or content from the computer and from Office Online (online).

Clicking the Search button arrow also provides a menu with commands for an online or offline search (Figure C–4a). These commands determine the source of information that Help searches for during the current Help session only. For example, assume that your preferred search is an offline search because you often do not have Internet access. You would set Connection Status to 'Show content only from this computer'. When you have Internet access, you can select an online search from the Search menu to search Office Online for information for your current search session only. Your search will use the Office Online resources until you quit Help. The next time you start Help, the Connection Status once again will be offline. In addition to setting the source of information that Help searches for during the current Help session, you can use the Search menu to further target the current search to one of four subcategories of online Help: Access Help, Access Templates, Access Training, and Developer Reference. The local search further can target one subcategory, Developer Reference.

In addition to searching for a word or string of text, you can use the links provided on the Browse Access Help area (Figure C–3 on page APP 10) to search for help on a topic. These links direct you to major help categories. From each major category, subcategories are available to further refine your search.

Finally, you can use the Table of Contents for Access Help to search for a topic the same way you would in a hard copy book. The Table of Contents is accessed through a toolbar button.

Toolbar Buttons

You can use toolbar buttons to navigate through the results of your search. The toolbar buttons are located on the toolbar near the top of the Help Window (Figure C–5). The toolbar buttons contain navigation buttons as well as buttons that perform other useful and common tasks in Access Help, such as printing.

Figure C–5

The Access Help navigation buttons are the Back, Forward, Stop, Refresh, and Home buttons. These five buttons behave like the navigation buttons in a Web browser window. You can use the Back button to go back one window, the Forward button to go forward one window, the Stop button to stop loading the current page, and the Home button to redisplay the Help home page in the Help window. Use the Refresh button to reload the information requested into the Help window from its original source. When getting Help information online, this button provides the most current information from the Microsoft Help Web site.

The buttons located to the right of the navigation buttons — Print, Change Font Size, Show Table of Contents, and Not on Top — provide you with access to useful and common commands. The Print button prints the contents of the open Help window. The Change Font Size button customizes the Help window by increasing or decreasing the size of its text. The Show Table of Contents button opens a pane on the left side of the Help window that shows the Table of Contents for Access Help. You can use the Table of Contents for Access Help to navigate through the contents of Access Help much as you would use the Table of Contents in a book to search for a topic. The Not On Top button is an example of a toggle button, which is a button that can be switched back and forth between two states. It determines how the Access Help window behaves relative to other windows. When clicked, the Not On Top button changes to Keep On Top. In this state, it does not allow other windows from Access or other programs to cover the Access Help window when those windows are the active windows. When in the Not On Top state, the button allows other windows to be opened or moved on top of the Access Help window.

You can customize the size and placement of the Help window. Resize the window using the Maximize and Restore buttons, or by dragging the window to a desired size. Relocate the Help window by dragging the title bar to a new location on the screen.

Searching Access Help

Once the Access Help window is open, several methods exist for navigating Access Help. You can search for help by using any of the three following methods from the Help window:

1. Enter search text in the 'Type words to search for' text box
2. Click the links in the Help window
3. Use the Table of Contents

To Obtain Help Using the Type Words to Search for Text Box

Assume for the following example that you want to know more about simple reports. The following steps use the 'Type words to search for' text box to obtain useful information about simple reports by entering the words, simple report, as search text. The steps also navigate in the Access Help window.

1

• Type simple report in the 'Type words to search for' text box at the top of the Access Help window.

• Click the Search button arrow to display the Search menu.

• If it is not selected already, click All Access on the Search menu to select the command. If All Access is already selected, click the Search button arrow again to close the Search menu.

Q&A

Why select All Access on the Search menu?

Selecting All Access on the Search menu ensures that Access Help will search all possible sources for information on your search term. It will produce the most complete search results.

Figure C–6

- Click the Search button to display the search results (Figure C–7).

Q&A

Why might my results differ?

If you do not have an Internet connection, your results will reflect only the content of the Help files on your computer. When searching for help online, results also can change as material is added, deleted, and updated on the online Help Web pages maintained by Microsoft.

Q&A

Why were my search results not very helpful?

When initiating a search, keep in mind to check the spelling of the search text; and to keep your search very specific, with fewer than seven words, to return the most accurate results.

Figure C–7

- Click the 'Create a simple report' link to open the Help document associated with the link in the Help window (Figure C–8).

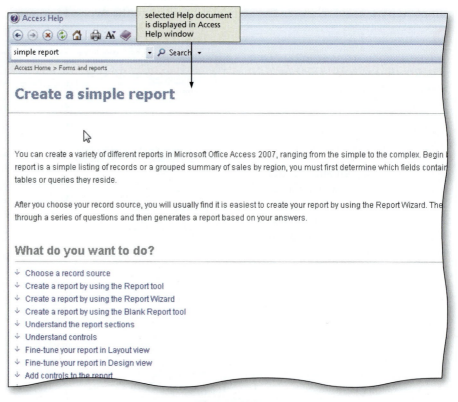

Figure C–8

4
- Click the Home button on the taskbar to clear the search results and redisplay the Access Help home page (Figure C–9).

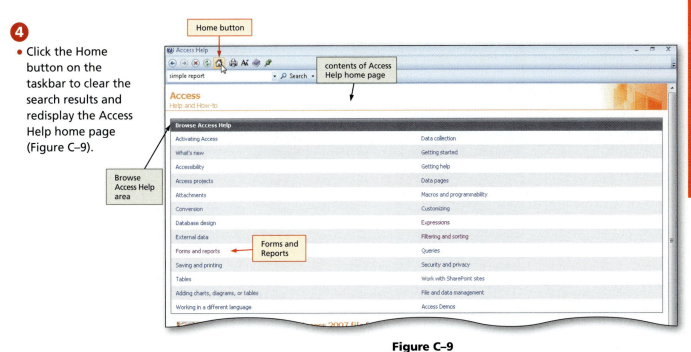

Home button

contents of Access Help home page

Browse Access Help area

Forms and Reports

Figure C–9

To Obtain Help Using the Help Links

If your topic of interest is listed in the Browse Access Help area, you can click the link to begin browsing Access Help categories instead of entering search text. You browse Access Help just like you would browse a Web site. If you know in which category to find your Help information, you may wish to use these links. The following steps find the simple report Help information using the category links from the Access Help home page.

1
- Click the 'Forms and reports' link to open the Forms and Reports page.

- Click the 'Create a simple report' link to open the Help document associated with the link (Figure C–10).

Q&A
What does the Show All link do?

In many Help documents, additional information about terms and features is available by clicking a link in the document to display additional information in the Help document. Clicking the Show All link opens all the links in the Help document that expand to additional text.

selected Help document displayed in Access Help window

Show All link

Figure C–10

To Obtain Help Using the Help Table of Contents

A third way to find Help in Word is through the Help Table of Contents. You can browse through the Table of Contents to display information about a particular topic or to familiarize yourself with Access. The following steps access the simple report Help information by browsing through the Table of Contents.

- Click the Home button on the toolbar.

- Click the Show Table of Contents button on the toolbar to open the Table of Contents pane on the left side of the Help window. If necessary, click the Maximize button on the Help title bar to maximize the window (Figure C–11).

Figure C–11

- Click the 'Forms and reports' link in the Table of Contents pane to view a list of Help subtopics.

- Click the 'Create a simple report' link in the Table of Contents pane to view the selected Help document in the right pane (Figure C–12).

Q&A

How do I remove the Table of Contents pane when I am finished with it?

The Show Table of Contents button acts as a toggle switch. When the Table of Contents pane is visible, the button changes to Hide Table of Contents. Clicking it hides the Table of Contents pane and changes the button to Show Table of Contents.

Figure C–12

Obtaining Help while Working in Access

Often you may need help while working on a database without already having the Help window open. For example, you may be unsure about how a particular command works, or you may be presented with a dialog box that you are not sure how to use. Rather than opening the Help window and initiating a search, Access Help provides you with the ability to search directly for help.

Figure C–13 shows one option for obtaining help while working in Access. If you want to learn more about a command, point to the command button and wait for the Enhanced ScreenTip to appear. If the Help icon appears in the Enhanced ScreenTip, press the F1 key while pointing to the command to open the Help window associated with that command.

Figure C–13

Figure C–14 shows a dialog box with a Get help button in it. Pressing the F1 key while the dialog box is displayed opens a Help window. The Help window contains help about that dialog box, if available. If no help file is available for that particular dialog box, then the main Help window opens.

Figure C–14

Use Help

1 Obtaining Help Using Search Text

Instructions: Perform the following tasks using Access Help.

1. Use the 'Type words to search for' text box to obtain help about the Navigation Pane. Use the Connection Status menu to search online help if you have an Internet connection.

2. Click Guide to the Navigation Pane in the list of links in the search results. Double-click the Microsoft Office Access Help window title bar to maximize it. Read and print the information. At the top of the printout, write down the number of links Access Help found.

3. Use the Search menu to search for help offline. Repeat the search from Step 1. At the top of the printout, write down the number of links that Access Help found searching offline. Submit the printouts as specified by your instructor.

4. Use the 'Type words to search for' text box to search for information online about keyboard shortcuts. Click the 'Keyboard Shortcuts for Access' link in the search results. If necessary, maximize the Microsoft Office 2007 Access Help window. Read and print the contents of the window. Close the Microsoft Office Access Help window. Submit the printouts as specified by your instructor.

5. For each of the following words and phrases, click one link in the search results, click the Show All link, and then print the page: multivalued field; Ribbon; wildcards; relationship; datasheet totals; and update. Submit the printouts as specified by your instructor.

2 Expanding on Access Help Basics

Instructions: Use Access Help to better understand its features and answer the questions listed below. Answer the questions on your own paper, or submit the printed Help information as specified by your instructor.

1. Use Help to find out how to customize the Help window. Change the font size to the smallest option and then print the contents of the Microsoft Office Access Help window. Change the font size back to its original setting. Close the window.

2. Press the F1 key. Search for information about tables, restricting the search results to Access Templates. Print the first page of the Search results.

3. Search for information about tables, restricting the search results to Access Help files. Print the first page of the Search results.

4. Use Access Help to find out what happened to the Office Assistant, a feature in the previous version of Access. Print out the Help document that contains the answer.

Appendix D
Publishing Office 2007 Web Pages to a Web Server

With the Office 2007 programs, you use the Save As command on the Office Button menu to save a Web page to a Web server using one of two techniques: Web folders or File Transfer Protocol. A **Web folder** is an Office shortcut to a Web server. **File Transfer Protocol (FTP)** is an Internet standard that allows computers to exchange files with other computers on the Internet.

You should contact your network system administrator or technical support staff at your Internet access provider to determine if their Web server supports Web folders, FTP, or both, and to obtain necessary permissions to access the Web server. If you decide to publish Web pages using a Web folder, you must have the Office Server Extensions (OSE) installed on your computer.

Using Web Folders to Publish Office 2007 Web Pages

When publishing to a Web folder, someone first must create the Web folder before you can save to it. If you are granted permission to create a Web folder, you must obtain the Web address of the Web server, a user name, and possibly a password that allows you to access the Web server. You also must decide on a name for the Web folder. Table D–1 explains how to create a Web folder.

Office 2007 adds the name of the Web folder to the list of current Web folders. You can save to this folder, open files in the folder, rename the folder, or perform any operations you would to a folder on your hard disk. You can use your Office 2007 program or Windows Explorer to access this folder. Table D–2 explains how to save to a Web folder.

Table D–1 Creating a Web Folder
1. Click the Office Button and then click Save As or Open.
2. When the Save As dialog box (or Open dialog box) appears, click the Tools button arrow, and then click Map Network Drive... When the Map Network Drive dialog box is displayed, click the 'Connect to a Web site that you can use to store your documents and pictures' link.
3. When the Add Network Location Wizard dialog box appears, click the Next button. If necessary, click Choose a custom network location. Click the Next button. Click the View examples link, type the Internet or network address, and then click the Next button. Click 'Log on anonymously' to deselect the check box, type your user name in the User name text box, and then click the Next button. Enter the name you want to call this network place and then click the Next button. Click to deselect the 'Open this network location when I click Finish' check box, and then click the Finish button.

Table D–2 Saving to a Web Folder
1. Click the Office Button, click Save As.
2. When the Save As dialog box is displayed, type the Web page file name in the File name text box. Do not press the ENTER key.
3. Click the Save as type box arrow and then click Web Page to select the Web Page format.
4. Click Computer in the Navigation pane.
5. Double-click the Web folder name in the Network Location list.
6. If the Enter Network Password dialog box appears, type the user name and password in the respective text boxes and then click the OK button.
7. Click the Save button in the Save As dialog box.

Using FTP to Publish Office 2007 Web Pages

When publishing a Web page using FTP, you first must add the FTP location to your computer before you can save to it. An FTP location, also called an **FTP site**, is a collection of files that reside on an FTP server. In this case, the FTP server is the Web server.

To add an FTP location, you must obtain the name of the FTP site, which usually is the address (URL) of the FTP server, and a user name and a password that allows you to access the FTP server. You save and open the Web pages on the FTP server using the name of the FTP site. Table D–3 explains how to add an FTP site.

Office 2007 adds the name of the FTP site to the FTP locations list in the Save As and Open dialog boxes. You can open and save files using this list. Table D–4 explains how to save to an FTP location.

Table D–3 Adding an FTP Location
1.   Click the Office Button and then click Save As or Open.
2.   When the Save As dialog box (or Open dialog box) appears, click the Tools button arrow, and then click Map Network Drive... When the Map Network Drive dialog box is displayed, click the 'Connect to a Web site that you can use to store your documents and pictures' link.
3.   When the Add Network Location Wizard dialog box appears, click the Next button. If necessary, click Choose a custom network location. Click the Next button. Click the View examples link, type the Internet or network address, and then click the Next button. If you have a user name for the site, click to deselect 'Log on anonymously' and type your user name in the User name text box, and then click Next. If the site allows anonymous logon, click Next. Type a name for the location, click Next, click to deselect the 'Open this network location when I click Finish' check box, and click Finish. Click the OK button.
4.   Close the Save As or the Open dialog box.

Table D–4 Saving to an FTP Location
1.   Click the Office Button and then click Save As.
2.   When the Save As dialog box appears, type the Web page file name in the File name text box. Do not press the ENTER key.
3.   Click the Save as type box arrow and then click Web Page to select the Web Page format.
4.   Click Computer in the Navigation pane.
5.   Double-click the name of the FTP site in the Network Location list.
6.   When the FTP Log On dialog box appears, enter your user name and password and then click the OK button.
7.   Click the Save button in the Save As dialog box.

Appendix E
Customizing Microsoft Office Access 2007

This appendix explains how to change the screen resolution in Windows Vista to the resolution used in this book. It also describes how to customize the Word window by changing the Ribbon, Quick Access Toolbar, and the color scheme.

Changing Screen Resolution

Screen resolution indicates the number of pixels (dots) that the computer uses to display the letters, numbers, graphics, and background you see on the screen. When you increase the screen resolution, Windows displays more information on the screen, but the information decreases in size. The reverse also is true: as you decrease the screen resolution, Windows displays less information on the screen, but the information increases in size.

The screen resolution usually is stated as the product of two numbers, such as 1024×768 (pronounced "ten twenty-four by seven sixty-eight"). A 1024×768 screen resolution results in a display of 1,024 distinct pixels on each of 768 lines, or about 786,432 pixels. The figures in this book were created using a screen resolution of 1024×768.

The screen resolutions most commonly used today are 800×600 and 1024×768, although some Office specialists set their computers at a much higher screen resolution, such as 2048×1536.

To Change the Screen Resolution

The following steps change the screen resolution from 1280×1024 to 1024×768. Your computer already may be set to 1024×768 or some other resolution.

- If necessary, minimize all programs so that the Windows Vista desktop appears.

- Right-click the Windows Vista desktop to display the Windows Vista desktop shortcut menu (Figure E–1).

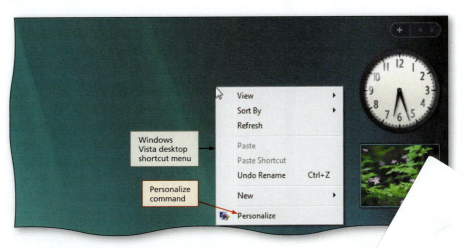

Figure E–1

2

- Click Personalize on the shortcut menu to open the Personalization window.

- Click Display Settings in the Personalization window to display the Display Settings dialog box (Figure E–2).

Figure E–2

3

- Drag the slider in the Resolution area so that the screen resolution changes to 1024 × 768 (Figure E–3).

Figure E–3

4

• Click the OK button to change the screen resolution from 1280 × 1024 to 1024 × 768 (Figure E–4).

Figure E–4

5

• Click the Yes button in the Display Settings dialog box to accept the new screen resolution (Figure E–5).

Q&A

What if I do not want to change the screen resolution after seeing it applied after I click the OK button?

You either can click the No button in the inner Display Settings dialog box, or wait for the timer to run out, at which point Windows Vista will revert to the original screen resolution.

• Click the Close button to close the Personalization Window.

Figure E–5

Screen Resolution and the Appearance of the Ribbon in Office 2007 Programs

Changing the screen resolution affects how the Ribbon appears in Office 2007 programs. Figure E–6 shows the Access Ribbon at the screen resolutions of 800 × 600, 1024 × 768, and 1280 × 1024. All of the same commands are available regardless of screen resolution. Access, however, makes changes to the groups and the buttons within the groups to accommodate the various screen resolutions. The result is that certain commands may need to be accessed differently depending on the resolution chosen. A command that is visible on the Ribbon and available by clicking a button at one resolution may not be visible and may need to be accessed using its group button at a different resolution.

Figure E–6

Comparing the three Ribbons, notice changes in content and layout of the groups and galleries. In some cases, the content of a group is the same in each resolution, but the layout of the group differs. For example, the same buttons appear in the Font group in the three resolutions, but the layouts differ. The buttons are displayed in three rows at the 800×600 resolution, and in two rows in the 1024×768 and 1280×1024 resolutions. In other cases, the content and layout are the same across the resolution, but the level of detail differs with the resolution. In the Clipboard group, when the resolution increases to 1280×1024, the names of all the buttons in the group appear in addition to the buttons themselves. At the lower resolution, only the buttons appear.

Changing resolutions also can result in fewer commands being visible in a group. Comparing the Records group, notice that the group at the 800×600 resolution consists of a Records button, while at the higher resolutions, the group has three buttons visible. The commands that are available on the Ribbon at the higher resolutions must be accessed using the Editing button at the 800×600 resolution.

Customizing the Access Window

When working in Access, you may want to make your working area as large as possible. One option is to minimize the Ribbon. You also can modify the characteristics of the Quick Access Toolbar, customizing the toolbar's commands and location to better suit your needs.

To Minimize the Ribbon in Access

The following steps minimize the Ribbon.

- Start Access.

- Maximize the Access window, if necessary.

- Click the Customize Quick Access Toolbar button on the Quick Access Toolbar to display the Customize Quick Access Toolbar menu (Figure E–7).

Figure E–7

• Click Minimize the Ribbon on the Quick Access Toolbar menu to reduce the Ribbon display to just the tabs (Figure E–8).

Figure E–8

Other Ways

1. Double-click the active Ribbon tab
2. Press CTRL+F1

Customizing and Resetting the Quick Access Toolbar

The Quick Access Toolbar, located to the right of the Microsoft Office Button by default, provides easy access to some of the more frequently used commands in Access (Figure E–7). By default, the Quick Access Toolbar contains buttons for the Save, Undo, and Redo commands. Customize the Quick Access Toolbar by changing its location in the window and by adding additional buttons to reflect which commands you would like to be able to access easily.

To Change the Location of the Quick Access Toolbar

The following steps move the Quick Access Toolbar to below the Ribbon.

• Double-click the Home tab to redisplay the Ribbon.

• Click the Customize Quick Access Toolbar button on the Quick Access Toolbar to display the Customize Quick Access Toolbar menu (Figure E–9).

Figure E–9

2

- Click Show Below the Ribbon on the Quick Access Toolbar menu to move the Quick Access Toolbar below the Ribbon (Figure E–10).

Figure E–10

To Add Commands to the Quick Access Toolbar Using the Customize Quick Access Toolbar Menu

Some of the more commonly added commands are available for selection from the Customize Quick Access Toolbar menu. The following steps add the Quick Print button to the Quick Access Toolbar.

1

- Click the Customize Quick Access Toolbar button to display the Customize Quick Access Toolbar menu (Figure E–11).

Figure E–11

• Click Quick Print on the Quick Access Toolbar menu to add the Quick Print button to the Quick Access Toolbar (Figure E–12).

Figure E–12

To Add Commands to the Quick Access Toolbar Using the Shortcut Menu

Commands also can be added to the Quick Access Toolbar from the Ribbon. Adding an existing Ribbon command that you use often to the Quick Access Toolbar makes the command immediately available, regardless of which tab is active.

• Click the Create tab on the ribbon to make it the active tab.

• Right-click the Table button on the Create tab to display a shortcut menu (Figure E–13).

Figure E–13

2

- Click Add to Quick Access Toolbar on the shortcut menu to add the Table button to the Quick Access Toolbar (Figure E–14).

Figure E–14

To Add Commands to the Quick Access Toolbar Using Access Options

Some commands do not appear on the Ribbon. They can be added to the Quick Access Toolbar using the Access Options dialog box.

1

- Click the Office Button to display the Office Button menu (Figure E–15).

Figure E–15

2
- Click the Access Options button on the Office Button menu to display the Access Options dialog box (Figure E–16).

Figure E–16

3
- Click Customize in the left pane.
- Click the 'Choose commands from' box arrow to display the 'Choose commands from' list.
- Click Commands Not in the Ribbon in the 'Choose commands from' list.
- Scroll to display the Split command.
- Click Split to select it (Figure E–17).

Figure E–17

4
- Click the Add button to add the Split button to the list of buttons on the Quick Access Toolbar (Figure E–18).

Figure E–18

5
- Click the OK button to add the Split button to the Quick Access Toolbar (Figure E–19).

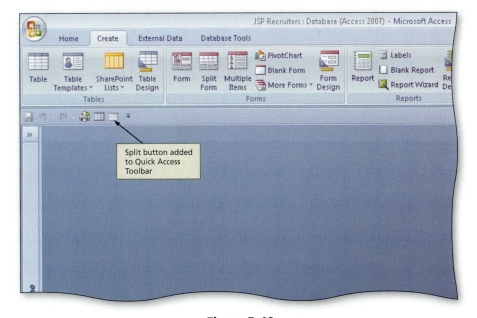

Figure E–19

Other Ways

1. Click Customize Quick Access Toolbar button, click More Commands, select commands to add, click Add button, click OK button

To Remove a Command from the Quick Access Toolbar

• Right-click the Split button on the Quick Access Toolbar to display a shortcut menu (Figure E–20).

Figure E–20

2

• Click Remove from Quick Access Toolbar on the shortcut menu to remove the button from the Quick Access Toolbar (Figure E–21).

Figure E–21

Other Ways

1. Click Customize Quick Access Toolbar button, click More Commands, click the command you wish to remove in the Customize Quick Access Toolbar list, click Remove button, click OK button

2. If the command appears on the Customize Quick Access Toolbar menu, click the Customize Quick Access Toolbar button, click the command you wish to remove

To Reset the Quick Access Toolbar

1

- Click the Customize Quick Access Toolbar button on the Quick Access Toolbar.

- Click More Commands on the Quick Access Toolbar menu to display the Access Options Dialog box.

- Click the Show Quick Access Toolbar below the Ribbon check box to deselect it (Figure E–22).

Figure E–22

- Click the Reset button, click the Yes button in the dialog box that appears, and then click the OK button in the Word Options dialog box, to reset the Quick Access Toolbar to its original position to the right of the Office Button, with the original three buttons (Figure E–23).

Figure E–23

Changing from Tabbed Documents to Overlapping Windows

In Access 2007, tables, queries, forms, reports, and other objects are displayed as tabbed documents rather than overlapping windows as they were in previous versions. You can change to overlapping windows if you wish. The following steps change the display from tabbed documents to overlapping windows.

To Change from Tabbed Documents to Overlapping Windows

- Click the Office Button to display the Office Button menu.

- Click the Access Options button to display the Access Options dialog box.

- If necessary, click Current Database in the left pane. Click the Overlapping Windows option button to select overlapping windows (Figure E–24).

- Click the OK button to change to overlapping windows.

- When Access informs you that you must close and reopen the database for the change to take effect, click the OK button.

- Close and reopen the database.

- Open both the Client and Recruiter tables to see the effect of overlapping windows (Figure E–25).

Q&A

How do I switch back to the tabbed documents?

Follow the steps for changing to overlapping windows, but click the Tabbed Documents option button.

Figure E–24

Figure E–25

Appendix F

Steps for the Windows XP User

For the XP User of this Book

For most tasks, no differences exist between using Access under the Windows Vista operating system and using Access under the Windows XP operating system. With some tasks, however, you will see some differences, or need to complete the tasks using different steps. This appendix shows how to Start Access, Create a Database, and Open a Database while using Microsoft Office under Windows XP.

To Start Access

The following steps, which assume Windows is running, start Access based on a typical installation. You may need to ask your instructor how to start Access for your computer.

1

- Click the Start button on the Windows taskbar to display the Start menu.

- Point to All Programs on the Start menu to display the All Programs submenu.

- Point to Microsoft Office on the All Programs submenu to display the Microsoft Office submenu (Figure F–1).

Figure F–1

- Click Microsoft Office Access 2007 to start Access and display the Getting Started with Microsoft Office Access screen (Figure F–2).

- If the Access window is not maximized, click the Maximize button next to the Close button on its title bar to maximize the window.

Q&A

What is a maximized window?

A maximized window fills the entire screen. When you maximize a window, the Maximize button changes to a Restore Down button.

Figure F–2

Other Ways
1. Double-click Access icon on desktop, if one is present
2. Click Microsoft Office Access 2007 on Start menu

To Create a Database

The following steps create a database, using the file name JSP Recruiters, on a USB flash drive.

- With a USB flash drive connected to one of the computer's USB ports, click Blank Database to create a new blank database.

- Repeatedly press the DELETE key to delete the default name of Database1.

- Type JSP Recruiters in the File Name text box to replace the default file name of Database1 (your screen may show Database1.accdb). Do not press the ENTER key after typing the file name.

Q&A

What characters can I use in a file name?

A file name can have a maximum of 255 characters, including spaces. The only invalid characters are the backslash (\), slash (/), colon (:), asterisk (*), question mark (?), quotation mark ("), less than symbol (<), greater than symbol (>), and vertical bar (|).

3

- Click the 'Browse for a location to put your database' button to display the File New Database dialog box (Figure F–3).

Q&A Do I have to save to a USB flash drive?

No. You can save to any device or folder. A **folder** is a specific location on a storage medium. You can save to the default folder or a different folder. You also can create your own folders, which is explained later in this book.

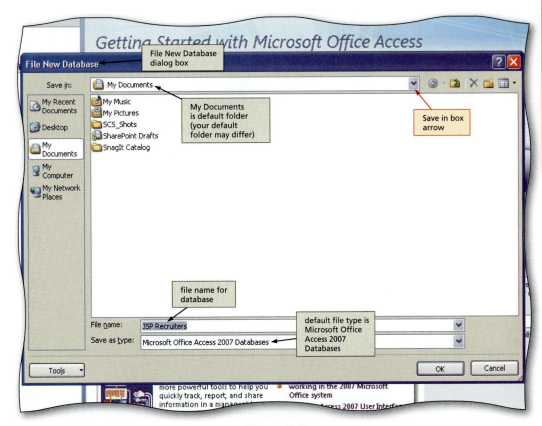

Getting Started with Microsoft Office Access

File New Database dialog box

File New Database

Save in: My Documents

My Music
My Pictures
SCS_Shots
SharePoint Drafts
SnagIt Catalog

My Documents is default folder (your default folder may differ)

Save in box arrow

file name for database

File name: JSP Recruiters

Save as type: Microsoft Office Access 2007 Databases

default file type is Microsoft Office Access 2007 Databases

Tools   OK   Cancel

more powerful tools to help you
quickly track, report, and share
information in a man...

working in the 2007 Microsoft
Office system

Access 2007 User Interf...

Figure F–3

4

- Click the Save in box arrow to display a list of available drives and folders.

Q&A Why is my list of files, folders, and drives arranged and named differently from those shown in the figure?

Your computer's configuration determines how the list of files and folders is displayed and how drives are named. You can change the save location by clicking shortcuts on the My Places bar.

Q&A How do I save the file if I am not using a USB flash drive?

Use the same process, but be certain to select your device in the Save in list.

5

- Click UDISK 2.0 (E:) in the Save in list to select the USB flash drive, Drive E in this case, as the new save location.

Q&A What if my USB flash drive has a different name or letter?

It is very likely that your USB flash drive will have a different name and drive letter and be connected to a different port. Verify that the device in your Save in list is correct.

6

- Click the OK button to select the USB flash drive as the location for the database and to return to the Getting Started with Microsoft Office Access screen.

7

- Click the Create button to create the database on the USB flash drive with the file name, JSP Recruiters.

Q&A How do I know that the JSP Recruiters database is created?

The name of the database appears in the title bar.

- If a Field List appears, click its Close button to remove the Field List from the screen (Figure F–4).

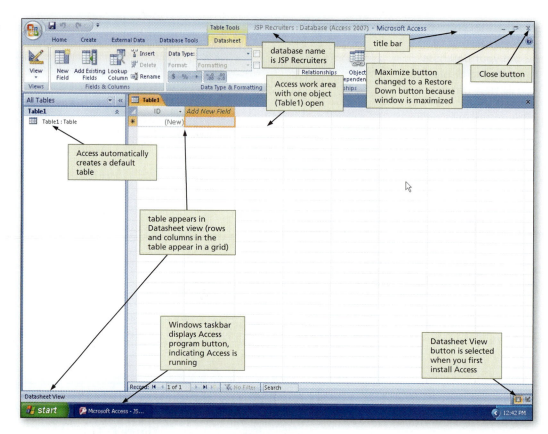

Figure F–4

Other Ways
1. Click Office Button, click Save, type file name, select drive or folder, click Save button   2. Press CTRL+S or press SHIFT+F12, type file name, select drive or folder, click Save button

To Open a Database

The following steps use the More button to open the JSP Recruiters database from the USB flash drive.

1

- With your USB flash drive connected to one of the computer's USB ports, click the More button, shown in Figure F–2 on page APP 36, to display the Open dialog box (Figure F-5).

- If necessary, click the Look in box arrow and then click UDISK 2.0 (E:) to select

Figure F–5

the USB flash drive, Drive E in this case, in the Look in list as the new open location.

- Click JSP Recruiters to select the file name.

Q&A How do I open the file if I am not using a USB flash drive?

Use the same process, but be certain to select your device in the Look in list. You might need to open multiple folders.

2

- Click the Open button to open the database (Figure F–6).

3

- If a Security Warning appears, as shown in Figure F–6, click the Options button to display the Microsoft Office Security Options dialog box.

4

- Click the 'Enable this content' option button.

- Click the OK button to enable the content.

Figure F–6

Q&A When would I want to disable the content?

You would want to disable the content if you suspected that your database might contain harmful content or damaging macros. Because you are the one who created the database and no one else has used it, you should have no such suspicions.

Other Ways

1. Click Office Button, double-click file name in Recent Documents list

2. Press CTRL+O, select file name, press ENTER

Appendix G
Microsoft Business Certification Program

What Is the Microsoft Business Certification Program?

The Microsoft Business Certification Program enables candidates to show that they have something exceptional to offer – proved expertise in Microsoft Office 2007 programs. The two certification tracks allow candidates to choose how they want to exhibit their skills, either through validating skills within a specific Microsoft product or taking their knowledge to the next level and combining Microsoft programs to show that they can apply multiple skill sets to complete more complex office tasks. Recognized by businesses and schools around the world, more than 3 million certifications have been obtained in more than 100 different countries. The Microsoft Business Certification Program is the only Microsoft-approved certification program of its kind.

What Is the Microsoft Certified Application Specialist Certification?

The Microsoft Certified Application Specialist certification exams focus on validating specific skill sets within each of the Microsoft Office system programs. Candidates can choose which exam(s) they want to take according to which skills they want to validate. The available Application Specialist exams include:

- Using Microsoft® Windows Vista™
- Using Microsoft® Office Word 2007
- Using Microsoft® Office Excel® 2007
- Using Microsoft® Office PowerPoint® 2007
- Using Microsoft® Office Access 2007
- Using Microsoft® Office Outlook® 2007

> For more information and details on how Shelly Cashman Series textbooks map to Microsoft Certified Application Specialist certification, visit scsite.com/off2007/cert.

What Is the Microsoft Certified Application Professional Certification?

The Microsoft Certified Application Professional certification exams focus on a candidate's ability to use the 2007 Microsoft® Office system to accomplish industry-agnostic functions, for example Budget Analysis and Forecasting, or Content Management and Collaboration. The available Application Professional exams currently include:

- Organizational Support
- Creating and Managing Presentations
- Content Management and Collaboration
- Budget Analysis and Forecasting

Index

Microsoft Office Access 2007 Quick Reference Summary *(continued)*

Task	Page Number	Mouse	Ribbon	Shortcut Menu	Keyboard Shortcut
Switch Between Form and Datasheet Views	AC 57	Form View or Datasheet View button			
Update Query	AC 162		Update button on Design tab | select field, Update To row, enter new value	Query Type | Update Query	
Use Advanced Filter/Sort	AC 155		Advanced button on Home tab | Advanced/ Filter Sort		
Use AND Criterion	AC 95				Place criteria on same line
Use Criterion	AC 81	Right-click query | Design View | Criteria row			
Use OR Criterion	AC 96				Place criteria on separate lines

Microsoft Office Access 2007 Quick Reference Summary *(continued)*

Task	Page Number	Mouse	Ribbon	Shortcut Menu	Keyboard Shortcut
Move to First Record	AC 39	First Record button			
Move to Last Record	AC 39	Last Record button			
Move to Next Record	AC 39	Next Record button			
Move to Previous Record	AC 39	Previous Record button			
New Item	various	Office button | Open			
Omit Duplicates	AC 100	Open Property Sheet, set Unique Values to Yes	Property Sheet button on Design tab | Unique Values	Properties | Unique Values	
Open Database	AC 37	More button | Open button or Office button | double-click file name			CTRL+O
Open Table	AC 26	Open button		Open	
Preview Table	AC 41	Office button | Print | Print Preview			ALT+F, W, V
Print Object	AC 41, 56	Office button | Print | Quick Print or Print			CTRL+P
Quit Access	AC 36	Close button			
Referential Integrity	AC 186		Relationships button on Database Tools tab		
Resize a Column	AC 175	In Datasheet view, double-click right boundary of the field selector		Right-click field name | Column Width	
Save Form	AC 58	Office button | Save			CTRL+S
Save Query	AC 91	Save button or Office button | Save			CTRL+S
Save Table	AC 27	Save button	Office button | Save	Save	CTRL+S
Search for Access Help	AC 62	Microsoft Office Access Help button			F1
Search for Record	AC 145		Find button on Home tab		CTRL+F
Select Fields for Report	AC 51		Report Wizard button on Create tab | Add Field button		
Simple Query Wizard	AC 78		Query Wizard button on Create tab		
Sort Data in Query	AC 98		Select field in Design grid | Ascending		
Sort on Multiple Keys	AC 101	Assign two sort keys			
Split Form	AC 57		Split Form button on Create tab		
Start Access	AC 12	Start button | All Programs | Microsoft Office | Microsoft Office Access 2007			

Microsoft Office Access 2007 Quick Reference Summary *(continued)*

Task	Page Number	Mouse	Ribbon	Shortcut Menu	Keyboard Shortcut
Create Query	AC 78		Query Design button on Create tab		
Create Report	AC 51		Report Wizard button on Create tab		
Create Table	AC 23	Office Button | Save button	Table button on Create tab		CTRL+S or SHIFT+F12
Customize Navigation Pane	AC 126	Navigation Pane arrow | Object Type			
Delete Record	AC 148	Click Record Selector | DELETE	DELETE button		
Define Fields in a Table	AC 24		Right-click Add New Field on Datasheet tab | Rename Column	Right-click Add New Field | Rename Column	
Exclude Field from Query Results	AC 112	Show check box			
Export Query	AC 221		Select query | desired application button in Export group on External Data tab		
Field Size	AC 46		Design View button on Design tab | select field | Field Size box		
Filter by Selection	AC 149		Selection button on Home tab | select criterion		
Format a Calculated Field	AC 116		Property Sheet button on Design tab		
Format a Field	AC 168	Select field | Format property box			
Group in Query	AC 121	Total row or include multiple fields in query			
Import Data	AC 212		Desired application in Import group on External Data tab		
Include All Fields in Query	AC 85	Double-click asterisk in field list	Query Design button on Create tab | Add All Fields button		
Include Field in Query	AC 85		Query Design button on Create tab | select field | Add Field button		
Join Tables	AC 105		Query Design button on Create tab | bring field lists for tables into upper pane		
Link Tables	AC 217		Access button on External Data tab | select database | OK button		
Lookup Field	AC 172	Data Type column for field | Lookup Wizard			

Quick Reference Summary

In the Microsoft Office Access 2007 program, you can accomplish a task in a number of ways. The following table provides a quick reference to each task presented in this textbook. The first column identifies the task. The second column indicates the page number on which the task is discussed in the book. The subsequent four columns list the different ways the task in column one can be carried out.

Microsoft Office Access 2007 Quick Reference Summary

Task	Page Number	Mouse	Ribbon	Shortcut Menu	Keyboard Shortcut
Add New Field	AC 24	Right-click Add New Field in Datasheet	Insert Rows button on Design Tab	Design View | INSERT	
Add Record	AC 30, 38	New (blank) record button	New button on Home tab	Open | Click in field	CTRL+PLUS SIGN (+)
Calculate Statistics	AC 118		Totals button on Design tab		
Change Colors and Font	AC 180		Alternate Fill/Back Color button arrow or Font Color button arrow or Font box arrow on Home tab		
Change Database Properties	AC 60	Office button | Manage | Database Properties			
Change Gridlines	AC 179		Gridlines button on Home tab		
Change Primary Key	AC 28	Delete field | Primary Key button	Design View button on Design tab | select field | Primary Key button		
Clear Query	AC 98				Select all entries | DELETE
Close Object	AC 35	Close button for object		Right-click item | Close	
Create Calculated Field	AC 113			Zoom	SHIFT+F2
Create Crosstab Query	AC 123		Query Wizard button on Create tab | Crosstab Query Wizard		
Create Database	AC 14	Blank Database button or Office Button | Save			CTRL+S or SHIFT+F12 or ALT+I
Create Form	AC 142		Form button on Create tab		

CONTENTS